– LLEWELLYN'S –
2024
HERBAL
ALMANAC

Cover Designer: Kevin R. Brown
Editor: Lauryn Heineman

Chapter opener art and illustration on page 43 © Melani Huggins
Illustrations on pages 23, 25, 210, 217, 218,
276, 277, and 279 by Llewellyn Art Department

You can order annuals and books from *New Worlds,*
Llewellyn's catalog. To request a free copy, call 1-877-
NEW WRLD toll-free or visit www.llewellyn.com.

ISBN: 978-0-7387-6895-3
Llewellyn Worldwide Ltd.
2143 Wooddale Drive
Woodbury, MN 55125-2989

Printed in China

Contents

DIY and Crafts

Plant Profiles

Gardening Resources

Introduction to
Llewellyn's Herbal Almanac

Holistic care for the mind, body, and soul starts in the garden. While adapting to the new normal, people around the world have sought out sustainable lifestyles and made greener choices, asking how to grow and preserve organic food for their family or how to forage for a nutritious bounty in their own neighborhood. Growing herbs enriches the soul, and using them in home-cooked meals, remedies, and crafts is natural, healthy, and just plain delicious.

There is no better time to grow, use, and eat herbs than now, and we hope you'll find inspiration for your own healthy life in this book. With sage advice appealing to novice gardeners and experienced herbalists alike, our experts tap into the practical and historical aspects of herbal knowledge—using herbs to help you connect with the earth, enhance your culinary creations, and heal your body and mind.

In addition to the twenty-two articles written by Master Gardeners, professors, homesteaders, and community herbalists, this book offers reference materials tailored specifically for successful growing and gathering. Use this book to plot this year's garden, practice companion planting, learn a new cooking technique, garden by the moon, find a helpful herbal remedy, and keep track of goals and chores.

Reclaiming our connection to Mother Earth in our own backyards can bring us harmony and balance—and a delicious, healthy harvest. May your garden grow tall and your dishes taste divine!

Growing
and
Gathering

Taming the Wild Plant

⤳ JD Walker ⤶

In late spring 2022, I was enjoying a bit of agritourism while on a short road trip. For those unfamiliar with the term, *agritourism* combines the working of a farm or other agricultural business with recreational activities open to the general public. In this case, I was at a small suburban garden center that also included a petting zoo, duck pond, craft beer and snacks area, and small music venue. While browsing the center's plant collection, I came across an old friend from the plant kingdom.

"Well, look at that," I thought to myself. "Someone has tamed the wild cow-itch vine."

People in the southern United States need no explanation of what a cow-itch or trumpet creeper vine is. Botanically speaking, it is *Campsis radicans*, a deciduous, wildly aggressive vining plant that will attach to anything that stands still long enough. The leaves can cause contact dermatitis in some people. Given the opportunity, the vine will grow thirty feet long with a lateral spread of four to ten feet. Pulling it up is not an option. It has a death grip on any land, post, barn, or house it grows in or around. Its saving grace is gorgeous, red-orange or yellow trumpet-shaped flowers that hummingbirds adore.

I have often thought when seeing it come into bloom around July along cornfields and road ditches that it would make a lovely garden specimen if you could reduce the height . . . and subdue its aggressiveness . . . and do something about the millions of seeds it produces . . . and maybe fix that mildly toxic dermatitis it causes. Basically, what any gardener would want is the lovely flowers without the overall boorishness of the plant.

Why Breed New Plants for the Garden?

The drive to find new introductions for the landscape is a major reason why researchers keep breeding or hybridizing new plants. In her 2008 book *Flower Confidential*, author Amy Stewart points out breeders are often looking for larger flowers, new colors, bigger (or smaller) versions of plants, and greater durability. In the case of cow-itch vine, it turns out people have been working on this North American native almost since Europeans first landed on the new continent. English botanist John Parkinson described the plant in his *Paradisi in Sole*, first published in 1629. From there, it spread in popularity to the rest of Europe. *C. radicans* 'Flamenco' is an example of a variety of the native vine that was bred in Germany. It helps to understand that in the cooler climates of northern Europe, cow-itch is a bit more restrained in growth.

Aesthetics aside, we are finding out that we need new plants for other reasons. As the climate changes, we may not be able to rely on the old standbys in commercial farming. Plants have to be more heat and drought tolerant. If we hope to cut down on the use of insecticides, we need plants to be more resistant to bug infestations. Of course, a big driver of crop development has always been greater harvests from the same acreage planted.

Going from Concept to Reality

The old-school way to get new plants is to control their sex lives. It sounds dirty, but it's not. Plants of the same family are selected that have desirable characteristics, such as a unique bloom or particular color or special growing habit. The plants are brought to bloom, often in a greenhouse or contained location. The breeder then carefully takes pollen from one plant flower and dusts it into the bloom of another plant.

This is a slow process that must be done two parent plants at a time. The breeder can't mix the pollen from multiple plants into one blossom. The bloom is then protected, usually with netting, to keep insects or air movement from introducing additional pollen from another plant. The plant sets seed: those seeds are collected and eventually planted. The new plant is monitored to see if the desired traits—any of the desired traits—are present in the offspring of the original cross.

This has been done with cow-itch vine. Breeders crossed the aggressive North American *C. radicans* with the more mild-mannered Asian *C. grandiflora*. The result was the new plant *C.* ×*tagliabuana,* a shorter vine with a more open flower that is still more resilient than its Asian parent.

A Labor of Love

When the process works and the breeder is lucky, the new plant delivers that bigger bloom or new color. Unfortunately, it's rarely that simple. Famed plant breeder Luther Burbank worked for years to develop the Shasta daisy (*Leucanthemum* ×*superbum*). This is the flower we immediately think of when someone says "daisy." It's a large, white-rayed flower with a bright yellow center, presented on strong stems that are perfect in a cottage garden or in a bouquet. Why did he do it? He just loved daisies.

Burbank started by growing wild ox-eyed daisies (*L. vulgare*) to get the best and strongest plants possible. Next, he crossed the result with the English field daisy (*L. maximum*). The result was considered better but not good enough. The new daisy was crossed with the Portuguese field daisy (*L. lacustre*). This gave Burbank the large flowers he wanted but a less-than-brilliant white color. The next cross was with the Japanese field daisy (*Nipponanthemum nipponicum*). Burbank ended up with bright white flowers that were smaller than desired. After several seasons of crossbreeding these last new plants with each other, Burbank finally ended up with the Shasta daisy we know today.

This process took seventeen years. But that is a drop in the bucket to the time some plants have undergone hybridization. The forerunners to our summer geraniums (*Pelargonium* ×*hortorum*) were first collected by Europeans in the early 1700s from South Africa (*P. sidoides*). Striking plants in their native environment, these predecessors look distinctly different from our zonal geraniums. The natives grow with red or white flowers. Modern geraniums come in nearly every shade except blue. This is due to busy breeders hard at work in the greenhouse. As is often the case, the South African plants tend to be smaller and more compact than our summer standards.

While humans have been manipulating plants (often accidentally) for thousands of years, Thomas Fairchild of London was the first person to scientifically produce a new plant in 1717 with methods still used today—the Dianthus caryophyllus barbatus, *a cross between the sweet william and carnation plants.*

Europeans did the same thing with North American deciduous azaleas. In my area of the country, we often think of the flame azalea (*Rhododendron calendulaceum*) or the Piedmont azalea (*R. canescens*) when we talk about the wild deciduous azaleas, but there are many natives in this group of plants. In the early 1700s, plant collectors took samples of all these new plants, bred them in English nurseries with the European *R. luteum*, and sent us back the Ghent, Knapp, and Exbury azaleas we find in garden centers today.

Of course, all this breeding and hybridizing does come with drawbacks. Old World explorers were introduced to maize (*Zea mays*) in the fifteenth century. At that point, researchers think maize had already been in cultivation for about 6,000 years. The plant the Spanish explorers saw was a tall plant (ten feet and higher) that produced small ears made up of cobs that had few kernels that could be white, yellow, red, purple, and even green. After hundreds of years of more hybridizing and crossbreeding, most of us enjoy *Z. mays* var. *saccharata,* or sweet corn, and *Z. mays* var. *everta*, or popcorn.

As tasty as they are, these varieties of corn would probably not survive in the wild, researchers tell us. All the domestication has resulted in corn kernels that don't easily detach from the cob without the help of human hands or hulling machines. The outer leaves or husks tend not to relax as the cob ages. Both traits keep birds and small animals from helping distribute the seeds.

New-School Breeding Techniques

As noted, the old way plants were improved or adapted to modern use can take years, even decades, to produce viable results. Even then, the changes may not be permanent. Anyone who has grown an F1 hybrid tomato knows they get a strong, disease-resistant plant that produces abundantly for a long growing period. However, if they save the seeds in the hopes of growing their own tomato sets next season, the result will likely not be the same.

The reason is that the hybridized plant doesn't come back "true to seed," as my grandmother would say. The offspring will tend to resemble one or the other of its parents—usually a smaller plant with smaller, cherry tomatoes. Grandma would buy new tomato sets each year to get tomatoes for sandwiches and for canning. But we never wanted for cherry tomato plants. We just went down to the pig pens around May and dug up any of the many tomato seedlings that sprouted from last year's wasted tomatoes.

Much discussion has been made of genetically modified organisms or GMOs. This is the process of taking the genes that result in a set of desired characteristics from one plant and inserting those genes into a different plant. Some people worry about the unintended consequences of "Franken-plants." Could GMO plants crossbreed with existing crops or even wild plants in waste areas around fields to produce a noxious weed that could not be controlled? Could GMO plants do harm to surrounding wildlife or even to humans who consume the plant (or its produce)?

These may be valid concerns, but not for the home gardener—at least not yet. The process to produce GMO plants is very expensive and mostly limited to commercial farming. Currently, the only GMO crops available in the United States are corn, soybeans, papaya, cotton, squash, canola, alfalfa, and sugar beets. These are not available "over the counter," so to speak, to the average homeowner. European breeders have come up with a handful of carnations and one rose for the flower markets there. However, again, the average homeowner can't buy GMO carnations or roses.

Growing Forward

Plant hybridizing is a labor-intensive process that requires true attention to day-to-day details. I've known several dedicated gardeners who started as avid hobbyists and morphed into plant breeders. It usually starts out as intense devotion to a particular species of plants, be that flower, vegetable, shrub, or tree. The result isn't always a desirable offspring. Even if the hobbyist does create an outstanding new plant, the chances are someone has already beat them to that particular combination and sent it off for patenting.

But for these special gardeners, the goal is not accolades. It is the joy of working with plants. Sometimes, that is reward enough.

Resources

Cash, R. Christian. "Exbury Azaleas—From History to Your Garden." Temple University. Accessed October 18, 2022. https://scholar.lib.vt.edu/ejournals/JARS/v40n1/v40n1-cash1.htm.

Favretti, Rudy J. "Colonial Gardens." *Arnoldia* 31, no. 4 (1971): 145–71. http://www.jstor.org/stable/42962477.

"Shasta Daisy." Luther Burbank Home & Gardens. Accessed October 18, 2022. http://www.lutherburbank.org/about-us/shasta-daisy.

Stewart, Amy. *Flower Confidential*. New York: Algonquin Books, 2008.

Fruit Tree Guilds

⇜ Jordan Charbonneau ⇝

If you've ever been apple picking in the fall, you're probably familiar with the traditional orchard setup: long, tidy rows of trees surrounded by trimmed grass dominate the landscape. They're essentially the fruit equivalent of monoculture gardens like the large fields of corn you'd see on any trip through the Midwest.

These neat monocultures are designed for ease of harvest and often for ease of maintenance on a large scale with machinery. They're not at all what you find in nature. Trees have various plants growing under and around them in a natural setting. Picture the forests that are around where you live.

Unfortunately, it isn't as simple as giving up on mowing, as most fruit trees will not outcompete the succession of native forests. However, there is a way to move away from monoculture and toward a more natural system.

The Benefits of Fruit Tree Guilds

Fruit tree guilds allow you to create a mini ecosystem around your fruit tree. Properly designed tree guilds help the tree thrive by planting other plants nearby that will benefit them in a few different ways.

A critical part of a productive orchard is pollination. Without pollination, a spring fruit tree loaded with blossoms will never produce a single piece of fruit. Some orchards have turned to renting honeybee hives to try to increase pollination. However, you can work with native pollinators. Fruit tree guilds help attract and provide habitat for native species. If you happen to have honeybees, they'll reap the benefits too.

Another consideration for most orchards is mowing or weeding. Fruit trees, especially young ones, may struggle to compete with other plants for light, water, and nutrients. Rather than encouraging constant maintenance, tree guilds attempt to solve this issue by using plants that will grow harmoniously with your tree.

Fruit trees are also susceptible to pests and diseases. Most large orchards turn to chemicals to cope with these issues. When planting a tree guild, you can use other plants to deter pests, attract predatory insects, add nutrients to the soil, and improve your tree's health and natural defenses.

Last, tree guilds slowly improve your soil year after year. Normally, you may add a little compost or attempt to improve your soil while digging a hole and planting your tree. Except for occasional mulching, for many growers, that initial investment is all the soil improvement a fruit tree will get. In a tree guild, plants mine nutrients from deep below the surface, capture nitrogen from the air, and add organic matter to build up the soil.

These incredible benefits make the initial investment of time and effort in starting a fruit tree guild well worth it.

What Should I Include in My Fruit Tree Guild?

There are no set rules for fruit tree guilds, and you can experiment to find what works best in your climate and local conditions. There are some basic categories many folks include:

The Tree

The first and most obvious is the tree. While permaculturalists often refer to them as fruit tree guilds, you don't have to use a fruit tree for your tree guild. You can create a guild with shade, nut, or ornamental trees. You may order a tree with this project in mind or select a tree you already have growing on your property.

Here are a few ideas:

- Almond tree
- Apple tree
- Cherry tree
- Eastern redbud tree
- English walnut tree
- Lemon tree
- Mulberry tree

- Peach tree

- Pear tree

- Plum tree

The list goes on! When planting fruit and nut trees, remember that many require a pollinator or another tree of the same type to produce. Some are labeled self-pollinated, but even these may produce better with a pollinator nearby. The nursery your tree comes from should provide this information.

Selecting a tree is the first step in building your fruit tree guild because it will allow you to do a bit of digging and find out what plants will work best with your chosen tree.

The plants that will accompany your tree are generally divided into a few categories: mulchers, accumulators, fixers, attractors, suppressors, and repellers. Many plants will fit into more than one of these categories.

Mulchers

Mulchers are plants that create abundant material that can be cut and used as mulch. Some mulchers are perennial and can be cut occasionally and regrown, while others are annuals, enabling you to choose each year.

Mulch is a great way to suppress weeds, keep the soil cool and moist, reduce erosion, and add organic matter, which is critical to improving your soil. It helps heavy clay soils drain better and helps light sandy soils hold water and nutrients.

Some mulchers include the following:

- Buckwheat

- Comfrey (perennial)

- Hosta

- Mint
- Rhubarb
- Rye
- Wheat

When selecting a mulch plant, consider how much maintenance you want to put into your tree guild. Comfrey is an easy-to-grow perennial; even if you forget to cut it, the leaves will die back each fall, providing organic matter, and regrow each spring. On the other hand, you may need to sow wheat each year. Buckwheat is also an annual but is a prolific self-seeder.

Accumulators

The plants in this category typically have deep root systems or taproots. The leaves of these plants have high mineral content because root systems allow them to "mine" minerals from the soil. When leaves of these plants die or you cut them back beneath your tree, they decompose and allow your tree to access some of these minerals more readily. Some excellent choices for accumulators to add to your guild include the following:

- Alfalfa
- Borage
- Chicory
- Comfrey
- Echinacea
- Tansy
- Sorrel

Fixers

Plants in this category are nitrogen-fixing, meaning they have a relationship with bacteria that colonize their roots and allow the plants to capture nitrogen from the air and use it. Many of these may be familiar from your vegetable plot or cover crops. They include these:

- Alfalfa
- Beans
- Crimson clover
- Hairy vetch
- Lupine
- Peas
- Red clover
- White clover

Nitrogen from these plants is added to the soil when the leaves or the entire plant dies and decomposes. For annuals like beans, this will happen naturally each fall. For perennials like white clover, this process occurs over time as parts of the plant decompose, or you can speed up this process by cutting them back.

Suppressors

While aiming for a more natural environment for your tree, it's essential to realize that many fruit and nut trees aren't tough enough to compete with our native species. Creating a tree guild aims to keep plants under them but not have to mow or weed often. Suppressors are plants grown under fruit trees to help suppress weeds without overtaking or competing with your tree. Many of these are vining plants. Some great suppressors include the following:

- Cucumbers
- Mint
- Nasturtiums
- Pumpkins
- Strawberries
- Thyme
- White clover
- Winter squash

Attractors

As the name suggests, these plants attract beneficial insects to your tree. When we think about beneficial insects, we often consider pollinators such as bees, butterflies, and flies. However, you can also plant attractors to draw in other beneficial insects: predators. Predatory insects feed on common pest insects. Some you may want to attract include spiders, wasps, assassin bugs, and lacewings.

- Bee balm (monarda)
- Buckwheat
- Calendula
- Cosmos
- Dara
- Dill
- Fennel

- Phlox
- Rudbeckia (black-eyed Susan)
- Salvia
- Sunflowers
- Sweet alyssum
- Yarrow

Repellers

Repellers are plants that deter certain pests from bothering your tree. Before selecting a repeller, try to research what pests usually affect your type of tree. If you have neighbors with the same trees or local orchards, it's great to find out what pests are a problem locally. Good examples of repellers include these:

- Chives
- Chrysanthemum
- Daffodil
- Garlic
- Lemon balm
- Lemongrass
- Marigold
- Mint
- Onions
- Oregano
- Wormwood

Creating an Apple Tree Guild

While there are many trees to choose from, few may be as iconic of the small American farm or homestead as the humble apple. In the Northeast, where I grew up, we commonly located old cellar holes and farms in the woods by spotting the gnarled branches of an apple still standing strong amidst the pines, maples, and birches that had sprung up around it.

There are different types of apple trees. Some apples are good for storage and others for fresh eating, while others make excellent cider. You may want to explore different varieties before purchasing a tree.

Apple Tree Mulcher

When I initially plant a fruit tree, one of my favorite mulcher plants is buckwheat. Buckwheat is a tree guild workhorse. It's fast-growing and great at outcompeting weeds that may pop up around my freshly planted tree, allowing it to double as a suppressor. The buckwheat flowers also attract tiny parasitic wasps and flies, which feed on aphids, caterpillars, and other pests, making buckwheat an excellent attractor.

You can treat it in a couple of different ways as a mulcher. One method is to cut buckwheat back just before it goes to seed. It's easy to cut; I use a scythe to make quick work of it. Alternatively, you can let it self-seed.

Unless you live somewhere very warm, buckwheat will be killed back by the fall frosts, but if it has gone to seed, you'll get some popping up next spring. Dead buckwheat is a good mulch, preventing weeds but also decomposing reasonably quickly to add organic matter to the soil.

Apple Tree Accumulator

Like all plants, apple trees can suffer from nutritional deficiencies. Aside from nitrogen, potassium deficiency is one of the most common deficiencies in apple trees. It's often seen as the yellowing of tissue along the leaf margins, particularly as the tree is developing fruit because the fruit requires large amounts of potassium.

Borage is excellent at accumulating potassium in its leaves from deep within the soil. When borage leaves are cut or die back, they decompose, making that potassium readily accessible to the apple tree.

Apple Tree Fixer

Nitrogen deficiency is typically the most common deficiency seen in apple trees. You may notice pale leaves and reduced growth (small new shoots each year). As I don't live in an area with particularly rich soil, I want a fixer that helps me add nitrogen to the soil each year, so I'm selecting white clover for my apple tree guild.

White clover is a low-growing perennial. It helps attract pollinators and is easy to maintain. While I don't often mow, cutting the white clover around my apple tree, using a bagger, and dumping the clippings around the tree's base provides a great boost of nitrogen.

Apple Tree Suppressor

As the white clover and buckwheat I chose also work as suppressors, this category isn't a huge concern for this guild. However, given any extra space, I would add strawberries.

Strawberries are an excellent choice for getting fruit out of your new home orchard long before any fruit trees are ma-

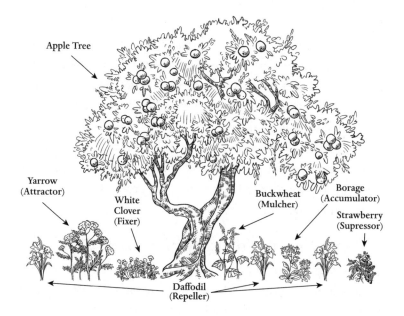

Apple Tree

Yarrow
(Attractor)

White
Clover
(Fixer)

Buckwheat
(Mulcher)

Borage
(Accumulator)

Strawberry
(Supressor)

Daffodil
(Repeller)

ture enough to produce. Their little white flowers also help support pollinators, and their vining, spreading nature helps suppress weeds and keep the soil cool and moist.

Apple Tree Attractor

In this guild, the attractor I'm going to use is yarrow, or *Achillea millefolium*. It's an easy-to-grow, hardy perennial that produces clusters of tiny, tightly packed flowers. It's native to North America, and in the wild, these flowers are typically white, though you can find red, pink, and yellow cultivars.

Yarrow is an ideal attractor for an apple tree guild because it attracts pollinators like bees and butterflies and predatory insects like lacewings and ladybugs. Both lacewings and ladybugs feed on aphids. While aphids seldom kill mature apple trees, they can do severe damage to seedlings, damaging twigs and preventing growth.

Apple Tree Repeller

Apple trees are susceptible to many pests, most of which are insects. However, one pest problem you may not notice until they've caused serious damage is rodents! Especially in the winter, when food supplies are limited, rodents may gnaw on the roots of apple trees.

A great, beautiful way to deter rodents is to plant daffodils among the roots of your tree. Daffodils are toxic to rodents and typically avoided. They're great for protecting fruit trees, tulips, and other rodent favorites.

Creating an English Walnut Tree Guild

English walnuts are a popular choice for homesteaders looking to add nuts to their orchards, and for a good reason. Compared to black walnuts, English walnuts are easy to harvest and shell. Depending on the variety, these trees reach heights of forty to sixty feet tall with crowns of equal width, making them excellent shade trees, something you'll also have to consider as your guild matures.

Note that English walnut trees produce a substance called **juglone**, which can prevent the growth of some sensitive plants. While they produce much less juglone than black walnut trees, this will still be a consideration as we plan our guild.

Walnut Tree Mulcher

One plant that seems immune to juglone is the humble hosta. Hostas are tough, drought tolerant, and shade tolerant, and they can be cut back, making them a good option for walnut tree mulchers. Plus, their scapes of flowers attract pollinators, including hummingbirds.

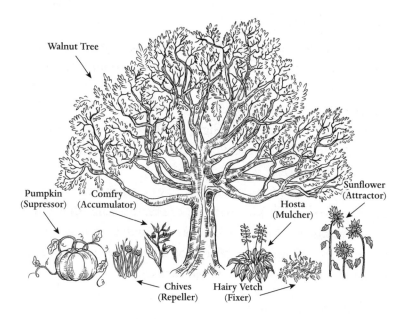

Walnut Tree

Pumpkin
(Supressor)

Comfry
(Accumulator)

Sunflower
(Attractor)

Hosta
(Mulcher)

Chives
(Repeller)

Hairy Vetch
(Fixer)

Walnut Tree Accumulator

While I've also listed comfrey as a mulcher, it's one of the best accumulators, in my opinion. Comfrey's large roots are excellent at pulling minerals from the soil into its leaves, which die back in the fall or can be cut back during the summer to decompose around your tree. Plus, comfrey is a tough, perennial plant that is maintenance-free and tolerates juglone.

Walnut Tree Fixer

Providing your walnut tree with adequate nitrogen levels is essential for good growth and production. Many commercial producers apply manure or fertilizer around their trees every two years.

To help provide this nitrogen, I recommend hairy vetch as a fixer. Hairy vetch has been shown to stimulate the growth of young walnuts. It also tolerates acidic soils that other fixers like clover and alfalfa will not.

Walnut Tree Suppressor

For a newly planted walnut tree, I recommend you use winter squash or pumpkins as a suppressor, as they both tolerate juglone. Their long vines and large leaves are excellent at shading the soil and preventing weeds once they get going. A smaller tree will still let in plenty of light for these crops to grow and produce. You'll get an excellent harvest from the space before your tree produces.

The shade your tree produces may be a significant consideration if you're working with a more mature English walnut. While not generally listed for fruit tree guilds, it may be appropriate to opt for ferns, hostas, or other shade-tolerant species under these trees spreading crowns.

Walnut Tree Attractor

English walnut trees are susceptible to several pests, including codling moths. Thankfully, codling moths are preyed on by nuthatches, woodpeckers, and creepers. These awesome birds feed on a number of other pests as well and are a welcome addition to the home orchard.

One plant great for attracting them is the sunflower. Leaving standing sunflowers with seed heads in the fall provides a great source of fat for these birds and will help encourage them to thrive in your area. Sunflowers also attract pollinators and are resistant to juglone.

Walnut Tree Repeller

Walnut trees are susceptible to mites and aphids. Most members of the *Allium* genus help repel both aphids and mites. They're also resistant to juglone and can be grown beneath walnuts.

I'd add chives to this guild as a low-maintenance, long-lived option. Chives have the added benefit of providing another edible harvest long before your walnut tree will begin producing.

A thoughtfully designed tree guild can help improve your soil, reduce pest and disease issues, reduce maintenance, and increase production. Use this basic guide along with your own research to add a beautiful guild to your property.

Resources

Glas, Adam. "Gardening Best Friends: Allium and Roses." The Scott Arboretum of Swarthmore College. July 22, 2015. https://www.scottarboretum.org/gardening-best-friends-allium-and-roses/.

"Hairy Vetch." The University of California, Davis. Sustainable Agricultural Research & Education Program. Accessed July 20, 2022. https://sarep.ucdavis.edu/covercrop/hairyvetch.

Hanson, Eric. "Apple Nutrition." Michigan State University. June 29, 2022. https://www.canr.msu.edu/uploads/files/Applenutrition-EricHanson.pdf.

Selmer, Jim. "Landscaping and Gardening around Walnuts and Other Juglone Producing Plants." Pennsylvania State University. Last modified October 22, 2007. https://extension.psu.edu/landscaping-and-gardening-around-walnuts-and-other-juglone-producing-plants.

Van Sambeek, J. W. "Site-Improving Intercrops for Black Walnut." USDA Forest Service. *Walnut Council Bulletin* 15, no. 1 (winter 1988): 2–6, 11. https://www.nrs.fs.usda.gov/pubs/jrnl/1988/nc_1988_vansambeek_001.pdf.

Over the Hedgerow:
Plant a Living Fence

~ Monica Crosson ~

When I say the word *hedgerow*, what comes to mind? For me, images of walking down a narrow country lane somewhere in the British Isles fill my imagination. I can just make out a hare as she peeks out from within her protective covering, and hawthorn and bramble blossoms quiver as bees help themselves to their sweet nectar. As a creative soul who tends to lose herself in the fantastical, traditional hedgerows transport me to a world where folktales are matter of fact and there is real danger of fairy retaliation if one partakes of the fruit of the bramble after October 31. And if you hear soft chanting from over the hedgerow, do not attempt to cross—for you might be swept away

by the Elder Mother, who weaves her magic with the herbs she knows so very well.

Hedgerows mimic the plants that grow naturally along the forest's edge and along country roads. In my region of the Pacific Northwest, natural hedges are made up of some classic hedge plants you may recognize, such as hawthorn, crab apple, wild cherry, and elderberry, as well as other native plants. Filbert, cascara, and vine maple along with Nootka rose, salmonberry, thimble berry, salal, and too many wildflower and fern species to name are also a part of woodland borders that separate the wild from what is tame.

When we purchased our property over twenty years ago, I liked how the hedge plants had grown over the remnants of fence posts that hinted to the property's former life as part of a large cattle farm. Instead of clearing them, we added cherry laurel and privet. And we lined emerald greens down our drive to add another layer of privacy. These "living fences" were created not only to keep noise levels down and work as a wind break and privacy screen, but also to act as home, byway, and food source to local wildlife. And to top it all off, we haven't had to replace one single part of it. In fact, it keeps getting better with time.

Hedge versus Hedgerow

Hedgerows are the country cousin of the formal hedge that is usually made up of one species, typically an arborvitae, and can be found trimmed to perfection around many a country estate. Hedgerows on the other hand, are a mixture of both evergreen and deciduous plantings and are typically made up of foundation plantings, such as small trees like hazel or hawthorn, supporting shrubs and bramble, and non-woody or flowering plants like yarrow or meadowsweet. Hedgerows were originally put into place to mark property lines and provide enclosures for livestock, and in many areas of Europe and North America, hedgerows still play a vital role in agricultural areas as a windbreak and as a natural fence. For many wildlife species, the intersecting hedgerows act as a corridor linking habitats, providing safety, food, and shelter in a world where wild spaces are diminishing.

The traditional hedgerow includes several layers of plantings and is at the minimum ten feet wide. Don't worry if you can't accommodate the space: you can easily add or drop layers of plantings to suit your property's dimensions.

Advantages and Disadvantages of a Living Fence

If you've been thinking about incorporating fencing into your landscape, you may want to think about a hedge or hedgerow. Here is a list of reasons why a living fence just makes sense.

Longevity: Once established, your living fence will last the lifetime of your plant species, which means your fence could last for centuries. One of the oldest known hedgerows in England is a section that is known as Judith's Hedge, located near Cambridgeshire, and is over 900 years old.

Cost: Living fences are typically less expensive than manufactured fences. And once your hedge or hedgerow is established, there are no maintenance fees for damaged or rotting boards or panels, paint, or stain.

Eco-Friendly: Instead of using our dwindling natural resources to enhance your property with a wood fence, a living fence will add to the environment by supporting ecological diversity, enriching the soil, decreasing wind erosion, and providing habitat, food, and fodder for wildlife.

Beauty: A living fence adds tranquility and beauty to your garden. The right plants can be adapted to suit any garden style. They can be pruned and controlled or left to grow naturally. They provide seasonal interest and may increase the value of your property.

Of course, with every advantage there is a disadvantage, so before deciding whether planting a living fence is for you, here are a few more things to consider:

Labor: Planting your living fence takes a bit of planning and, initially, will be labor intensive.

Time: Since hedges and hedgerows take time to become established, you need to be patient. They most likely won't start "filling in" until the third season.

Upkeep: Depending on the variety of trees and formality of your hedge, there may be pruning involved as part of its upkeep.

Let's Get Started

What is the intention of your living fence? This is the question that will help you decide what kind of plants you may want to incorporate. First, are you wanting to keep it to a single layer of hedge plants that can be trimmed to your liking? Species such as boxwood or the classic American arborvitae are perfect. Or maybe you're wanting a traditional hedgerow with multiple layers that benefits both you and your local wildlife. That's where the planning comes in.

If you're new to gardening, the first thing you need to do is familiarize yourself with your region's hardiness zone. Next, take a look at the area in which the living fence is being placed and note how many hours of sun the area receives. These two things will be the most important steps in helping you to determine which plants will grow best for you. Another thing to consider, if adding fruit trees, is whether they are self-fertile or if you will need more than one plant for pollination to occur.

Create a sketch of your property and add the length of your living fence. Mark out areas of full sun, partial sun/shade, and full shade and choose your plants accordingly. Add shapes to your map that represent small trees, shrubs, and flowering plants. The small trees are your foundation plantings and will be planted as your first layer, followed by supporting plants like shrubs, bramble, or vines. Then your last layer will include ferns, flowering plants, or ground cover.

The distance you space your plants apart really depends on both their final height and their natural width. But because we're planting small trees, the rule of thumb is to plant each tree approximately ten feet from another. If you have a fifty-foot length that you need to plant, you will need five trees. Shrubs should be spaced half of their mature width apart. Perennials, ferns, and ground cover can be tucked in and look nice planted in groups of three.

Planting Your Hedgerow

There are two ways to prepare your soil. You can till the entire area that you are planting and then follow with a heavy layer of compost; this is the fastest method. Or you can sheet mulch right over the top of your lawn. This approach is a little more time consuming and takes some planning, as it should be done several months before you plant, but ultimately, it is better for your soil, because you are building the soil up with nutrients rather than plowing it down.

To sheet mulch, lay cardboard over the entirety of your planting area, followed by several inches of straw, dried leaves, or wood chips. Follow this with several inches of compost. Give it four to six months before you begin planting.

The best time to plant your living fence is in the autumn or in early spring. You will need to start with your tallest foundation plants and work your way forward to the shortest plantings. Once you have planted your tallest trees or shrubs along the fence line, you want to place the second layer of shrubs slightly in front of and staggered between your first layer of trees. Follow this with any perennials, ferns, grasses, or ground cover.

Depending on the types of plants you have chosen, your hedgerow may take three to five years to fill in. Make sure to water your new hedgerow once a week or more during times of drought, during its first year. Adding a ground cover such as wild garlic, bugleweed, or trailing blackberry may help with weed suppression.

Living fences are as unique as the gardeners who grow them. Whether you need a privacy fence or want to add interest to your landscape, once established, your living fence will be a self-maintaining ecosystem that will be a benefit to you and your local wildlife for generations.

How to Plant a Tree or Shrub

1. Take off any protective packaging and gently untangle the root system.
2. Soak it in water for approximately three to six hours before planting.
3. Dig a hole that is at least double the size of the root spread. Break up the sides of the hole to accommodate growth.
4. Mix equal parts garden soil and good compost and partially fill in the hole.
5. Place the tree in the hole and fill soil in around the roots. Make sure the root collar (where the roots meet the base of the tree) is level with the ground. Pack the soil in well.
6. Build up the soil a little around the tree to form a water basin and give your tree a good watering.
7. Cover a three-foot-wide and two-inch-deep area around the base of your tree with mulch to hold in moisture.
8. Water every seven to ten days until well established.

Foundation Plants to Consider

Apple (**Malus domestica**): Great semi-dwarf or dwarf varieties include 'Cortland', 'Goldrush', and 'Arkansas Black'. Zones 3 to 8.

Cherry (**Prunus avium**): Try 'Stella', a semi-dwarf tree that is self-fertile and produces dark sweet fruit. Zones 5 to 9.

Dogwood (**Cornus *spp.***): Ranging from to small shrubs to trees, the beautiful dogwood thrives in dappled shade. Zones 2 to 9.

Elderberry (**Sambucus *spp.***): This common deciduous hedgerow shrub is both versatile and highly productive. It is also easy to grow if you're new to gardening. Zones 3 to 8.

Hawthorn (**Crataegus *spp.***): The quintessential hedgerow tree produces lovely white blossoms in the spring, turning to bright haws in the autumn—perfect for jams or jellies. Zones 5 to 9.

Peach (**Prunus persica**): Try the semi-dwarf variety 'El Dorado' for early summer peaches. Zones 5 to 9.

Plum (**Prunus domestica *subsp.* insititia**): Try 'Damson', a semi-dwarf, self-fertile heirloom that boasts dark-blue-skinned plums with yellow flesh. Zones 5 to 8.

Quince (**Cydonia oblonga**): A lovely small tree whose fruit is wonderful in jams, jellies, and wine. Zones 4 to 9.

Rowan Tree (**Sorbus *subg.* Sorbus**): A frost-hardy tree that is characterized by its compound leaves and bright red berries in late summer. Zones 3 to 6.

Support Plants to Consider

Blueberries (**Vaccinium *spp.***): A lovely member of the rhododendron family that offers tasty blueberries in the summer and bright red foliage in the fall. Zones 3 to 7.

Cow Parsley (**Anthriscus sylvestris**): Commonly seen growing along the forest's edge, this member of the carrot family has impressive umbrellas of small white blooms. Zones 7 to 10.

Honeysuckle (**Lonicera *spp.***): A beautiful vining addition to your hedgerow that will attract nectar-loving hummingbirds and butterflies. Zones 4 to 8.

Meadowsweet (**Spiraea alba**): An upright shrub with clusters of creamy flowers, perfect for areas that may retain moisture. Zones 3 to 8.

Yarrow (**Achillea millefolium**): With dome-shaped clusters of tiny flowers, this lovely plant in the aster family is a care-free bloom that self-sows easily. Zones 3 to 9.

Hedgerow Plants for Warmer Zones

Meyer Lemon (**Citrus ×meyeri**): The best of a lemon and mandarin orange. It will yield fruit in just two years after planting. Zones 8 to 11.

Natal plum (**Carissa macrocarpa**): A thorny, fast-growing variety that produces small fruit whose flavor is reminiscent of cranberries. Zones 9 to 11.

Pineapple guava (**Feijoa sellowiana**): Prefers filtered sunlight and is drought tolerate. A great addition to an edible landscape, as both the flowers and the fruit can be enjoyed. Zones 8 to 11.

Pittosporum (**Pittosporum tobira**): Dwarf evergreen with fragrant flowers, this variety is perfect as a loosely mounded foundation plant. Zones 8 to 11.

Pomegranate (**Punica granatum**): Fast growing, drought tolerant, and produces wonderful fruit. Zones 8 to 10.

Satsuma Mandarin (**Citrus reticulata,** *syn.* **C. unshiu**): A cold-hardy citrus that provides tasty fruit in early winter. Zones 8 to 11.

Valencia Orange (**Citrus ×sinensis**): Bursting with flavor, this popular orange prefers warm days and cool nights for optimum flavor. Zones 8 to 11.

Quick-Growing Shrubs

Cherry Laurel (**Prunus laurocerasus**): This glossy-leaved evergreen shrub is sometimes called English laurel. It has creamy white flowers that smell amazing in late spring. It likes a temperate climate. Zones 6 to 8.

Diablo Ninebark (**Physocarpus opulifolius**): If you want to add something dark and mysterious to your hedge plantings, try this shrub with deep purple-black leaves that turn a brilliant red in the autumn. Zones 2 to 8.

Forsythia (**Forsythia**): The old-fashioned favorite that heralds spring. With bright yellow blooms, this deciduous shrub will add cheeriness to your hedgerow. Zones 5 to 8.

Mock Orange (**Philadelphus coronarius**): A deciduous shrub known for blossoms that release a wonderfully citrus scent. Zones 4 to 8.

Red Twig Dogwood (**Cornus sericea**): This tree is not only quick growing but also a standout in a winter landscape, as it boasts beautiful red bark. Zones 2 to 7.

Resource

For more information on hedgerows, check out CPRE, a non-profit focused on protecting the English countrysides, at https://www.cpre.org.uk/discover/hedgerows-through-the-seasons/.

Mushroom Foraging
for Beginners

৯ Lupa ৯

Mushroom hunting has been part of the human experience for thousands of years—and possibly millions, if you consider our hominin ancestors were also curious and resourceful omnivores likely to have sampled edible fungi as well. Today there are still communities around the world for whom wild mushrooms are an essential part of their diet, and even many people who have access to grocery stores will forage recreationally. The COVID-19 pandemic saw a surge of interest in foraging classes, both for food security and something to do during shutdowns.

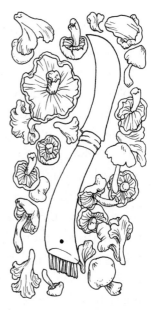

Most mushrooms are harvested for culinary use; however, some do have medicinal qualities, and others may be utilized for spiritual purposes. Some mushrooms, especially in autumn, make excellent natural decorations, though they are prone to decaying rather quickly.

So there are plenty of good reasons to go mushroom hunting! Consider this an introductory guide to get you started.

This article is only for mushrooms for culinary or medicinal use; I have zero experience with and therefore zero authority on hallucinogenic mushrooms, many of which are prohibited in multiple locations, and I also do not have sufficient experience to write about medicinal mushrooms. You are 100 percent responsible for whatever you ingest, including verifying the exact species of mushroom you have in your possession and whether it is safe for human consumption. Always check multiple sources, and err on the side of caution if you have any doubts.

What Is a Mushroom?

Let's clear up a common misconception: mushrooms are not plants, though they are used in similar ways to herbs and vegetables. They are fungi, which means they belong to an entirely different kingdom than plants. In fact, we animals are more closely related to fungi than the fungi are to plants, so much so that when pharmaceutical companies develop new antifungal medications, they have to be sure that our cells don't metabolize them the same way that the fungal cells do.

More specifically, a mushroom is the temporary reproductive structure of a fungus. What you see pop up after a good rain is not the main body of the fungus. Instead, the mushroom is grown by the **mycelium**. This mycelium is made of many tiny filaments called **hyphae**, which grow throughout whatever substrate that particular fungus likes, whether soil, rotting wood, manure, or that moldy block of cheese in the back of your fridge.

A fungus needs to be sufficiently hydrated before it can produce mushrooms. It needs water to move around the nutrients needed to grow these reproductive structures, which is why you so often see mushrooms after rain. Mushroom hunters taken note: if there's been a drought, it may take longer for mushrooms to appear after the rain returns since the fungus may need more hydration.

Once the mushroom appears (this is called **fruiting**), it spreads spores on the wind, which, if they fall on a suitable substrate, will become new fungal colonies. The spores usually fall out of specialized structures like gills or pores on the underside of the mushroom's cap, though some species have even more unusual spore-spreading structures. Once the spores have been disseminated, the mushroom will decay; in most species you'll see, the mushrooms only last a few days to a few weeks at best.

Tools for Mushroom Hunting

Mushroom hunting doesn't require a lot of specialized equipment. You'll want to take a field guide or two with you; these are books that have pictures and other information about various mushrooms and how to identify them. I highly recommend getting field guides specific to your region, as they will have more species local to you when compared to a more general guide that tries to cover, say, all of North America. You may only be able to carry one or two with you out in the field, but my philosophy is that the more books and resources I have to verify my identifications once I'm back home, the better.

You also need something to carry your mushrooms home in. The very best thing is a mesh bag, like a produce bag or laundry bag. You want the holes big enough to see, but not so big that the mushrooms fall out. As you're carrying them down the trail, you'll be scattering spores wherever you go, which makes it more likely that you may find more mushrooms in future years.

You might find a magnifying glass helpful for looking at small structures on mushrooms like gills, especially if your eyes (like mine) aren't as good as they used to be. Make sure you dress for the weather and terrain and have both a GPS unit and a map and compass if you're going to be going off-trail, especially in more remote areas.

Gloves are useful if you're going to be digging around in the underbrush anywhere there may be thorns, poison ivy, angry insects, and the like. Contrary to popular belief, you will not be harmed if you handle a poisonous mushroom with your bare hands. There are even experienced mushroom hunters who will break a piece off of an unidentified mushroom, chew it up, and spit it out to use its flavor to help with identification (novices should *not* attempt this). Unless you are one of those rare people with a mushroom allergy that's severe enough to cause dermatological reactions, the only way a poisonous mushroom can harm you is if you eat it and digest it fully.

Where to Find Mushrooms

My approach to mushroom hunting is to look for them everywhere! Whether I am in the middle of a city or out in the woods and fields, I am always watching for mushrooms around me. There's one particular species of edible morel, *Morchella*

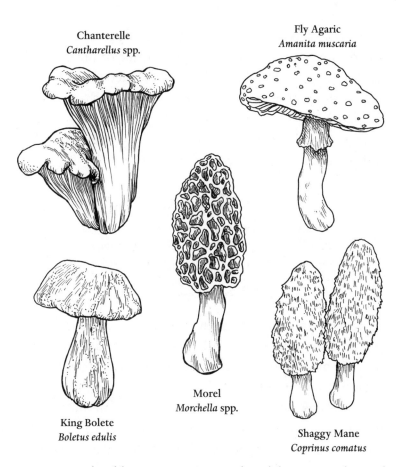

Chanterelle
Cantharellus spp.

Fly Agaric
Amanita muscaria

Morel
Morchella spp.

King Bolete
Boletus edulis

Shaggy Mane
Coprinus comatus

importuna, that likes to grow in wood mulch commonly used in urban landscaping, and my very first morels were picked behind an apartment complex in Portland. Most of the time, though, you'll need to go to an area that's a little more open, like a large park, hiking trail, or other natural area.

If you're mushroom hunting on public land, make sure that it's legal to do so. For example, it is against federal law to take anything, mushrooms or otherwise, from any National Wildlife Refuge in the United States. However, many State and

National Forests allow foraging, often with a permit and a limit on how much you can take in a given period of time. Always get permission before foraging on private land, and don't tell others what you've found there unless you have the landowner's permission so that they don't end up with a bunch of trespassers. Also take care to avoid foraging along public roadsides, which may be affected by runoff and pesticides.

A fairy ring of mushrooms is formed as nutrients at the center are depleted and the mycelium underground grows outward in a circle looking for more nutrients!

Many edible mushrooms have **mycorrhizal** relationships with certain plants, particularly trees. *Myco* means "fungus," and *rhizo* means "root," and this describes the way that the mycelium of certain fungi will grow around the roots of their partner plants. As the fungus decomposes matter in the soil and frees up nutrients, it feeds some of those nutrients to the plant. And as the plant photosynthesizes sunlight into sugars, it shares some with the fungus. Because certain fungi prefer certain plants, looking for those plants can help you locate mushrooms if it's their fruiting season. Many field guides will mention if a particular fungus species is mycorrhizal with a plant.

I wish I could tell you, "Well, just go to any place with a hemlock tree during fall and you'll automatically find chanterelles." Unfortunately, it's not that easy. Not every fungus will produce mushrooms each year. And even if a place seems perfect for a given species of fungus, it simply may not grow there at all. This is why so many people spend entire days stomping around the woods during their local mushroom hunting seasons, hoping to stumble across something worth taking home.

If you've been lucky enough to find edible mushrooms somewhere, make sure you take note of when you found them so you know to go back there next year. It's also helpful to visit throughout the year, as some species, like oyster mushrooms, may have more than one fruiting season. Many foragers tend to be secretive about where they've found mushrooms before, especially high-demand species like morels and chanterelles. This is because there are commercial mushroom hunters out there who won't hesitate to completely clean out an area of every single edible mushroom, year after year, leaving nothing for anyone else to find. So it's up to you whether you want to share the location with someone else or not.

Harvesting Mushrooms

Please don't take more than 25 percent of a given mushroom in an area. Yes, if you find three chanterelles all alone, take them. But if you find an entire stream valley full of chanterelles, don't clean it out. Leave some for other foragers, and leave some for wildlife and the ecosystem.

There's a big debate about whether you should pick mushrooms by hand or cut them with a knife. After doing a fair amount of reading up, I've found that there really isn't any major difference. Mushrooms, again, are not plants, and they don't have roots to be pulled up. If you pick the whole mushroom, the mycelium can still produce more of them. And often when a mushroom is cut, the portion left behind simply decays away; it can also leave the fungus vulnerable to disease. The Oregon *Cantharellus* Study Project showed a slight increase in mushroom growth in patches that were consistently picked rather than cut, but it really wasn't enough to make a major difference. You probably don't need a tailor-made mushroom knife, but it won't hurt if you decide you want one anyway.

Mushroom Identification

If at all possible, do your identification in the field; that way you don't end up wasting time picking a bunch of inedible mushrooms, and you can leave them there to continue their life cycle. Please don't deliberately destroy poisonous or otherwise inedible mushrooms; these fungi still have very important ecological roles to play that are more important than our appetites.

The first thing you want to do is take a really good look at each species of mushroom you've found. Here are some of the things to look for:

Color: This includes obvious colors like the top of the cap and also smaller details like the colors on the stipe (stem), gills, and so on.

Shape: Look at both the overall shape (this mushroom looks like an open umbrella) and individual details (the underside of the cap has little spines instead of gills).

Size: Compare the sizes of all the mushrooms of one species you've found, and compare that to the average size of the suspected species listed in field guides and other resources.

Hollow or Solid: When you cut the mushroom in half, notice if part or all of it is hollow, or whether it is solid all the way through.

Spore Print: Each mushroom species has its own color of spores; you won't find multicolored spores in one mushroom! To take a spore print, remove the entire stipe so all you have is the cap. Put the cap gills or pores side down on a white sheet of paper and place them in a cool, dry place. Put a mixing bowl over the mushroom to prevent drafts from blowing the spores around. Leave it for twenty-four to forty-eight hours, then carefully lift the bowl and mushroom cap, and you should have a nice spore print that clearly shows the color. If you want to preserve it, carefully spray it with acrylic paint sealer or hair spray, and once dry the spores will be held in place.

Arrangement: Note whether the mushrooms are growing as isolated individuals or in clusters.

Substrate: Many mushrooms prefer only one substrate; common substrates include soil, rotting wood, or manure. Pay close attention to what each mushroom you pick is growing on. If a mushroom is growing very close to a log or stump, dig around its base to be sure it isn't growing on part of the wood under the soil.

Location: When researching, notice whether your sources say the species you think you may have found is actually found in your area or not; if it isn't, you may need to see if there's a similar mushroom that is.

Season: Similarly, pay attention in your research to whether the mushroom you think you found normally fruits this time of year or not.

Often the difference between two similar species of mushroom may come down to small details; species A and B may look similar, but species A bruises blue when damaged and species B doesn't. Or species A may be commonly found in your area according to your research, but species B isn't. If species A usually fruits right now but species B almost always fruits in the other half of the year, you probably don't have species B (though exceptions do happen!).

Identification Tools

You have a lot of information gathered; now you need to use it to narrow down what you have. Field guides, as I mentioned previously, are an excellent resource, and the more you have access to the better. I've found the best ones have clear, full-color photos, as well as thorough descriptions of the physical characteristics, typical habitat, and other identifying markers of each species. If a given mushroom has a look-alike, especially a poisonous one, the book will often mention how to tell the difference or at least mention the similarities. Your local library or bookstore should have some recommendations.

Some field guides also have a **dichotomous key**. This is basically a series of questions about different traits of the mushroom, such as color, size, shape, and so on. Some of them can be very technical and may be difficult for laypeople to use. This is because they aren't limited to only edible mushrooms, and often the difference between two similar species may literally come down to microscopic features. With practice (and a lot of vocabulary additions), a layperson can learn to use these, but it takes time and patience.

There are also lots of foraging and other websites dedicated to mushrooms. Those run by federal and state natural resources entities are often quite solid, as they are run by biologists and other naturalists in their employ. Mycology clubs and similar organizations also often have good, referenced websites. I find that if I don't have a particular website to go to, I'll use a search engine and search for, say, "Oregon mushroom species" and then peruse the websites I find for information.

I also really like talking to other foragers, both in person and online. If you have a local mycology club, it can be a really useful resource to connect you with other people, and help you learn more about local mushrooms. If there's no one local, there are plenty of groups on sites like Facebook and Reddit. These have the advantage of allowing you to post photos as well as ask questions. And I also find it very valuable to scroll through and see what other people have posted pictures and questions about, as it's often a great way to learn about things I'd never heard of. Other foragers are often happy to share titles of field guides and other resources they really like too.

Let's talk a moment about phone apps. There's an increasing number of apps that are designed to help you identify a mushroom simply by taking a photo of it. These vary in quality and price. All of them rely on algorithms that draw from a database of photos, locations, and seasonal data to help find mushrooms that look like the one you just took a picture of, in the same area, and at the same time of year. Unfortunately, if your photo isn't clear or if the mushroom is rather nondescript, these algorithms may not find a suitable match. I am a big advocate of the app iNaturalist. It's free, it works on all smartphones, and in addition to the initial identification through algorithms, it also allows other iNaturalist users to look at your observations and suggest identifications.

Always use multiple sources when trying to identify a mushroom! Some people prefer to only pick one new-to-them mushroom species at a time to make identification simpler. Also, I strongly recommend that even if you find a mushroom that you've read is edible, but you haven't eaten it yourself, triple-check through all those resources just to be sure new information hasn't come to pass or that you aren't misremembering.

Eating Mushrooms

Now, if you're just looking for seasonal decorations, you can plunk those mushrooms on your table for a few days and then put any unused portions back outside. But most people looking for mushrooms are interested in edible ones.

I want to reiterate that you need to be absolutely, 100 percent sure that whatever mushroom you are planning to eat is in fact the species you think it is and that that species is in fact edible by humans. Just because you saw a slug or squirrel eating a mushroom doesn't mean it's safe for us. Also, even some commonly edible mushrooms can give individual people problems if their bodies just don't tolerate them. And some edible mushrooms, like *Coprinopsis* species, react badly with alcohol, so don't drink or cook them with any spirits of any sort.

If you are sure beyond any doubt of what you have and its edibility, then cut up a small amount of the mushroom—just a few small bites at most—and cook it up. I like to do a simple sauté in butter or olive oil, as this helps preserve the flavor of the mushroom and doesn't take much prep work. Then I eat this small amount and wait for any signs of gastrointestinal distress. Do not cut up every single mushroom you have; keep at least one mushroom of each species you eat intact so that if you need medical help, it will be easier for professionals to identify what you ate.

Usually symptoms will show up within the first twelve hours and often include things like painful abdominal cramps, vomiting, and diarrhea. The advantage of only eating a small amount at first is that the reaction will be proportionately smaller, compared to eating an entire plateful. If you are experiencing severe symptoms, like dizziness and other neurological issues, bleeding from any orifices, or significant vomiting, get medical care immediately. If you are feeling a little off but not horrible, contact your doctor, or call Poison Control (in the US, 1-800-222-1222, or visit poison.org). When in doubt, err on the side of caution.

If you get through a couple of days with no symptoms, then you're probably okay to go ahead and eat more of that mushroom. Make sure every person who tries the mushroom for the first time just has a small amount, even if you can eat pounds of it with no problem. And if a species you've eaten before suddenly starts giving you symptoms, stop eating it and consult your doctor.

Thankfully, most poisonous mushrooms will just cause some really unpleasant gastrointestinal issues. Some, like death cap (*Amanita phalloides*) and *Pholiotina rugosa,* syn. *Conocybe filaris*, can do severe damage to your liver, kidneys, or other internal organs. Make sure you familiarize yourself thoroughly with the poisonous mushrooms found in your area; that way you'll be more likely to recognize them out in the field before you even have a chance to pick them.

Done with care, mushroom hunting can be an exciting and enjoyable excuse to go out into nature, as well as a source of good food. If I can help you with any book recommendations or other resources, feel free to email me at lupa.greenwolf@ gmail.com.

Resource

Norvell, Lorelai, and Jugy Roger. "The Oregon *Cantharellus* Study
Project: The 'Pacific Golden Chanterelle'—Preliminary Observations and 1986–1997 Productivity Data." *Inoculum* 49, 2 (1998):
n.p. https://www.researchgate.net/publication/255719094_The
_Oregon_Cantharellus_Study_Project_Pacific_Golden
_Chanterelle_preliminary_observations_and_productivity
_data_1986-1997.

Cultivating a Hobbit Garden

≫ Natalie Zaman ≪

Many people think that J. R. R. Tolkien was a wizard, but he saw himself quite differently. He wrote in a letter, "I am, in fact a Hobbit (in all but size). I like gardens, trees, and unmechanized farmlands; I smoke a pipe, and like good plain food (unrefrigerated) . . . I am fond of mushrooms (out of a field)."[1] Like his creation Bilbo Baggins, he was also fond of flowers, if his writing is to be believed. Middle Earth is populated by a rich flora-filled landscape. My favorite is that which can be found in the Shire. Hobbits are very much country dwellers, fond of woodland copses and well-tilled fields. Even "townie" hobbits like Bilbo Baggins take pride in their gardens. For hobbits, plants

are practical and pretty, being cultivated for food (obviously, potatoes being a particular favorite), fun (vineyards for wine and fields for pipeweed), physic (herbal remedies), and floral beauty.

Plot and plant a hobbit garden to honor the stories (if you're a fan) and enjoy the lovely leaves, flowers, vegetables, and fruits it produces—woolly toes not required!

The Shire

The Shire is divided into four sections or "farthings." Plants of all kinds are found throughout the Shire, but each farthing has its own particular specialty:

Westfarthing

The Westfarthing, where Bilbo lives in Hobbiton, is more village than farm, but here too there is a great love of plant life, particularly flowers. In *The Hobbit*, Bilbo remarks on the floral quality of Gandalf's fireworks, "Not the man that used to make such particularly excellent fireworks! I remember those! Old Took used to have them on Midsummer's Eve. Splendid! They used to go up like great lilies and snapdragons and laburnums of fire and hang in the twilight all evening!"[2]

Northfarthing

Farm fields populate the Northfarthing. In *The Fellowship of the Ring*, Gaffer Gamgee speaks to Sam about where he should focus his energies: "Elves and dragons? Cabbages and potatoes are better for me and you."[3]

Eastfarthing

The Eastfarthing is where, apparently, the best mushrooms can be found. Farmer Maggot, on meeting Frodo, Sam, Merry, and Pippin traveling over his fields in *The Fellowship of the Ring*, comments, "'And you, Mr. Baggins—though I daresay you still like mushrooms.' He laughed. 'Ah yes, I recognized the name. I recollect the time when young Frodo Baggins was one of the worst young rascals of Buckland.'"[4]

Southfarthing

Finally, the Southfarthing is famed for its vineyards and fields of pipeweed. One of the presents Bilbo leaves behind after he departs from his birthday party in *The Fellowship of the Ring* is labeled, "Old Rory Brandybuck, in return for much hospitality, got a dozen bottle of Old Winyards: a strong red wine from the Southfarthing and now quite mature, as it had been laid down by Bilbo's father."[5]

Lay of the Land

Looking at maps of the Shire drawn by J. R. R. Tolkien, you'll see that it is boxy in shape. For the purposes of this work and for ease of calculations, I've laid our Hobbit Garden out in a square, but this can be adapted to your space. The suggestions that follow are for planting directly into the ground and assume that you have a six-foot-by-six-foot space with which to work. This plan can be downsized if you don't have this much ground for planting (or any at all). All the suggested plants can be grown in pots; simply arrange them in the same order as the in-ground garden.

Plot out a patch of ground approximately six feet by six feet in size. This area will accommodate a modest crop of each of the suggested plants. When planning where to place your garden, situate it so that the Eastfarthing is in the shadiest available area, as this is where you will cultivate mushrooms. They like a good bit of shade.

Do a preliminary prep of the soil: turn it, weed, remove any debris, and add a neutral fertilizer of your choice before marking out the square plot with a border. I usually manage to forage a hodgepodge of stray bricks and stones to use for this purpose.

Next, plot out the beds. Each bed will represent one of the four farthings. Starting at the northwest corner of the plot lay your border through the middle of the square across to the southeast corner. Do the same from the northeast corner to the southwest corner. Your garden should look like a square with an X through it from corner to corner, and you should have four beds. Now you're almost ready to begin planting—but before you dig in . . .

- Note that planting will be done at different times of the year. Plot and prepare the ground for your hobbit garden in the autumn and then build as the year progresses. Weed and turn the soil as necessary during this time. Covering plant beds with cardboard weighed down with bricks or stones keeps weeds at bay.

- Cabbages, grapes, and lilies like well-drained soil. Mushrooms and lobelia love moist soil. This has been taken into account with placement—but just be aware when you are watering which plants like to be wet (none needs to be standing in water!).

- I've planned out this garden based on my location, the northeast coast of the United States. You may need to adjust the plan depending on your growing zone. Refer to the USDA Plant Hardiness Zone Map on pages 217 and 218 to assist in plotting out this or any garden for the best results!

Now, let's create a bit of the Shire in our back gardens!

The Westfarthing

Bilbo's luxurious hobbit hole is located in the village of Hobbiton. Though Bilbo was not a farmer, Bag End did have a "bit of garden" in which flowers featured heavily.[6] In the Westfarthing of our hobbit garden, we'll plant one of his favorite flowers, lilies, and one that might make him cringe a bit—but only because of the name: lobelia. It is noteworthy that many female hobbit names are flower names; Frodo points this out to Sam in *The Return of the King* when Sam is thinking of what to name his newborn daughter.[7]

Of the thousands of varieties of lilies available, I chose the Asiatic lily for our hobbit garden as it's hardy, easy to grow, and colorful, like our hobbits: "Hobbits dress in bright colors (chiefly green and yellow)."[8] Our lilies will live in the narrower, back half of the Westfarthing. Install your lily bulbs in the late fall; being nestled in the cold winter soil will make for big blooms in the spring. Plant the bulbs at a depth approximately three times the size of the bulb. How big are your bulbs? Space them out about three times the size of their diameters. You should be able to plant five to six bulbs in this garden section. Use a bowling pin formation: one bulb in the top corner of the bed, a row of two beneath that, and then, if space allows, a third row of three bulbs (see the garden plan on page 278 for guidance). Asiatic lilies typically bloom in May and June and should continue to bloom for about a month after the first flowers show their faces.

Bilbo's cousins Otho and Lobelia Sackville-Baggins were famously deprived of inheriting Bag End when Bilbo returned alive from his adventure with the dwarves, and they proceeded to be a thorn in his side for decades. Lobelia does manage to plant herself at Bag End for a time, so we can safely place lobelia in the Westfarthing in the company of our lovely lilies.

Lobelia is a low-growing ground cover, so we'll keep her to the broader, front portion of the Westfarthing bed. She can be installed as an established plant or by seed. Seeds planted once warm weather is well established should pop up in a couple of weeks and grow quickly thereafter. Lobelia loves the sun but will grow in the shade as well. She'll also serve a second purpose in providing protective cover for the lilies as they grow. Your lilies should return every year, but your lobelia will only return if it's a perennial (there are annual lobelia plants)—check with your nursery or your seed supplier to determine which category your lobelia falls under.

The Northfarthing

Reflecting the well-tilled fields of the Northfarthing of the Shire, we'll plant a favorite hobbit vegetable: the cabbage. The triangular bed should accommodate about six cabbages, arranged in a bowling pin format (see page 278).

Cabbages require full sun and well-drained neutral soil (not acidic). There are several varieties from which to choose; for the hobbit garden, I've gone with traditional head cabbage. Plant your seeds or seedlings in the spring, about twelve inches apart in three rows: three across the broadest part of the bed, then two, and then one in the corner near the center of the plot. The plants can be installed closer together; just keep in mind that the smaller the distance between the beds, the smaller your cabbage heads will be. It will take about two months for your plants to grow to maturity. Cabbages are also generous plants—when harvesting, cut off the head, leaving as many outer leaves intact as possible, and your plant will start making a new baby cabbage!

The cabbage is a versatile vegetable that can be eaten cold (coleslaw) and hot (sauerkraut), but think about trying a distinctly British dish, bubble and squeak, that was probably enjoyed by hobbits and contained another favorite ingredient—potatoes! Originally, I was going to suggest growing cabbages and potatoes together, but as potatoes require more acidic soil than cabbages, they probably would not have worked in the same bed. Bubble and squeak is made by combining chopped cabbage and crushed boiled potatoes, then frying it in a pan with lard. Clarissa Dickson Wright of *Two Fat Ladies* said that if you're not going to use lard for this recipe, don't bother, as it's not proper bubble and squeak.[9] Keep turning sections of the mixture in the pan until a lovely brown crust forms on both sides. There are two potential roots to the name "bubble and squeak": either it's the sound that the cabbage and potatoes make while cooking in the pan or . . . it's the sound you make after you've eaten some!

The Eastfarthing

When Frodo, Sam, Merry, and Pippin set out to move Frodo from Hobbiton to Buckleberry, they cross the lands of Farmer Maggot in the Eastfarthing. Frodo was no stranger to the Maggot farm, having snuck in as a hobbit boy to steal mushrooms—mushrooms being a minor obsession with hobbits.

Tolkien (who, as seen previously, loved mushrooms out of a field) never specified the type of mushrooms the hobbits were eating or how Farmer Maggot grew them, but the king oyster mushroom can be grown in gardens outdoors. Try cultivating a batch in the Eastfarthing garden bed. Growing mushrooms is a bit more complicated than "regular" planting but not difficult.

You will need:

Some extra border material. You will make a mini border within the main bed to help retain moisture.

King oyster mushroom spawn

Substrate such as straw and wood chips. This layer will nourish the mushrooms as they grow.

Before you begin, remember that this area of the garden must be in as little direct sunlight as possible; it can even be under a tree. First, dig a mini-bed inside the larger Eastfarthing bed. This will be the same triangular shape but about five to six inches in. This bed should be about six inches in depth. Save the soil you removed and outline the mini bed with your border material.

Next, mix your spawn with the substrate. According to mushroom grower Tony Shields at FreshCap, straw and wood chips make an excellent substrate for king oyster mushrooms. Shields suggests that "spawn should be added at 5–10% to the substrate. (Spawn weight to wet weight substrate)."[10] Combine the spawn and the substrate evenly, then distribute it evenly in the mini bed. Finally, top the mixture lightly with the reserved soil. This will act as a protective layer for your mushrooms and help keep the spawn moist.

Observe your mushrooms as they fruit. The size and appearance of your mushrooms will vary depending on the environment. Shields notes that while king oyster mushrooms can be grown indoors and out, those grown indoors have a significantly different appearance than those grown outside.[11]

Important: know what you've planted and know what king oyster mushrooms look like! Turn to page 46 for identification tips, and consult a proper mushroom identification guidebook. If mushrooms that are not what you planted crop up (it happens), do *not* consume!

The Southfarthing

The Southfarthing is famous for its wine and pipeweed (making it the fun farthing?). Grapes are hardy plants and can grow in a variety of regions. In wine making vineyards, grapevines are planted in rows and trained on horizontal wires, which allow the fruit to imbibe air and moisture. These, the soil, the container in which the wine is aged, and the length of time it is aged determine the wine's flavor.

What kind of grapes should you plant to get the most authentic taste of Old Winyards? This topic is discussed on the *Tolkien Geek* blog: The anonymous writer suggests that the idea that such a wine could be produced in the temperate Shire is unlikely. Because Old Winyards is described as "a 'strong red wine' that takes many years to mature . . . this indicates that the yield from Old Winyards is a wine that is full-bodied and high in tannin. . . . The grapes in question would have to be thick-skinned and require a long, hot growing season. Such conditions only really exist well between the 30th and 50th parallels in either hemisphere."[12] In other words, a warm climate—but this is, after all, fiction. According to the Grape Community of Practice, Cabernet Sauvignon grapes are high in tannins and hardy and easy to grow—so worth a try in replicating Bilbo's famous wine.[13]

Install two sturdy four-foot stakes vertically down the center of the Southfarthing bed. Run two wires or lengths of strong string from one stake to the other, the first about six inches from the top and the second about twelve inches from the first wire. These will be supports for the vines once they grow. Install a single grape plant at the center point between the two stakes. The plant will be the central vine from which branches will grow—you will train these to grow along the wires and string.

I installed my grape plants in the spring after the last hard frost. As they grow, select shoots and start training them along the string or wires. Trim back any shoots that are excessive of the ones you are training. One plant might produce up to two bottles of wine: it takes about two and a half pounds of grapes to make a single bottle of wine. Ideally, a single grape plant produces seven pounds of fruit a season. However, you might be waiting a bit. It can take up to three years for a vine to produce fruit, and then figure you have to process and age the wine . . . so at least a good five years before you get a taste of the Southfarthing!

Endnotes

1. J. R. R. Tolkien, *The Letters of J.R.R. Tolkien,* ed. Humphrey Carpenter (New York: Houghton Mifflin Harcourt, 2000), 288.

2. J. R. R. Tolkien, *The Hobbit,* rev. ed. (New York: Ballantine, 1982), 19.

3. J. R. R. Tolkien, *The Fellowship of the Ring* (New York: Ballantine, 1994), 24.

4. Tolkien, *Fellowship*, 105.

5. Tolkien, *Hobbit*, 105.

6. Tolkien, *Fellowship*, 76–77.

7. J. R. R. Tolkien, *The Return of the King* (New York: William Morrow, 2004), 1026.

8. Tolkien, *Hobbit*, 16.

9. Jennifer Paterson and Clarissa Dickson Wright, *Two Fat Ladies: Gastronomic Adventures (with Motorbike and Sidecar)* (London: Ebury Publishing, 1998), 97.

10. Tony Shields, "Growing Mushrooms in the Garden: The King Oyster," FreshCap, accessed July 18, 2022, https://learn.freshcap .com/growing/growing-mushrooms-in-the-garden-the-king -oyster/.

11. Tony Shields, "Growing Mushrooms in the Garden."

12. "FOTR: Bk1, Ch1," *Tolkien Geek* (blog), September 3, 2005, http:// tolkiengeek.blogspot.com/2005/09/fotr-bk-1-ch-1.html.

13. "Growing Cabernet Sauvignon Wine Grapes," Grape Community of Practice, June 20, 2019, https://grapes.extension.org /growing-cabernet-sauvignon-wine-grapes/.

More Information, Recipes, and Reading!

Boeckmann, Catherine. "Growing Cabbages from Sewing to Harvest." *Old Farmer's Almanac*, May 15, 2020. https://www.almanac .com/video/how-grow-cabbages-planting-harvest.

"Four Farthings." Encyclopedia of Arda. Last modified December 6, 2010. https://www.glyphweb.com/arda/f/fourfarthings.php.

"FOTR: Bk1, Ch1." *Tolkien Geek* (blog), September 3, 2005. http:// tolkiengeek.blogspot.com/2005/09/fotr-bk-1-ch-1.html.

Gerling, Chris. "Conversion Factors: From Vinyard to Bottle." *Appellation Cornell Newsletter* 8 (2011). https://grapesandwine.cals .cornell.edu/newsletters/appellation-cornell/2011-newsletters /issue-8/conversion-factors-vineyard-bottle.

"Growing Cabernet Sauvignon Wine Grapes." Grape Community of Practice. June 20, 2019. https://grapes.extension.org/growing -cabernet-sauvignon-wine-grapes/.

"Lilies." *Old Farmer's Almanac*. Accessed July 20, 2022. https://www .almanac.com/plant/lilies.

Paterson, Jennifer, and Clarissa Dickson Wright. *Two Fat Ladies: Gastronomic Adventures (with Motorbike and Sidecar)*. London: Ebury Publishing, 1998.

Shields, Tony. "Growing Mushrooms in the Garden: The King Oyster." FreshCap. Accessed July 18, 2022. https://learn.freshcap.com/growing/growing-mushrooms-in-the-garden-the-king-oyster/.

Tolkien, J. R. R. *The Fellowship of the Ring.* New York: Ballantine, 1994.

———. *The Hobbit.* Rev. ed. New York: Ballantine, 1982.

———. *The Letters of J.R.R. Tolkien.* Edited by Humphrey Carpenter. New York: Houghton Mifflin Harcourt, 2000.

———. *The Return of the King.* New York: William Morrow, 2004.

Bucket Garden Dos and Don'ts

⤞ Diana Rajchel ⤝

As I write this, sixteen buckets sit in my backyard, filled with potting soil and good intentions. They are more aesthetically pleasing than some bucket gardens because I bought stands for them. Even so, they lack the prettiness of ceramic containers or even utilitarian black greenhouse pots. Yet what I get from them—high-yield vegetables and herbs and lower-effort gardening—makes up for the absence of pretty. They are easy to plant, easy to move, and forgiving when you must plant later in the season than you like.

Even with all this convenience, I am experiencing the troubles you can still have with any garden. My homemade insect soap appears to be hailed by certain bugs as a vinaigrette to their broccoli salad, and the kohlrabi in the next bucket appears to be a favored palate cleanser. Fortunately, the insect mafia ignores the rest of my plants. If one of them bites into the rue, it's a self-correcting problem, and it seems like squash, dill, and beans appeal solely to a bipedal audience. My Michigan home saw a late frost break, meaning I had to plant later than I would have liked. That means that the plants might still be at peak harvest when the first frost visits in the fall—just in case, I may need to design an indoor setup with my buckets since I don't have any container plant shelters ready at my new home just yet.

A new issue? I see urbanized deer can hop the neighbor's fence and may make short work of my lettuce if I don't put netting over the leaves.

In the rush of planting, I also forgot to put burlap with seed holes poked in it over the top of the soil. Because of my absentmindedness, I must weed my bucket garden far more often than I have in past years.

Next year I plan to buy a large roll of burlap, wrap it around each bucket, and tie it with twine, so I can have a touch of rustic loveliness to offset the utilitarian look.

What I just described with bucket gardening is, as experienced gardeners know, minor. Aside from persnickety plants—shallots demand coaxing to grow anywhere—bucket gardening removes the hardest labor of gardening and replaces it with almost houseplant convenience. While you can spend hours on your buckets if you wish, once you get them started, they only call for a little work every day, and you can reap the benefits.

For those unfamiliar, a bucket garden is what it sounds like: a garden made from plants you grow in buckets. It requires the same things you may need for container gardening: potting soil, drainage holes, and perhaps a little pea gravel at the bottom to improve drainage and water retention. It has the same advantages as any other container garden: it's portable, and you can have one even in a rental home that disallows digging up a yard. If the plant doesn't get enough light or needs shade, you can move the bucket where it needs to go.

You can find bucket planter plans free or for low cost online if you want to build your own.

The greatest boon of bucket gardening is that you can grow medium to large crops in them, a much higher yield than most people get with traditional garden pots. The average five-gallon bucket has enough depth for even a tap root to reach the nourishment it needs and ample room for a miniature crop to spread. The buckets are light enough that you don't need to worry about your knees and back while weeding. Except for ones that have held certain plants, you need not replace the soil in them each year. Just change the plant in that bucket, add new fertilizer or plant food, and continue to enjoy the lower-effort micro-agriculture experience.

I've used my bucket garden to grow food since I bought my first bucket garden planter, built by a bored carpenter during the first pandemic lockdown. Since then, it has continued to be a staple of my garden plans, and its portability and relative affordability have come in handy when relocating. Even though I now have enough land for a traditional garden, I start with my containers and expand from there. The buckets maximize my land use without taking away from other places I can grow.

As someone who works with plants closely, I especially like that bucket gardening gives me a hands-on tutorial on a given plant. I can more easily discern what a plant looks like from sprout to seed, become far more intimate with its life cycle and phases, and bring that knowledge to raising it in the future. I am still learning quite a bit from each of my bucket plants.

While bucket gardening is container gardening by any other name, the subtle differences matter, especially in urban farming. The main difference is that you can grow more in less land space than you get with a traditional garden bed, and you can do so at a lower cost than you might other methods of container gardening. Given what I've learned thus far (and will continue to discover for years to come), here is my list of dos and dont's for bucket gardening.

Container Choice

Do consider purchasing food-grade buckets from a restaurant supplier if you or your family have chemical sensitivities. Most hardware store buckets are plastic. Exposed to the sun over months and years, the chemicals will slowly break down into the soil. Certain plants absorb that material, and your family might then ingest those chemicals when eating the fruits of your garden.

Chemical extraction can happen faster than you might expect. I cultivated some climbing spinach in my first year with this growing style. The crop grew quickly, and in addition to entangling my tomatoes, it somehow sucked in material from the bucket. When my kids ate it, they complained of a "chemical" taste. Since children have more sensitive taste buds than adults, I trusted that they weren't just trying to get out of eating their vegetables, and I set aside that spinach. Upon looking into it later, it turns out that spinach is a lesser-known phytoextractor, meaning it can leach chemicals such as metals and plastics from the soil.

Another option, if you prefer the hardware store buckets, is to line the inside. While it is a common practice to line wood planters with plastic, you can select liners from an array of other materials as long as you can poke holes in the bottom for drainage. For example, landscape fabric, burlap, coconut fiber, and moss make great bucket liner options that allow plenty of drainage.

Don't worry about the color of your bucket unless you live in a region where high temperatures and dryness guarantee fried roots. If that is a concern, stick with white or lighter colors—and pay attention to your weather reports. On especially hot days, placing your bucket in a tub of water in the shade helps the plants stay cool and healthy.

Healthy Soil and Drainage

Do make sure you drill holes in the bottom of the bucket. Plants need some way to self-regulate their water retention, and without drainage, you risk root rot, mold, and a host of other plant-killing problems. I skip the common advice to add small rocks to the bottom to slow excess drainage, but they don't hurt.

If you're not sure you want to use a power drill, or if you have a rental home and thus have limited use for a power drill, you can purchase a mini battery-operated one intended for crafters. Plastic is soft and pierces easily, so you don't need anything fancy. You can also try making holes by hammering the top of a Phillips screwdriver, but the process is slow and frustrating compared to using an electric drill. You also run the risk of cracking the bottom of the bucket so much you can't use it.

Do put coffee grounds and eggshells in your buckets. Pests still find their way into potted plants, albeit much less so than in a traditional garden. The eggshells keep the slugs down, and the coffee grounds repel certain insects while giving the plants a perky nutritional pick-me-up. If you practice small-space composting, your bucket plants love it just as much as in-ground plants. Of course, always check first: while most plants like coffee, occasionally someone will have a plant that prefers something else for fertilizer.

Do use any countertop composting as fertilizer for your bucket garden. Whether you use a countertop bin or a machine that dehydrates and grinds your leftover food, bucket garden plants respond well to the extra nutrition.

Do add extra fertilizer in rainy climates. Overwatering can happen easily in buckets, and you will be able to tell when the leaves of your plants yellow. When I see this happening, I add a bit of dirt from my kitchen composter or dump in coffee grounds every few days. You can also purchase liquid iron for under twenty dollars at a garden supply store.

Do rotate the plants and add compost if you plan to use the same soil in the buckets each year. Different plants absorb different nutrients from the soil—unless you want to restart with new potting soil each year (which can get expensive!), keep track of what bucket you planted what crop in, and make sure it has a different plant the next year. For example, if one had squash, plant snapdragons in it next year.

Do change the soil on anything from the nightshade family once a year. Tomatoes, eggplants, and most peppers will drain the potting soil of vital nutrients. Add the used dirt to your compost heap.

Don't use manure to fertilize bucket gardens. Manure compacts and hardens, making cleaning the bucket or allowing the plant to grow difficult.

Don't use heavy-duty pesticides on your bucket garden plants. While they have more ample growing space compared to other containers, they are still in a limited space with limited drainage. In addition, inorganic chemicals have a way of accumulating and lingering no matter how well you rinse your plants before you eat them.

I use three types of vinegar-based sprays instead of insecticides. I have one spray bottle filled with half food-grade white vinegar and half water. On most plants, I don't need to do more than spray, and it doesn't seem to cause any harm to the plant stalks. If pests still snack on the leaves, I switch to spicy apple cider vinegar. I prepare this by soaking cayenne pepper, dried hot chilis, and rosemary in the liquid, then straining before I pour it into the sprayer with water. If I receive continued defiance from the bugs, I will then reluctantly add about a tablespoon of dish soap to the apple cider vinegar mixture. Usually, at that point, the insects back off.

What to Plant

Do label your outdoor plants, so you know early what grows where and so you can anticipate what that plant might need. I track my plants by writing on some small bamboo planter labels with a Sharpie, and then I cover the label with glue to waterproof it for a season. The label does wear away throughout the summer, but by the time the glue and ink are gone, I can easily identify the plant. If necessary, I can reuse the label for a different plant next year.

Do employ companion planting if you use a bucket planter stand. It's a touch of superstition on my part, but I've found that putting plants next to each other that are known to get on well seems to garner better results, even when they do not share soil. For example, keeping tomatoes next to basil seems to cut down on certain tomato-eating worms, and I swear the tomatoes produce more when provided a friend.

Do plant flowers in at least one bucket to draw pollinators. A popular choice is echinacea. Not only is this flower pretty, but you can also harvest the roots for medicine in the fall. Also, consider planting milkweed, as it draws the endangered monarch butterfly. Some nature preservation organizations give away the seeds for free as part of their pollinator rescue efforts.

Do expect to replant certain crops within a single season. For example, lettuces and microgreens grow fast, so you can harvest them sooner. I have found that with strategic planting, I can get up to four lettuce harvests between May and October. You need not use your entire seed packet each planting.

While buckets do well for one-and-done planting on fruit-bearing vines, other plants taste best before they go to seed. In that case, plant just part of your seed packet at the beginning of your season and replant a few days after your first harvest.

Do supplement your kitchen herb selection and your cat's happiness. Catnip, mint, and basils grow especially well in bucket gardens. Right now, I am enjoying lush dill and chervil, along with the thyme. In summer, I can harvest just a little as dinner cooks; in September, I will harvest down to the bottom of the stalk and dry the herbs for use as a cooking aid through the winter.

Don't plant edible cabbages or sunflowers in non-food-grade buckets if you intend to eat them. Both extract metals and other chemicals from the soil easily, and you could accidentally end up eating your bucket in the form of a brassica. If you did this, then burn the plant at the end of the season as it will carbonize and eliminate from the environment whatever it absorbed from the plastic.

Don't give your plants any roommates without a compelling reason to do so. One plant per bucket gives the space it needs to spread out and prevents cross-pollination. The basil can sit next to the tomatoes, rather than in the same bucket with them.

Maximize Your Harvest

Do expect to weed, especially if you don't put any ground cover fabric down on the top of your bucket. Plants are mysteriously ambulatory and have a way of finding spots exactly where you don't want them. In prior years, I reduced my weeding time by cutting holes in pieces of burlap, placing the burlap on top of the soil in my bucket, and planting the seeds of the plant I want through the burlap hole. It doesn't stop all the intruders—they are tricky—but it reduces work compared to years when I forget to put the porous fabric cover on top.

Also, because of my waste-not-want-not mentality, I use phone apps like Seek and PlantFinder to identify the weeds in my buckets. Then, if the wandering plant is nutritious or has a medicinal application, I often toss it in a labeled paper bag and tape it to a wall to dry.

Do add poles and towers for vining plants. My cucumbers, beans, and squash plants climb right up the poles I planted in the bucket with less training than expected. I also increase my crop yields by giving the plants more air space. Cucumbers and zucchini respond as well to cages as tomatoes do. Adding plant obelisks and towers over your buckets can be as cheap or expensive as you like. Right now, I am using an old bed headboard to train cucumbers and squash; you can also place pallets behind your buckets or mount them on top of your bucket planter to add greater vertical gardening space to your setup.

Do check your frost dates before the planting season and try to organize your crops accordingly. Sometimes unexpected late-season frosts happen. When they do, either move the plants indoors or do your best to cover and insulate the buckets to maintain an above-freezing soil temperature. Yes, wrapping your buckets in blankets or a tarp can work for this. These coverings can also help protect from damage when hail appears in the weather forecast.

Do pay attention to the expected number of days to germination listed on your seed packet. I allow a latitude of about five to seven days, up to fifteen if a cold snap happens right after planting. Sometimes seeds don't germinate. If you catch that growth hasn't started for what you put down soon enough, you have time to plant something else or reseed.

Do consider taking your bucket gardens indoors if you can set up adequate shelving in your home. All you need is enough space for the bucket, a pan for water to drain in, and a plant light. While you can purchase expensive plant light and tray setups, I have worked successfully with a plant lightbulb from a hardware store, a reading lamp I found at a thrift store, and a light timer. Most plants need nine hours or less of direct light each day; make sure you check for each plant because overexposure to light may cause them to generate free radicals, potentially making them toxic.

The wonderful thing about bucket gardens is that they have so many more dos than don'ts—and the affordability of the container and the portability of the entire garden opens so many delightful possibilities for what you can grow. If you're beginning on the gardening path, I recommend using buckets. You can learn the ins and outs of individual plants easily, and it can help you decide if you want to grow a specific crop in a larger space. On the other hand, even if you're a seasoned gardener, I recommend them, as you can eke out that much more food from your land and space.

While my bucket garden isn't perfect, watching it grow brings me joy—and it's helping me learn how to work with my new climate, bugs and all. So much of gardening is about learning to live with the foibles of nature, and you can't beat buckets for a low-cost way to discover all you need to know!

Resources

Alia, N., K. Sardar, M. Said, K. Salma, A. Sadia, S. Sadaf, A. Toqeer, and S. Miklas. "Toxicity and Bioaccumulation of Heavy Metals in Spinach (*Spinacia oleracea*) Grown in a Controlled Environment." *International Journal of Environmental Ressearch and Public Health* 12, no. 7 (2015): 7400–7416. doi:10.3390/ijerph120707400.

Avasti, Amitabh. "Too Much of a Good Thing: Plants Have a Defense Mechanism to Protect Them from Too Much Sunlight." *Science,* January 21, 2005. https://www.science.org/content/article/too-much-good-thing.

"Bucket Gardening 101." Idaho State University. Accessed July 15, 2022. https://www.isu.edu/media/libraries/rural-health/microgreens/Bucket-Gardening-101.pdf.

"Do I Need to Line My Planter Box?" Gardening Mentor. Accessed July 15, 2022. https://gardeningmentor.com/do-i-need-to-line-my-planter-box/.

Cooking

Pasta, the World's Favorite Food

❧ Dawn Ritchie ❧

The origins of pasta have been hotly debated for centuries. While Italy and China argue most passionately for the honor, new evidence regularly turns the tables on those theories. Marco Polo may have brought pasta back from his travels in Asia, but ancient pasta unearthed in the tombs of the Etruscan civilization temporarily gave ancient Italy a leg up. Then, primitive pasta from Arabia was discovered to have traveled the Silk Road. Even Syria, Spain, Greece, and Sardinia have claimed a place in the pasta origin story. Whichever land birthed pasta, the fact is whence grains grow, people have found a way to turn them into a myriad of edibles. From buckwheat soba noodles to heavenly melt-in-your-mouth gnocchi to plain old mac and cheese, pasta is hands down the number one comfort food worldwide.

Fill It, Float It, Dress It, or Dunk It

One thing we do know about pasta's origins. Those ancient long flat ribbons, known as *laganum*, started out being eaten without sauce or fillings. That addition came later and transformed the dish into the diverse assortment of pleasures we now enjoy.

The marriage of noodle and sauce brings the garden into a wholeness of the occasion. Add the fruits of the sea or farm to the mix and you have a more complex picture. From beef stroganoff to vegetable lasagna, the best part is that both vegans and carnivores can enjoy pasta at the same event. Two sauces, one pasta base, and a large bowl of grated parmesan or vegan cheese will delight all.

Moderate Your Saucing

At the core of most sauces you will generally find olive oil, minced garlic, onions, and herbs. From there, you branch out to add vegetables, fungi, meats, seafood, and dairy, especially the obligatory parmigiano reggiano (or perhaps vegan cashew ricotta).

The one downfall of saucing is that we tend to use too much of it and suffocate the pasta so that the fulsome flavor of the noodle is lost. It may be due to those unfortunate cans of mushy spaghetti we were served in our youth. They did nothing to develop our palates. But pasta is more than a sauce carrier. It has a very distinct flavor and toothsome texture that is immensely enjoyable if you give it a chance. Sauce should be addressed with the same restraint as a dressing on a salad. It should complement but not dominate.

Al Dente

The toothsome texture I am referring to here is called *al dente*. When reading directions on those packages of dried pasta, you will often see the words "Cook to al dente." Al dente literally means "to the teeth." It refers to the slight resistance your teeth will meet from an al dente–cooked noodle before it submits to the bite. Not hard, but not too soft. A texture, not a mush. The secret to reaching that al dente texture lies in the cooking. Never boil noodles past the indicated time on packaging. Stick religiously to the allotted time and you will achieve al dente and grow to appreciate it.

This chapter will show you how to make a fresh pasta dough, but frankly, every home pantry should have a box or two of dry pasta at the ready—penne, farfalle, linguini, capellini, or tortellini that can be boiled up in three to ten minutes and plated within fifteen minutes is a life saver.

The Basics of Fresh Pasta

You need no special equipment or ingredients to make fresh pasta from scratch. The five primary ingredients are generally found in most pantries: flour, eggs, salt, olive oil, and water. Not all are necessary to make a dough, however. You can make pasta with merely flour and water, or flour and oil, or flour and eggs. Salt is optional but recommended. That's because the finished product cooks quickly and spends less time in your salted boiling water, so pre-seasoning helps.

Vegetable enrichments are another addition to consider. Red peppers, beets, greens, and any other vegetable you choose, even carrots, will add flavor and lively color. Squid ink delivers an exciting black stripe to a bowtie pasta and turns a dish into a work of art. First you will want to precook your vegetable and puree it, then add it to the dough as a wet ingredient as you mix it together. What you are going for is a firm yet pliant dough. Not a sticky one. Remember, *pasta* figuratively means "paste." Which is what you will get if you add too much water to the flour, as children who have made papier-mâché volcanos know. If your dough gets too sticky, add more flour.

Common Dry Ingredients	Wet Options
Flour	Eggs
Salt	Water
	Olive oil
	Vegetable puree
	Squid Ink (and other flavorings)

Choosing Your Flour

Semolina: Semolina is a coarse grind of durum wheat with a grainy texture, yellowish hue, and earthy flavor. It possesses a high gluten content. It is the preferred pasta flour used in the southern region of Italy where it grows. A little water or oil is all you need to produce a hearty dough.

All-Purpose or 00 Flour: Unbleached all-purpose and 00 flour are more popular in the northern region of Italy because that's where that flour is produced. 00 flour is a finer grind that produces a silky and tender pasta. Both all-purpose and 00 flour require extra protein to get that gluten going. Adding an egg achieves that and makes for a nice elastic pasta with a springy, smooth texture that suits many palates.

Low- or Gluten-Free Flours: You can make pasta dough from spelt, kamut, buckwheat (which has no gluten properties), and other nut flours, but often they break apart in the rolling process. Buckwheat especially has this tendency. You have to be quicker and more precise while working those doughs. There are work-arounds, like adding tapioca starch to help it hold together or crushed flax seed and chia seeds, but for our purposes an all-purpose flour or, even better, half all-purpose and half semolina is the sweet spot for dough making.

Equipment

Your hands, a rolling pin, and a knife and fork are all you really need, but you can utilize a cluster of pasta-making specialty tools if you have the cabinet room to store them. After you mix the dough with your hands, the classic Italian pasta roller is a good choice to gradually thin your pasta sheets to your desired width. You run an oblong strip of dough through the machine's rollers, adjusting the thickness in gradations to make the pasta thinner and thinner with each pass. Next you draw it through the cutter for fettuccine, linguine, lasagna, or ravioli.

I own the cheapest version of the Imperia hand crank pasta roller from Italy, and it does the job beautifully when making larger amounts. The roller has six settings and a cutting attachment. Stand mixers also offer motorized attachments that do the job. They run a little higher in price, but if you make pasta dough regularly, the investment is worth it.

A *chitarra* pasta cutter is a wooden tray with guitar-like strings strung across lengthwise. This cuts a thin sheet of pasta dough into perfectly sized spaghetti noodles. Pasta stamps and crimping wheels will also slice out rounds and squares in innumerable forms, and ravioli molds reduce your prep time by making several uniform raviolis all at once. There are also wooden gnocchi paddles to set those creases in your gnocchi dumplings that attract sauce (I use a fork) and pasta drying racks to hold your spaghetti as it dries for storage. I use a wooden spoon hanging across two pots. I don't own a ravioli mold because I prefer to make my raviolis by hand with a larger, uneven noodle that has a rustic look to it, but if you want a uniform look you could always use an ice tray in a pinch.

You can invest in any of these products, but more often than not, I find myself digging out my rolling pin and a knife and going to town. If you do choose to use elbow grease, roll your sheets of pasta as thin as you can, until you see light through the other side.

Making Your Dough

The steps to making dough are virtually the same, whether you use all-purpose flour and egg, semolina and oil, flour and water, or flour, egg, and a vegetable additive.

Start with a mound of flour on your working board. (A generous cup of flour will make enough pasta dough for two servings.) Make a well in the center and add your liquid ingredients to the well. Then you slowly draw the flour into the liquid with your fingers, incorporating bit by bit and hydrating the dry ingredients. Continue to add flour as needed until you have a ball of stiff dough. Then you can begin to knead it.

Knead the dough for at least ten minutes, adding flour as necessary. Kneading mindfully is a very satisfying meditative activity. You become one with your dough and establish a rhythm: pressing the dough away from your body with the heel of your palms, flipping one side of the dough over top of the other, then giving it a quarter turn and pressing with the heel of your palm again. Press, flip, quarter turn. Press, flip, quarter turn. Kneading combines all the ingredients fully while developing the gluten, which gives you the elasticity you want. It also relaxes you. Next time you find yourself annoyed with customer service, don't call for the manager. Make pasta and knead it out.

If your dough gets too dry, add water to your hands, not to the dough, and continue kneading to work it in.

Shaping Your Pasta

Once you have a standard dough ball, wrap it in plastic wrap, let it rest for forty-five minutes, and then begin to shape. Consider your dough your modeling clay for the innumerable shapes, sizes, thicknesses, and ridges you can create. Each one will affect the pasta's chewing texture and sauce adherence differently. Ridged tubular penne will have more heft and thus fare better for a cold picnic pasta salad, whereas hair-thin angel hair pasta is a fine choice for a quick, light meal that is ready in a flash. Flat sheets allow for layering of heavier fillings like meat sauce and cheese (lasagna), and twisted and hollow shapes also permit those creamy sauces to penetrate inside and provide more interest in the chewing.

Experiment with different shapes by cutting out small circles and then pressing a thumb into them to form little ears of orecchiette. Or roll out a long thin ribbon and then twist it to create spirals of fusilli. Cut squares and pinch them in the center to create little bowties of farfalle. To make fettuccine, roll the wide sheet of dough up and use a knife to slice your noodle strips off the end of the roll.

Recipes

✎ Egg-Based Pasta Dough

All ingredients should be at room temperature before combining. You'll want 1 large egg per every 1¼ cups all-purpose flour. Expect to add additional flour, as needed. Create a mound of flour with a dash of salt and make a well in the center. Crack an egg into that well, whisk the egg with your fingers, and gradually pull flour into the yolk, mixing and hydrating the flour as you go. Do a bit at a time. Do not rush this process. Large eggs vary greatly in size so there's a little winging it when it comes to measurements. The type of flour, the humidity in the air, and even the ambient temperature will all affect your proportions of ingredients, so paying attention to the feel of the dough is where you put your energy. Add flour as needed to get a stiff yet pliant dough.

✎ Semolina Pasta Dough

Follow the same procedure as described above. Make a mound of 1¼ cup semolina with a dash of salt, create a well in the center, and this time add a drizzle of olive or water to the well and begin to incorporate the flour with your fingers. Continue to add oil or water until all the flour is fully hydrated, then knead, rest, and roll out. (You can also add an egg, if so desired.)

⚘ Spinach Pasta Dough

1 cup fresh spinach leaves, packed

Pinch of salt

Light drizzle of olive oil

2½ cups all-purpose flour

2 large eggs

Wash the spinach leaves and pat them dry. Sauté the spinach in a dry hot pan over medium heat, stirring continuously until the spinach wilts, about 1–3 minutes. Do not burn.

Place the spinach in a food processor (or blender) and whiz it until pureed. Add a pinch of salt and a very tiny drizzle of olive oil at this stage to help the spinach pull away from the sides of the food processor. Then add 1 egg and continue to puree until smooth.

Place 2½ cups all-purpose flour on your counter and make a well in the center. Gradually add 1 spoonful of the spinach puree to the well, pulling the dry flour into the center with your fingers to hydrate the flour. Continue adding a spoonful at a time until all the spinach is incorporated. Now add the second egg, whisked, to the well and continue to mix. Shape the dough into a ball and knead for 10 minutes. The dough should be stiff and not sticky. Add flour as needed.

The beauty of this dough is the bright green hue with tiny flecks of real spinach that elicit a homemade rustica look. Wrap it in plastic wrap and let it rest for 45 minutes at room temperature before rolling into form.

Unwrap the dough. Divide the ball into 4 parts. Return 3 parts to the plastic wrap while you work 1 part. Roll it into a ball, then flatten it to make an oblong rectangle as best you can. Now you can roll your pasta into whichever form you choose, using either a rolling pin or a pasta roller.

This recipe yields 4 servings of pasta.

⤳ Butternut Squash Ravioli Filling

This filling pairs well with the spinach pasta dough.

You will need:

4 cups finely cubed butternut squash

4 roughly chopped shallots

4 cloves garlic

Drizzle of olive oil

1 tablespoon butter

Salt and freshly ground pepper

¼ cup grated parmesan (⅓ cup for more cheesiness)

½ teaspoon minced thyme

1 teaspoon minced fresh parsley

⅛ cup chopped pancetta or bacon bits (optional)

Drizzle squash, shallots, and garlic with olive oil and dab with small bits of butter as needed. Salt lightly and add a grind of fresh black pepper. Place on a baking sheet in a 375°F oven for 35–40 minutes. Keep an eye that it doesn't burn. Once fork tender, puree the roasted mix in a food processor while still warm, adding ¼ cup parmesan and the thyme and parsley.

Let the squash mix cool before filling the ravioli. If you choose to add some pancetta or bacon bits to the filling, stir them into the mixture at this stage. Do not puree.

There are many ways to fill ravioli. Dollop your filling in a row on a sheet of fresh pasta and fold it over, pressing all the air out around the filling and pinching a seal so it will not burst when cooking in the water. You can use a ravioli mold or use two sheets of pasta. I lay one sheet on top of the other because I prefer to make larger, imperfect ravioli with floppy artistic sides. It may have something to do with my brief stint working in the kitchen of a fine restaurant, where dishes with a mere three raviolis floating in a broth came at a hefty price. But I also like the texture of the floppy sides of the ravioli that fan out around the filling and produce a better mouthfeel. This way you experience the noodle as much as the filling.

⤳ White Wine Sauce

Because the butternut filling is so rich and creamy (the cheese effect), I prefer a lighter sauce for this dish. A white wine and vegetable broth with some fresh tomato cubes as a finisher mitigates the heaviness of the filling.

You will need:

- 2 slivered shallots
- 2 cloves sliced garlic
- 2–3 tablespoons olive oil
- ¼ cup white wine
- ¼ cup vegetable or chicken broth
- Basil leaves for garnish
- ⅛ cup finely chopped tomato (seeded)

Sweat the finely slivered shallots and garlic slices in a generous amount of olive oil. As they turn translucent, add ¼ cup white wine and reduce. Add an additional ¼ cup vegetable or chicken broth. Simmer. Spoon over the ravioli. Garnish with basil and the handful of fresh tomato.

⇗ Gnocchi

Gnocchi are potato-and-flour-based heavenly pillows of pasta that resemble tiny dumplings about the size and shape of the tip of your thumb to the first knuckle. They have a sticky, starchy, unctuous quality that make them immensely satisfying as a side dish or entrée. Gnocchi pair well with many sauces, from pesto and cream sauce to tomato. Choose dry, floury russets or Idaho potatoes for this recipe. Because potatoes don't come in uniform sizes, your flour-potato ratio should approximately be 1:3.

You can make gnocchi with or without egg. One medium egg is sufficient for a standard household batch (enough to serve 4 to 5), unless you are making enough gnocchi to serve a banquet, then double or triple up as needed. The same goes with salt. Per a standard batch, 1½ to 2 teaspoons salt should suffice. Gnocchi is a notoriously difficult recipe to unwind, because generally it is all about the feel of the dough, which should hold together but remain springy.

Make sure your hands are clean and dry because you'll be using them a lot.

You will need:

    Idaho potatoes

    Flour

    Eggs

    Salt

Boil unpeeled potatoes whole in a large pot of water until fork tender. Once cool enough to the touch, scrape the peel off with a knife and run the cooked potato through a potato ricer or food mill (or simply mash it with a fork). Let cool. You want the potato cool before you incorporate the flour to keep your gnocchi light and springy. Begin to add flour, mixing with your hands. Crack an egg into the mixture and continue mixing by hand, adding flour as needed. Bring the dough together into a firm but springy mound. Let it rest for 5 minutes, then divide it into smaller portions and roll each lump out into a long rope. Cut the rope of dough into little knobs the size of your thumb (to first knuckle), about ½ inch. Then quickly slide each knob down the back-side tines of a fork. This creates grooves in the gnocchi that help hold the sauce. Dust lightly with flour as you work.

Bring a large pot of well-salted water to a rolling boil. Boil your fresh gnocchi until they float, about 2 minutes. Scoop them out with a slotted spoon and add to a pan of warm cream sauce briefly to coat. Plate, sprinkle with grated parmesan and fresh parsley, and serve.

✎ Sage Cream Sauce

  2 cloves garlic

  2 tablespoons butter

  2–3 tablespoons sage

  1 tablespoon parsley

  Dash of cooking wine (or dry white wine)

  ¼–⅓ cup heavy cream

  Grated pecorino romano cheese

  Freshly ground pepper to taste

Mince 2 cloves garlic and sauté in 2 tablespoons butter. Add a small handful of fresh sage leaves and your parsley. Add the dash of wine. Simmer on low for about 2 minutes, add ¼ cup heavy cream, and grate pecorino cheese over it. Grind pepper in. The cheese is salty, so no need for additional salt. If you don't have heavy cream on hand, don't sweat it. I have even made this sauce with skimmed milk, which was more buttery than creamy but just as tasty.

⤞ Emergency Pasta for One

Had a bad day? Eating alone? I often make a quick lemony capellini pasta with sautéed scallions, chopped garlic, olive oil, lemon juice, and lemon zest, sprinkled with dried parsley and parmesan that is literally ready in 10 minutes. A pot of salted water goes on, and in the time it takes to boil water and cook the noodles (3 minutes for these noodles), the fixings are done and everything is plated.

Alternatively, a bright margherita angel hair pasta with cherry tomatoes, basil, garlic, green onion, and dash of olive oil will feed you in minutes and leave you with a clean, refreshed palate. Optionally, add a few chopped stems of broccoli rabe sprinkled with chili peppers to boost excitement.

Don't think about measurements here for either of these meals for one. You don't have to be precise—1 slice of an onion, 1 clove of garlic, a splash of olive oil, and 2 shakes of the spice jar, and you are good to go.

It's Greek to Me: A Few Greek Salads

⤞ James Kambos ⤝

The Greeks love salads. But the majority of salads served in Greece aren't like the Greek salads you'll find in Greek restaurants in America. Yes, you'll find that type of lettuce-based salad in Greece, but it's primarily served in larger hotels and resorts. Most salads served in Greek homes or cafes catering to the locals omit the lettuce. Instead they rely more on sliced vegetables, olives, cheeses, and even beans. The salads are then dressed with olive oil (of course) and some type of vinegar or lemon juice. Then the salads are usually seasoned with plenty of herbs. Favorite herbs are parsley, dill, oregano, mint, and basil. Salt and pepper are also used frequently.

Growing up in a Greek home, I can remember many of these salads being prepared hastily at the dinner table. Someone would mix the salad, then someone would run out to the garden to snip a few sprigs of the desired herbs. The herbs were quickly chopped and added to the salad. These salads were simple, fresh, and easy to prepare. The scents and flavors of the fresh herbs were heavenly. I can still remember the colors, textures, and fragrance of these "country" salads.

One of the reasons they may have tasted so good is that nothing was measured. Oil, vinegars, lemon juice, herbs, salt and pepper were mixed without measuring. The cooks in my family didn't know what a measuring spoon was. Everything was measured by a dash, a couple of leaves, or a handful. Even the vegetables weren't measured exactly. We'd use a "couple" of tomatoes or "one or two" cucumbers.

That said, the measurements in the salad recipes that follow are educated guesses. Or they're close to how I remember my mom, aunts, or grandmother did it.

✒ A Traditional Greek Salad

This is the typical salad people think of when they hear the term "Greek" salad. This is just one of many variations. It includes endive lettuce for its nutty, slightly bitter flavor. The romaine lettuce gives it a nice crunch.

You will need:

  1 head curly endive lettuce

  1 head romaine lettuce

  2 medium cucumbers, peeled and sliced

  2 tomatoes, sliced into wedges

  2 dozen pitted kalamata olives

2 green onions, chopped

½ cup olive oil

3 tablespoons red wine vinegar

½ teaspoon salt

Dash of freshly ground black pepper

6–8 anchovy fillets, chopped if desired

½ cup cubed feta cheese

½ teaspoon dried oregano

Rinse and dry the lettuce, and tear it into bite-size pieces. Place the lettuce, cucumbers, tomatoes, olives, and onion into a large salad bowl. Whisk the olive oil, vinegar, salt, and pepper together in a small bowl until frothy. Pour over the salad, mixing well. Place the anchovy fillets on top. In a plastic sandwich bag, place the cheese cubes and oregano. Shake until the cheese cubes are coated with the oregano. Garnish the salad with the cubed feta and serve. Serves 6–8.

⤞ Summer Vegetable Salad

This fresh vegetable salad is a great side dish on a warm summer day. My grandmother would serve it when company came. It goes well with fish, chicken, or lamb.

You will need:

4 tomatoes, sliced into wedges

1 cucumber, peeled and sliced

1 green pepper, seeded and sliced into strips

1 bunch radishes, thinly sliced

1 clove garlic, minced

Salt and pepper to taste

1 teaspoon dried mint, or 1 tablespoon chopped fresh
mint

½ cup olive oil

Juice of 2 lemons

Sprig of fresh mint for garnish

Combine the tomatoes, cucumber, green pepper, and radishes in a serving bowl. Whisk together the garlic, salt, pepper, mint, olive oil, and lemon juice in a small bowl. Pour over the vegetables and mix well. Cover and refrigerate for 1–2 hours. Garnish with a sprig of mint and serve. Serves 6.

✎ Green Bean and Tomato Salad

Serve this salad chilled or at room temperature. Try it on the side with your favorite pasta or meat.

You will need:

½ pound green beans, cleaned with ends removed

1 dozen cherry tomatoes, sliced in half

½ cup crumbled feta

Salt and pepper to taste

1 teaspoon dried basil, or 4–6 fresh basil leaves, chopped

⅓ cup olive oil

2 tablespoons white wine vinegar

Leave the beans whole or cut them in half. Place the beans in a medium saucepan, and barely cover with water. Bring to a boil, cover, and simmer for 8 minutes. Drain the beans, rinse in cold water, and drain again. Place the beans in a serving bowl. Combine with the tomatoes, feta cheese, salt, pepper, and basil. Mix well. Add the olive oil and vinegar, tossing to coat. Serve at room temperature, or cover and chill. Serves 5–6.

ᔍ Black-Eyed Pea Salad

The Greeks enjoy black-eyed peas. Black-eyed peas originated in Africa, and since Greece is close to the North African Coast, it's easy to understand how they made it into Greek cuisine. I've never eaten this salad anywhere else, but my aunt Athena would frequently mix it up at the dinner table.

It also goes well with American-style main dishes. I've enjoyed it on the side with pork chops or fried chicken.

I never add salt to this salad since I use canned black-eyed peas. They usually contain enough sodium, but add it if you wish.

You will need:

1 15.5-ounce can of black-eyed peas, drained and rinsed

2 medium tomatoes sliced into wedges, or 12 cherry tomatoes sliced in half

1 medium red onion, thinly sliced

¼ cup flat-leaf Italian parsley, chopped

Salt to taste (optional)

Black pepper to taste

¼ cup olive oil

2 tablespoons apple cider vinegar

Place the black-eyed peas, tomatoes, onion, parsley, salt (if you're using it), and pepper in a serving bowl. Mix well. Pour in the olive oil and vinegar, turning to mix well. Serve immediately. It can be served chilled also. Serves 4–5.

⤞ Greek-Style Potato Salad

My mother would make this frequently in the summer. It goes with any meat dish. Serve it chilled. If you can, use fresh dill.

You will need:

- 3–4 potatoes, boiled, cooled, peeled, and cut into bite-size pieces
- 2 tomatoes, cut into wedges
- 1 stalk celery, chopped
- 1 bunch green onion, chopped
- 1 hard-boiled egg, sliced
- Salt and pepper to taste
- 3–4 stems fresh dill, chopped, or 1 tablespoon dried dill
- ½ cup olive oil
- 3 tablespoons apple cider vinegar
- 2 stems fresh dill for garnish

Combine the potatoes, tomatoes, celery, onion, egg, salt, pepper, and dill in a salad bowl or large serving bowl. Mix gently. Pour in olive oil and vinegar, turning to coat the ingredients. Cover and chill 1–2 hours. To serve, uncover and garnish with fresh dill. Serves 6.

⤞ Tomato and Cucumber Salad

This simple salad shows up on the table in many Greek homes but also in fine restaurants and hotels. There are a ton of variations—all of them are good. It's a great way to use up tomatoes and cucumbers from the summer garden. It's good cold or at room temperature. Serve it the way they do in Greece: Bring it to the table with olive oil and a selection of different vinegars. Let each guest dress their serving themselves.

You will need:

  2–3 tomatoes, sliced into wedges

  1–2 cucumbers, peeled and sliced

  About 1 dozen pitted Greek or Sicilian olives

  ½–¾ cup crumbled feta cheese

  1–2 tablespoons dried or fresh oregano or basil

  Olive oil

  Your favorite vinegars

To serve, arrange the tomato and cucumbers on a plate. Scatter the olives over the tomatoes and cucumbers. Sprinkle the feta cheese over all. Garnish with the chopped herbs. Serve at room temperature or cold. Let guests help themselves and add their own olive oil and vinegar of their choice. Serves 4–6.

———

The salads of Greece are fresh and simple. The ingredients may vary from region to region, but they have one thing in common: the salads of this sun-drenched land are usually packed with bright herbal flavors.

Desserts with Herbs

❧ Sara Mellas ❧

There is a common misconception among culinary hobbyists that baking is an exact science, while cooking allows for limitless improvisation. In truth, the techniques and ratios indicated in baking and cooking require similar levels of precision to produce the desired results. Reciprocally, the ease with which one can adjust flavors when cooking savory recipes through spices, herbs, and other additives applies to dessert recipes as well. Desserts lend themselves to endless exploration of flavors through extracts, spices, zests, fruits, chocolates, nuts, and—as you'll find here—herbs.

In modern Western cultures, we use an array of culinary herbs in their various forms. Dried and ground herbs hold a place in nearly every spice cabinet collection, and fresh herbs are available in grocery stores year-round. We associate certain herbs with regional cuisines (basil for Italian dishes, cilantro for Mexican, tarragon for French), but we rarely think to incorporate herbs into desserts.

There are two primary ways to utilize herbs in dessert recipes. Fresh leaves can be finely minced and added directly to batters, dough, or fillings, or leaves and sprigs can be simmered in milk or cream to infuse their flavor, then strained from the liquid before use. It's always wise to start with small amounts of an herb when experimenting with a recipe, as most are quite powerful. Fresh herbs typically yield the best results, but when working with floral herbs like lavender and chamomile, dried is preferable.

There are countless desserts that lend themselves well to the addition of herbs. With a bit of exploration, herbs can bring dimension and uniqueness to classic flavors and transform traditional recipes into novel and inventive delights.

Common Herbs to Use in Desserts

Basil

Once referred to as "the royal plant," basil is a member of the mint family that grows with blooms of delicate purple flowers in hot, dry climates. It is thought to be anti-inflammatory, adaptogenic, and antioxidant. Basil is popularly used as the main ingredient in pesto and in traditional Italian dishes like caprese salad. Many Asian cultures feature the green leaves in sautés and soups. While incorporating the pungent flavor of basil into desserts may seem unusual, its seeds are commonly used to create sweet puddings and drinks in South Asia. Just a few leaves impart a great deal of flavor that pairs wonderfully with berries; use it in jams, compotes, berry pies, or cobblers.

Chamomile

A flowering herb of the daisy family, chamomile has been used medicinally since ancient times. Today, it is most often dried and brewed as a tea, which is taken to aid with sleep, easing anxiety and digestive distress. With a mildly floral, earthy flavor, chamomile is complemented well by honey, lemon, and berries. In baking, the dried leaves can be steeped in milk to be used in cake and muffin batters.

Lavender

Like basil, lavender is a flowering herb belonging to the mint family. Its luxurious scent is instantly recognizable and readily associated with cosmetic and home fragrance products. The dried buds are often used in blends of herbal tea for relaxation. While all lavender is edible, it is best to use culinary lavender in any kind of recipe. Culinary lavender is prepared from many cultivars of true lavender, which are less bitter and resinous than other varieties, and is specially sifted to be free of stems and debris. The crushed buds can be used in very small amounts in fruit preparations, cookies, cakes, and frostings.

Mint

Of all herbs, mint is the one most often found in sweets. Whether it's featured in ice cream, candy, cake, or chocolate or as a simple garnish on a plate, its refreshing flavor is a widely popular addition to desserts. The fresh leaves are typically infused into milk and cream to make ice cream, puddings, and chocolate ganache, while peppermint extract is a highly concentrated ingredient of which just a few drops can be used to flavor batters and doughs. Mint is also a powerful antinauseant, decongestant, digestive, and antioxidant.

Rosemary

Rosemary is an evergreen shrub with thin, pointed leaves that grow with blooms of white, pink, purple, and indigo flowers. The plant was sacred in ancient cultures and continued to hold significance through to medieval times. It was a primary ingredient in the first recorded perfumes, and the sprigs were revered as a symbol of remembrance. Today, we often associate fresh rosemary with the winter months and use the dried leaves year-round in a variety of recipes. Small amounts or infusions of the fresh leaves add a woodsy depth to desserts with caramel, chocolate, citrus, cranberries, and vanilla.

Thyme

Thyme is an aromatic herb indigenous to the Mediterranean, once believed to bear and symbolize courage. In ancient cultures it was used as incense, an antibiotic, and even for purification and embalming. Today, thyme is popular in its fresh and dried forms in the preparation of savory dishes. While it's not commonly used in sweets, the fresh leaves offer an earthy flavor that pairs well with stone fruits, lemon, and vanilla.

Recipes

⚞ Strawberry Basil Shortcakes

Few desserts evoke summer more than homemade strawberry shortcake. The combination of flaky, buttery scones, juicy fresh-picked berries, and lightly sweetened whipped cream makes for the perfect seasonal indulgence. This recipe elevates traditional strawberry shortcake by adding thin ribbons of basil leaves to the berries, imparting a subtle but unique flavor into every bite. Yields 8 servings.

For the basil-sweetened strawberries:

32 ounces (about 5 cups) fresh strawberries, washed

8–10 fresh basil leaves

Juice from ½ lemon

¼ cup (50 grams) granulated sugar

For the buttery scones:

2 cups (250 grams) all-purpose flour

⅓ cup (65 grams) granulated sugar

2½ teaspoons baking powder

½ teaspoon salt

½ cup (115 grams) unsalted butter, very cold

1 large egg

⅔ cup (165 milliliters) heavy cream, cold

1 teaspoon vanilla extract

Flour, for dusting

For the whipped cream:

1½ cups (375 milliliters) heavy cream, cold

¼ cup (50 grams) granulated sugar

1½ teaspoons vanilla extract

Remove the tops from the strawberries and discard. Roughly chop the berries into ½-inch pieces. Stack the basil leaves on top of one another. Tightly roll the leaves into a small log. With a sharp knife, slice the log very thin, creating ribbons of basil.

Place the strawberries and basil in a large bowl. Squeeze the lemon juice into the bowl and sprinkle with sugar. Mix gently to combine. Cover the bowl and refrigerate for at least 1 hour and preferably no more than 4 hours.

Preheat the oven to 400°F. Line a baking sheet with parchment paper.

Place the flour, sugar, baking powder, and salt in a large mixing bowl and stir to combine. Using the coarse side of a box grater or hand grater, grate the butter directly into the bowl. Mix gently with a rubber spatula to coat the shreds.

In a separate bowl, whisk together the egg, ⅔ cup heavy cream, and vanilla extract. Pour the mixture into the bowl of flour. Fold gently with a rubber spatula, working until the ingredients combine into a crumbly dough that just holds together when pinched.

Turn the dough onto a floured surface and gently pat it into a 1-inch-thick disk. Use a sharp knife to cut the dough into 8 triangles.

Arrange the scones 2 inches apart on the baking sheet and transfer to the middle rack of the preheated oven.

Bake for 19 to 22 minutes, until the scones are lightly golden and feel firm when tapped. Remove from the oven and allow to cool for at least 30 minutes.

Shortly before serving, make the whipped cream. Pour the 1½ cups of heavy cream into a large mixing bowl. Using an electric hand mixer or stand mixer, beat the cream for 2 to 3 minutes, or until soft peaks form. Add the sugar and vanilla extract. Continue beating for 1 to 2 minutes longer, just until the cream holds firm peaks.

To assemble, cut a scone in half crosswise and place the cut sides up onto a plate. Top with the macerated strawberries, followed by a few tablespoons of whipped cream. Serve immediately.

⤳ Chocolate Sheet Cake with Minted Chocolate Whipped Cream
For those who love the classic combination of chocolate and mint, this cake uses fresh mint and peppermint extract for double the flavor. The decadent chocolate cake batter comes together in one bowl, before being baked and cooled in a single pan. Topped with a light and airy mint-infused chocolate whipped cream, it's a welcome treat for any occasion. Yields one 9 × 13-inch cake, about 15 to 18 servings.

For the minted chocolate whipped cream:
⅓ cup fresh mint leaves, loosely packed

2 cups (500 milliliters) heavy cream

⅓ cup (65 grams) granulated sugar

⅓ cup (32 grams) unsweetened cocoa powder

½ teaspoon vanilla extract

1–2 drops peppermint extract

For the chocolate mint cake:
Nonstick cooking spray

1¾ cups (350 grams) granulated sugar

½ cup (125 milliliters) canola oil

2 large eggs, at room temperature

¼ cup (60 grams) sour cream, at room temperature

1 teaspoon vanilla extract

⅛ teaspoon peppermint extract

¾ cup (80 grams) unsweetened cocoa powder

¾ cup (185 milliliters) whole milk, at room temperature

1 cup (250 milliliters) hot brewed coffee or water

1¾ cups (210 grams) all-purpose flour

1 teaspoon baking soda

½ teaspoon salt

Fresh mint leaves, for garnish (optional)

Fresh berries, for serving (optional)

Place the mint leaves in a saucepan and pour in the heavy cream. Set the pan over medium-low heat and bring the cream to a simmer. Gently simmer for 10 to 15 minutes, until the mint is fragrant. Remove the pan from the heat and pour the cream into a large mixing bowl. With a fork, lift the mint leaves from the cream and discard. Cover and refrigerate until fully chilled, at least 4 hours.

Preheat the oven to 350°F. Spray a 9 × 13-inch baking pan with nonstick cooking spray.

Place the sugar, canola oil, eggs, sour cream, vanilla extract, and peppermint extract in a large mixing bowl and whisk vigorously to combine. Add the cocoa powder, milk, and hot coffee (or water), and continue whisking until smooth.

Add the flour, baking soda, and salt, and whisk gently until the ingredients are combined into a smooth, medium-thin batter.

Pour the batter into the prepared pan. Transfer to the middle rack of the preheated oven. Bake for 28–32 minutes, until a toothpick inserted in the center of the cake comes out clean.

Remove the cake from the oven and set aside to cool completely, at least 2 hours.

Remove the bowl of cream from the refrigerator. Using an electric hand mixer or stand mixer, beat the cream for 2–3 minutes, or until soft peaks form. Add the sugar, cocoa powder, vanilla extract, and peppermint extract. Continue beating for 1–2 minutes longer, just until the cream holds firm peaks.

Spread the whipped cream over the cooled cake. Refrigerate until ready to serve. Serve garnished with fresh mint leaves and berries, if desired.

➷ Lemon Lavender Sugar Cookies

These bright, subtly floral cookies taste like springtime. Buttery lemon cookie dough is rolled and cut into circles or shapes, baked until soft and golden, then finished with a zingy-sweet glaze. Not only are they fun to make, but they're sure to bring smiles when shared at any warm-weather gathering, picnic, or bake sale. Yields about 2 dozen cookies.

For the cookies:

¾ cup (172 grams) unsalted butter, at room temperature

¾ cup (150 grams) granulated sugar

1 large egg

½ teaspoon vanilla extract

Zest of 1 large lemon

1 teaspoon culinary lavender leaves, crushed

2¼ cups (275 grams) all-purpose flour

½ teaspoon baking powder

½ teaspoon salt

For the lemon glaze (optional):

1¼ cups (150 grams) powdered sugar

Pinch of salt

½ teaspoon vanilla extract

Juice of 1 lemon

Line 2 large baking sheets with parchment paper and set aside.

Place the butter and sugar in a large mixing bowl. Beat with a hand mixer on medium-high speed for 1 to 2 minutes, until smooth and creamy. Add the egg, vanilla extract, lemon zest, and lavender, and continue beating for about 1 minute more, until the mixture is pale and light.

Add the flour, baking powder, and salt. Beat on medium speed, scraping down the sides of the bowl with a rubber spatula as needed, until a smooth dough forms.

Turn the dough onto a floured surface. Gently roll with a floured rolling pin to ¼-inch thickness. Use a 2-inch cookie cutter to stamp out the dough, collecting and rerolling the scraps until all has been cut into about 24 cookies. Arrange the cookies 2-inches apart on the baking sheets.

Transfer the baking sheets to the freezer for 15 to 20 minutes. Preheat the oven to 350°F.

When the cookies are nearly solid, transfer the baking sheets from the freezer to the middle rack of the preheated oven.

Bake for 11 to 14 minutes, until the cookies are lightly golden around the edges. Remove from the oven and allow to cool completely.

If you'd like to add a lemon glaze, whisk together the powdered sugar and salt in a large mixing bowl. Add the vanilla extract and lemon juice and whisk until very smooth. The glaze should drizzle slowly from the whisk but not be runny. If too thick, add a bit more lemon juice. If too thin, whisk in a few tablespoons of powdered sugar.

Drizzle the glaze over the cooled cookies. Allow to set for about 20 minutes, or until dried.

☙ Rosemary Caramel Sauce

Salted caramel sauce is a luscious addition to a range of desserts and drinks and is one of the most rewarding things to make from scratch. Traditionally made from just sugar, butter, cream, and salt, this version uses fresh rosemary and a touch of vanilla to create a deep, earthy sauce that's irresistible drizzled over ice cream, paired with dark chocolate, or served alongside fall and winter spiced desserts. I love to make a few batches of this recipe and seal it in mason jars to give as gifts around the holidays. Yields 1 cup.

You will need:

  ½ cup (125 milliliters) heavy cream

  3 sprigs fresh rosemary

  1 cup (200 grams) granulated sugar

  3 tablespoons (42 grams) salted butter, at room temperature

  ¼ teaspoon vanilla extract

  ⅛ teaspoon salt

Pour the heavy cream into a small saucepan and add the rosemary sprigs. Set the pan over medium-low heat and bring the cream to a slow simmer. Gently simmer for 10 to 15 minutes, until the rosemary is fragrant. Remove the pan from the heat and discard the rosemary. Set the warm cream aside.

Place the sugar in a heavy-bottomed saucepan and set it over medium-low heat. Heat the sugar without stirring, swirling the pan by the handle every 30 seconds or so, until it is fully melted into a deep golden liquid. This may take several minutes.

Add the butter in pieces to the melted sugar. It will bubble aggressively. Slowly stir the butter into the sugar with a heat-resistant rubber spatula until mostly combined.

Stream the warm cream into the pan while continuing to stir. Again, the mixture will bubble. Once the ingredients are combined, allow it to bubble without stirring for 30 seconds longer.

Remove the pan from the heat. Stir in the vanilla extract and salt.

Carefully pour the caramel into a glass jar (or jars). Allow to cool completely before sealing the jar(s).

Keep the caramel stored in the refrigerator for up to 1 month. Reheat for 15 to 20 seconds in the microwave to loosen. Alternately, jars may be sealed in a water bath and stored at room temperature before opening.

Natural Food Colorings

Elizabeth Barrette

Natural food colorings appeal to people for different reasons. Some dislike artificial colors on principle. Others dislike the flavor or other effects. Many people just prefer natural ingredients in general. Gardeners and cooks often enjoy experimenting to see how much use they can get from natural foods. Appealing colors make food more interesting, which can boost appetite.

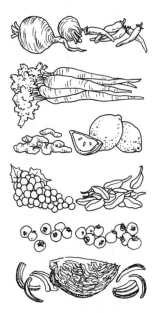

Benefits

Using natural food colorings conveys many benefits. First, you avoid the dangers of ultraprocessed foods. Chemical additives aren't always as "safe" as claimed, and the more artificial ingredients are eaten, the more likely they are to cause problems of some sort. Indigestion and restlessness are among the more common complaints. Second, the overbright hues of artificial food colorings undermine the ability to associate colors with nutrient categories and, thus, the mind's ability to regulate eating. Third, some artificial colors taste terrible—usually bitter or metallic—and some people have this problem with most artificial colors, thus making natural ones preferable. This seems to be worse with paste icing colors than liquid food colors, but any food tinted to a very strong hue can have unfortunate flavors.

Natural food colorings rely on real food ingredients, such as fruit or spices. Some are whole, while others use only part of a food, such as the juice. They customarily include nutrients and sometimes fiber. A few "superfood" powders have brilliant colors, like the yellow to orange of turmeric. These pack a lot of valuable nutrients into a very small amount of food.

Don't be afraid to get creative. You can use real spices to color as well as flavor spiced cookies or bread. Icing with a savory, sour, salty, or even bitter note can make a great contrast to a sweet cookie or cake when sweet-on-sweet icing might become overwhelming.

Colorful Nutrients

Colors in foods, especially phytochemicals, show their benefits with their appearance, hence the term **phytonutrients**, which divide into several types. They are often sorted into red, orange/yellow, green, and blue/purple groups. This is the source of the advice "eat the rainbow." By eating foods with different, vibrant colors, you get a wide range of vitamins and minerals.

Anthocyanins: These produce red, purple, or blue hues; when diluted, they can look pink. A quirk is that they turn red in an acid, purple when neutral, and blue in a base: nice for "unicorn" recipes. Benefits include antidiabetic, anticancer, anti-inflammatory, antimicrobial, and antiobesity effects, as well as supporting cardiovascular health.

Chlorophyll: This produces the vivid green color of plants, sometimes appearing as yellow-green. Benefits include antioxidant, anti-inflammatory, anticancer, and antiaging effects, as well as boosting energy, cleansing, and healing. Green foods also tend to contain vitamins A, C, E, and K, along with calcium, iron, magnesium, and potassium.

Carotenoids: These produce primarily yellow to orange colors, occasionally red or yellow-green. They promote vision and cardiovascular health; they also have antioxidant and anticancer effects.

Colorful Ingredients

Many natural colorings come in several formats. Wet and dry colorings behave differently. Wet ones will affect recipe behavior much more than dry ones, don't keep as long, and have softer colors, but they have much lower impact on flavor. Dry ones have less impact on recipe behavior, often store well, and have brighter colors, but they also have much stronger flavors, which may be desirable or undesirable. Some colorings only come in one version, but others, like most fruits, can be used wet or dry.

Because natural food colorings come from actual foods, they all have some amount of flavor. This can be beneficial, as in chocolate; neutral, as in purple sweet potato; or challenging, as in squid ink. Often a trace flavor can be covered up with a much stronger flavor, such as eclipsing baby spinach (bright green) with lime (nearly colorless, but associated with the color green). You will get the best results working with natural flavors rather than against them. For instance, use briny colorings like squid ink or chlorella in savory recipes or salty-sweet ones.

Furthermore, colors can change based on the pH or temperature of food. The pH can be controlled by adding small amounts of acid (such as lemon juice) or base (such as baking soda) to a food. Temperature-sensitive colors may be used in cold foods, such as icing. However, baked goods may be colored *after* cooking by soaking them with a colorful and flavorful syrup: you can make a vivid "poke cake" using fruit juices poured over a yellow or white cake.

Pink

Raspberries: Most raspberries are pink to red and produce pink coloring. However, black raspberries produce purple and yellow raspberries produce yellow to peach colorings. They grow on low, arching canes often at the edges of a forest. For coloring, raspberries are most often used in puree or freeze-dried powder form.

Red Currants: These tiny berries make pink to almost red coloring. They grow on low bushes in sun to part shade. Red currant concentrate or syrup can be found in some stores, and it's a popular flavor in the United Kingdom.

Strawberries: These red berries produce pink coloring. They grow on small plants with spreading runners, which benefit from mulch to keep the berries off the ground. Strawberries can be used as puree or freeze-dried powder.

Red

Beets: This root crop is typically red to purple and produces purple to nearly neon pink colors. Beets also come in yellow to orange and can be used for those colors. Beet color is very staining; you can put hard-boiled eggs in the liquid from pickled beets and they will turn pink. Beets grow underground as large round or cylindrical roots. Use the juice, puree, or freeze-dried powder.

Cranberries: These small berries make pink to red shades. They grow on medium bushes; some types like marshy areas. Cranberry puree tends toward pinkish, but cranberry juice is a deep jewel-red color with hints of purple.

Pomegranate: The large fruit opens to reveal many small red arils that give red to purple colors. It grows on a small tree that thrives in tropical, subtropical, and subtemperate areas. Pomegranate juice, with its dark ruby color, is becoming more available. It is deeply staining and needs only a tiny amount for coloring.

Tomatoes: While usually red, these vegetables also come in shades of yellow, orange, pink, purple, brownish to almost black, and even green. They typically yield red to orange colors, but different colored tomatoes may give different results. Commercial products are almost exclusively red-orange, but you can make a bright yellow to orange sauce or paste from yellow paste tomatoes. Large garden vines need full sun and plenty of water, but the tomatoes come in diverse sizes, shapes, textures, and flavors. Many available forms for coloring include juice, puree, paste, and freeze-dried powder. Tomato is widely used to color rice and pasta, and it mixes well with many other red to yellow colorings.

Orange

Carrots: Typically bright orange, carrots can also be yellow, red, or purple. Dark orange carrots tend to produce the best orange coloring. This root crop usually has long triangular roots, but some are chunkier or even radish-shaped. It grows best in light sandy soil because heavy soil can distort the roots. Carrot can be used as puree, juice, or freeze-dried powder. The juice blends well with many other yellow to orange colorings and makes a great base for them.

Paprika: This spice ranges from orange to red to almost brown. It can be mild, smoky, or spicy. It comes from a type of pepper that grows as a small plant. Paprika is almost always found as a powder but occasionally as a paste. It works best in savory recipes and combines well with other warming spices. But don't underestimate its use in sweet recipes, where a pinch can enhance both colors and flavors. It is widely used with tomato in coloring rice or pasta.

Pumpkin: This type of winter squash ranges from yellow to deep orange, and when cooked, it tends to take on deeper hues of orange to almost brown. Its color can be brightened with yellow or deepened with red or brown ingredients; it works well in sweet or savory recipes. Pumpkins grow on big rambling vines in full sun. Easiest to find as puree, it also comes as freeze-dried powder.

Sweet Potato: Usually deep orange, it can be yellow to almost red, occasionally pinkish. It produces mostly orange colors. Sweet potato is a vining crop that produces large pointed roots. It works well in sweet or savory recipes. Most often used as a puree, it can also be found as freeze-dried powder.

Yellow

Mango: This large tropical fruit comes in shades of yellow to orange and grows on a huge tropical tree. It blends well with similar colors. Mango is typically used as juice, puree, or freeze-dried powder. Occasionally, you can find paste that is a darker orange to brown.

Saffron: This rare spice produces yellow to light orange shades. It comes from the stamens of the saffron crocus—expensive, but a tiny bit goes a long way, as it is very staining. It has a dusty, buttery, golden flavor. Saffron is available as whole stamens or as a powder. It is widely used to color rice, bread, pasta, and desserts.

Turmeric: Turmeric yields shades of yellow to orange. This tropical root grows as a small plant, related to ginger. It has an earthy, spicy flavor. The fresh root can be made into puree or juice, but turmeric is more often available as a powder. It is deeply staining. Turmeric is popular for coloring rice, bread, and curries.

Green

Matcha: Matcha makes a light creamy green or yellow-green. This is a type of powdered green tea, made from the leaves of the camellia bush. It is very popular in Asian ice cream, mochi, or cookie recipes. If you need liquid, simply make a cup of matcha tea; the color will be lighter but still in the same range.

Peas: Peas yield a medium to pale green. Peas have the mildest flavor of green colorings; fresh spring peas can be blended into a paste that makes excellent dip. You can also find freeze-dried pea powder.

Spinach: This produces medium to dark shades of green, lighter when young or raw, darker when old or cooked. Baby spinach leaves are quite mild, while the large mature leaves are stronger; canned or frozen spinach is nearly black and often very bitter. It's a popular garden green. The flavor can often be covered by something stronger, such as lime or mint. For food coloring, it's usually used as a puree or powder, but it can be juiced.

Spirulina: This gives fresh green to yellow-green colors. An algae, it has a leafy, briny flavor. It works best in savory recipes or used in small amounts to brighten other colorings. It comes as a powder.

Chlorella: This gives spruce-green to teal colors or, when more diluted, turquoise. A type of blue-green algae, it is readily available as a powder. The briny-green flavor is easier to blend with savory dishes but can also keep sweet ones from getting insipid. It's ideal for "mermaid" recipes.

Blue

Butterfly Pea Flower: This makes a bright sky blue. It is the dried flower of a particular pea vine. It usually comes as a flower but can be made into tea if you need a liquid.

Red Cabbage and Baking Soda: What starts as purple to red becomes a medium blue with the addition of a base. Many anthocyanins do this trick, so it works with a number of purple foods. Red cabbage is usually pureed or juiced for use as a color. Alone it tends to stay purple, and acid pushes it toward red or pink.

Purple

Blueberries: Blueberries give shades of purple, blue, pink, and almost red. Like many berries, their colors can vary and separate in use. They grow on small to medium bushes, some in marshy areas. Blueberries may be used as puree, juice, or freeze-dried powder. Most dark berries mix well with each other. Their colors tend to be quite staining and readily tint things like batter or icing.

Dragonfruit: Dragonfruit has a vivid red-violet color. This is the fruit of a cactus. It can be used as juice, puree, or powder. The powder is sometimes a super-saturated pink more than purple. The flavor is less strong than most other red to purple colors.

Grapes: For color, use red to purple grapes, which yield similar colors. Much of the color comes from the skin and its pulpy lining. Grape juice is usually bright red to blue-violet. The powder can be lavender, pink, or mauve and typically gives softer results.

Purple Sweet Potato: Also known as ube, purple sweet potato gives medium purple to lavender shades. This is the large pointed root of a vine. It can be used in puree form, but is most often sold as a powder. It has one of the mildest flavors among the purple colorings.

Brown

Black Tea: It produces shades from tan to brown, sometimes with reddish tints. Made from the fermented leaves of the camellia bush, it comes as tiny dried shreds that can be powdered or steeped into tea. The flavor is tangy and bitter, but excellent for adding complexity to sweet or savory dishes. Eggs and fruit can be soaked in tea to give them color and flavor.

Cinnamon: This is brown to dark red and imparts similar colors to food. It comes from the bark of several related tropical trees, available as curled bark sticks or powder, but it readily steeps into tea as well. The flavor is strong and spicy. It combines well with most brown or red foods.

Cocoa: Typically brown, it can turn reddish or black depending on treatment. It has a strong earthy, bitter flavor that is usually sweetened. It comes from the fermented beans of a small bush. Cocoa works both in sweet and savory recipes. It blends well with most brown, red, or black foods. It is available as a powder and candy chips; if you need liquid, make it into hot chocolate.

Whole Wheat or Rye: These flours produce light brown to almost black baked goods. They can deepen yellow to red colors too.

Black

Activated Charcoal: This carbon powder turns things gray to black. It can have a bitter or burnt flavor.

Squid Ink: Squid ink produces gray to black shades. This natural ink is usually sold as a liquid and has a briny flavor. It's used to tint pasta, rice, and other foods.

Easy-to-Color Recipes

Buttercream Icing

    1 cup unsalted butter, softened

    3 cups powdered sugar

    1 teaspoon vanilla extract (or other liquid flavor)

    1–2 tablespoons almond milk

    Natural food coloring powder

Beat the butter until fluffy. Add powdered sugar, mix in slowly, then beat until fluffy. Beat in the extract and 1 tablespoon almond milk. Other flavor options include almond extract, peppermint extract, citrus cordial, floral water, and so on. Add more almond milk if needed to reach spreading consistency.

To color a small amount of icing, start with ¼ teaspoon natural food coloring powder. To color a whole batch, start with 1 tablespoon. Stir and taste, increasing gradually to get desired color. Good coloring options include powdered berries (pink, red, or purple), carrot (orange), turmeric (yellow), matcha (green), and spirulina (turquoise).

⋙ Glossy Glaze

- 2 cups colorful juice
- 1 cup water, plus 2 tablespoons, separated
- 1 cup sugar
- 2 teaspoons lemon juice
- 2 tablespoons tapioca starch

Measure 2 cups of colorful juice. You can mix and match multiple juices to get a desired color. A little turmeric juice will enrich yellow to orange ones. A little pomegranate can strengthen red to purple ones. Most fruit (like blackberry) and a few vegetable (like carrot) juices will yield vivid jewel-toned glazes. For a more transparent glaze, dilute a deeper-colored juice (like cranberry) with a lighter one (like orange).

In a pot, combine fruit juice, water, sugar, and lemon juice. Stir constantly and bring to a boil. Reduce heat to a simmer. Stir and cook until the mixture begins to thicken.

In a small bowl, whisk 2 tablespoons tapioca starch and 2 tablespoons water until smooth. Pour into the hot juice mixture and stir to combine. Turn up the heat and cook for 3–5 minutes, stirring constantly, until the mixture thickens into a glaze. It should coat the spoon.

Pour the glaze into a bowl to cool. When cool, cover and place in the refrigerator. It will be fairly thick when cold, and it will cling heavily to cold things like fruit. Spooned over warm baked goods, however, it will melt and run down.

✎ Basic Cookies

½ cup puree in the color of your choice

⅓ cup unsalted butter, softened

½ cup sugar

1 teaspoon vanilla extract (or other liquid flavor)

1⅓ cups flour

½ teaspoon baking soda

Pinch of salt

Preheat the oven to 350°F. Spray a cookie sheet with non-stick spray.

Measure ½ cup puree. Berry puree will make purple to red. Pumpkin offers orange. Mango will give orange to yellow. Baby spinach is green. You can tweak the color with spices. Saffron will deepen yellow or brighten green, cinnamon will deepen orange to red, and so on.

Cream the butter and sugar until fluffy. Beat in the puree and extract.

Whisk together flour, baking soda, and salt. Add the dry ingredients to the wet ingredients, then stir to combine. Cover the dough and chill for 30 minutes.

Scoop the dough by tablespoons. Roll into balls. Place on cookie sheet and flatten slightly. Bake the cookies for 8–10 minutes, until the edges set and start to change color. Cool on the tray for a few minutes, then shift the cookies to a cooling rack.

An Italian-American Family Garden

⁂ Marilyn I. Bellemore ⁂

The sun beamed brightly on my three-year-old body as I crawled on hands and knees between the sugar snap pea vines in my Grandma Isabel's garden, picking yet eating what was meant to be part of our evening dinner with Grandpa Anthony.

When I returned to the back door, empty handed and covered in dirt, my gentle grandmother was not pleased that I ate the entire crop. But she still managed to make a delicious beef braciole for us to enjoy.

Instilled in all my childhood memories at Brown Avenue in North Providence, Rhode Island, is a majestic Rainier cherry tree and the Italian family garden in my grandparents' backyard, abundant and brimming with colorful

rows of vegetables and herbs. My grandma Isabel also let their tenant Charlie have part of the plot to plant for himself. Although the soil was the same, her vegetables seemed to grow a bit richer and more plentiful, and oftentimes Charlie could be seen sneaking a cucumber or two or three into his back pocket to enjoy in his lunchtime salad.

Gardens and fruit trees were a mainstay for Italian-American families who emigrated to the United States through Ellis Island as early as the 1880s. They were skilled at adapting what they grew to a different climate, although southern Florida and coastal California have tropical climates similar to the Mediterranean.

My grandparents were married in the 1930s and still had a garden forty years later. Zucchini, summer squash, tomatoes, cucumbers, spinach, lettuce, peppers, and string beans were staples. Rosemary, basil, oregano, sage, mint, and thyme were grown and used in everyday cooking. Popular fruit trees were fig, plum, cherry, and peach along with grape arbors. Every inch of space was used to plant, and the healthy gardens were a way to save money. For people who didn't own homes, many landlords generously allowed them to plant on their property. It was primarily a woman's job to tend to the garden, although the men helped with the digging and fencing.

I was fortunate to have a great-grandmother named Crescenza with peach and Italian plum trees in the yard of her little home where she lived alone into her early nineties. When I went there to visit with my grandparents, it seemed she was almost always outside planting, watering, or harvesting her fruits and vegetables.

Crescenza made a delicious dessert of wine-soaked peaches that I would be able to eat when I "got older." Until then, I could pick and devour all her Italian plums to my heart's content.

Back at Grandma Isabel's kitchen table, I would sit for hours watching her wash, prepare, and can vegetables or make a huge family dinner to feed a table of twelve. She did her work meticulously and effortlessly, and this was an integral part of a homemaker's life. I often had the task of rinsing the string beans in a colander and snapping off the ends before they were cooked and made into a salad.

Italian-American cooking varies by the region in Italy where people came from. My grandfather was from Castelpizzuto in Molise, and his father was from San Vittore in Lazio. The regions are only about fifty miles apart, yet the style of meal preparation was varied. Castelpizzuto is in a remote mountain range where lamb ragu, pork fritters, and pasta dishes are predominant. Both cavatelli and fusilli pasta originated in this region. It's more rustic than San Vittore cuisine. San Vittore has rich soil that produces excellent artichokes, cauliflower, and lentils. As it is less than thirty miles from Rome, there is definitely a cosmopolitan influence with gourmet ingredients more readily available. Castelpizzuto, in my opinion, has more meat-based cooking compared to San Vittore's emphasis on lots of fresh vegetables.

My grandmother and mother cooked with a keen eye and instinct. If someone asked them for a recipe, they'd usually say they didn't have one. Both women cooked by feel and knew when something was ready to eat. This would often cause frustration with my mom's friends who wanted a handwritten recipe, but she'd invite them over when she was cooking their favorite meal so they could "watch her." You'll see the recipes that follow sometimes lack quantities for this reason.

As adults, my twelve first cousins and I reminisce about not just holiday meals and Sunday dinners that Grandma Isabel prepared but also the everyday dishes she cooked. We were always welcome around the table, no matter what time of day or night. The kitchen was filled with laughter, love, and something to eat from our family garden.

Recipes

I inherited Grandma Isabel's gardening skills. No matter where I live, there are always herbs and vegetables growing in my yard or on my patio. I happily make do with the space I have. At this moment, there are cilantro, basil, thyme, rosemary, oregano, and tomatoes growing in pots on my patio that I cook with at every meal.

The following are recipes from my great-grandmother, grandmother, and mother that I enjoyed as a child and still make today. They incorporate fresh vegetables, fruits, and herbs and are easy to make and healthy to eat.

⋙ *Grandma Isabel's Squash Soup*

This was my absolute favorite dish made by my grandma. It includes just about everything found in an Italian-American family garden. She cooked it in a large pot on the back of the stove as I waited patiently for it to be ready. I am still fascinated that there is no water in this recipe.

You will need:

Vegetable oil

1 medium squash (summer or zucchini)

1 green pepper

1 medium potato

1 cup fresh string beans

2 fresh tomatoes

1 medium onion

Basil to taste

Parsley to taste

Salt and pepper to taste

Coat the bottom of a saucepan with vegetable oil. Chop and add all the vegetables and herbs. *Do not add water!* Cover and simmer until the vegetables are soft. Season with salt and pepper to taste.

✎ Grandma Isabel's Escarole Soup

My dad was six feet tall and weighed 128 pounds when he began dating my mom in the early 1950s, and her family always wanted to feed him. He was from a French-Canadian family that didn't have the elaborate Italian meals like the Feast of the Seven Fishes on Christmas Eve. Grandma Isabel's escarole soup was the first course for most special occasions. My dad always ate four or five bowls because it was so delicious, but then he'd be too full to eat anything else. You be the judge!

You will need:

1 whole raw chicken of a good size

2–3 carrots

1–2 onions

3 stalks celery

Seasonings

Escarole

Rice

Ground beef

Parsley

Garlic

3 eggs

½–1 cup bread crumbs

Boil a good-size chicken with carrots, onions, celery, and seasonings of your choice, skimming when necessary. Boil until the meat falls off the bones. Strain, discarding the vegetables and any scum, and refrigerate the chicken and broth.

The next day, skim off the fat and cube up the chicken. Heat the soup. Boil the escarole, drain, cut it up, and add it to the soup. Prepare your desired amount of rice according to its packaging and add it to the soup. Make tiny meatballs using the ground beef, parsley, garlic, 1 egg, and bread crumbs, and drop them in boiling soup until done. Hard boil 1–2 eggs, peel off the shells, mush the eggs, and add them to the soup. Season to taste.

⇝ Grandma Isabel's Squash Flowers

As a child, the swirls of yellow and orange squash flowers were fascinating to look at as I held the fried dough in my hand and even better to eat! Grandma Isabel made these as an annual treat. It was a big deal because there was only a small window of time to pick the squash flowers.

You will need:

1 egg

1–2 cups squash flowers

2 cups flour

1 teaspoon baking powder

Salt and pepper

Water to moisten

Beat the egg. Add remaining ingredients. Add water so it is liquidy. Drop the flowers by spoonfuls into a cast-iron pan coated with heated oil. Brown on both sides until cooked through. Place them on a large plate that is covered with a paper towel. Sprinkle with salt and pepper to taste.

⇗ Grandma Isabel's Stuffed Peppers

To this day, I've yet to find anyone who can make this recipe the way my grandma did. I imagine the seasoning of her heavy baking pan had a lot to do with it. We often had stuffed peppers for lunch, but they also served as an appetizer at larger evening meals. To me, almost synonymous with Italian-American cooking is the Italian-American slang word for heartburn, *agita*. My mom always said the red bell peppers didn't cause heartburn.

You will need:

  Red or green bell peppers
  Old bread, preferably Italian
  Minced garlic
  Chopped black olives
  Grated cheese of your choice
  Olive oil
  Salt and pepper to taste

Slice the peppers in half. Mix all the other ingredients together in a bowl with your hands, then fill the peppers. You'll want the stuffing to be about ½ bread, and I usually fill the peppers with about ½ cup stuffing. Put the peppers into a heavy baking pan that has been drizzled with olive oil. Add a little water to cover the bottom of the pan. You can cover the pan with foil before putting it in the oven. Bake at 350°F (do not preheat) until the peppers are soft.

✎ Grandma Isabel's Eggs and Tomatoes

My grandmother would whip this up quickly if anyone stopped in with a fresh loaf of Italian bread. The color always reminded me of salmon. It's an easy recipe to follow, and yet I long for the way Grandma Isabel and Mom made it.

You will need:

> 2–3 tablespoons vegetable oil
>
> 1 small onion
>
> 8 ounces tomato sauce
>
> 2 eggs

Saute the onion in oil. Add the tomato sauce or your own sauce made with fresh tomatoes. Cook down for approximately 20 minutes. Beat the eggs and cook them in the sauce. Serve on fresh Italian bread.

✎ Mom's Italian String Bean Salad

This salad could be found on Grandma Isabel's table almost every day in season. Although it may not appeal to many people, I especially liked to eat it day-old because the string beans would be soft and soggy. Italian string beans are wider and flatter than the standard ones. I call this "Mom's" because my mother tweaked the recipe by adding fresh mint.

You will need:

> 1 pound Italian or standard green beans
>
> 1 clove garlic, crushed
>
> 2 tablespoons fresh mint, if desired

1 tablespoon fresh oregano

1 tablespoon balsamic vinegar

2 tablespoons fresh parsley

3 tablespoons olive oil

Salt and pepper to taste

Bring a large pot of water to a boil. Trim the ends of the beans, rinse, and place in boiling water until tender. Drain the beans and put in a serving bowl. Add all the ingredients, toss, and put in the refrigerator until chilled.

⇗ Great Grandma Crescenza's Peaches in White Wine

My mother made this in the summer months, as I now do. It's refreshing and delicious. In addition to making peaches in white wine, my great grandma also soaked peeled plums and peeled and chopped cherries in wine. She used whatever wine was available, whether white or red.

You will need:

2–3 very ripe peaches

White wine of your choice

Fresh mint leaves for garnish

Peel the peaches, slice them into wedges, and place them in wine glasses. Pour white wine over the peaches to cover and allow them to sit in the refrigerator for 24 hours. The peaches will soak in all the wine and be chilled. Garnish with mint leaves. Serve with a fork and eat right from the glass.

The Italian Garden Project

The Italian Garden Project, whose mission is "to celebrate the joy and wisdom inherent in the traditional Italian American vegetable garden," hosts a gallery of photos, videos, and stories of gardens around the country.

No matter what part of Italy our ancestors were from, I feel a close bond with other Italian-Americans, in part because so many of us had grandparents with Italian-American family gardens and fruit trees. I continue on the tradition myself by growing and tending to vegetables, herbs, and fruit trees at my summer home on Prince Edward Island and where I live in Rhode Island. Canning vegetables and making jams, jellies, and pickles is a way for me to share the wealth with family and friends.

So many of us are doing our part through writing articles, telling stories, and sharing memories of what these gardens mean to us. The Italian Garden Project preserves the heritage of the gardens by "reconnecting food, family, and the earth." More information about the project is available at https://theitaliangardenproject.com.

Health
and
Beauty

Pollen

✥ Suzanne Ress ✥

Pollen is made by all seed plants and is used to transfer male genetic traits from a flower's anther to the stigma of the same or another flower. In very simplified anthropocentric terms, pollen is to plants what sperm is to animals. Many insects, not only bees and butterflies, eat plant pollen. Some types of spiders catch wind-blown pollen in their webs to feed their babies with!

Pollen has been called a superfood for humans. It is loaded with vitamin C, potassium, magnesium, and calcium, antioxidants (which fight free radicals), amino acids, phenolic compounds, and protein, and there are various claims about its ability to protect against aging, chronic disease, inflammation, and infection, as well as to boost sexual potency, athletic ability, the immune system, strength, and endurance.

There are four forms of pollen that you can incorporate into your diet without resorting to supplements: bee pollen, honey, plant pollen, and whole edible flowers. I will discuss a little bit about each of these.

Bee Pollen

Bee pollen is more than just pollen. It also contains flower nectar and enzymatic bee secretions, which hold it together into the tiny gold nugget shape.

There are many claims about the benefits of eating bee pollen; however, it is important to know that one generic bee pollen will differ widely from another. Bees collect pollen from many plants, and depending on the time of year and the place where the pollen was gathered from the bees, there will be differences in the nutritional value and taste of the pollen.

In general, your best bet is to obtain fresh bee pollen from a local beekeeper, making certain that the pollen you are getting actually came from that beekeeper's bees. In some cases, even your trusty local beekeeper may have bought pollen from a second or third party to fill their clients' demands, which could mean it is neither fresh nor local. Some bee pollens produced on a larger commercial scale may have come from plants that were sprayed with chemicals in a distant locale a few years ago, and these are not going to give you the same benefits as really fresh local pollen. Even when bee pollen is labeled as being organic, there is no way that the organic (or any) beekeeper can control where his bees gather pollen, so you may be getting a small amount of toxic chemicals such as herbicides and pesticides too.

Bee pollen is supposed to help protect people from cancer, high cholesterol, bacterial diseases, and infections. It follows that it also possibly contributes to longevity. Personally, I really enjoy the way it tastes and looks, on its own or added to yogurt, fruit salads, and even peanut butter sandwiches.

Honey

All raw honey contains some plant pollen, so if you choose to eat raw, guaranteed-local honey, you will be consuming some pollen from your local pollen-producing plants, and it is thought that seasonal pollen allergy sufferers may benefit from this. It's a way to help your body get used to the offending pollen in small amounts over time, with the idea that eventually your system will no longer signal these pollens as being enemies, and your allergic reaction will diminish or disappear altogether. It is probably safer for allergy sufferers to start out by consuming only a teaspoon or two of raw local honey per day and, after some time, to try small amounts of local bee pollen. In some cases, allergic people may have extreme reactions to bee pollen, so it's best to proceed with caution.

Locally produced raw honey is often labeled as **monofloral**, which means it is primarily made up of only one type of flower nectar and pollen, but even monofloral honeys do contain pollens from other plants in bloom in your area at the same time. Probably, if you are aiming to alleviate seasonal allergies, selecting a raw local honey produced during the season your allergies flare up (spring, late summer, autumn) is your best bet.

There are analysts who specialize in identifying the plant pollens in honey and in bee pollen. They are called **melissopalynologists**, and the general field of pollen and spore study is called **palynology**. Under a microscope, single grains of pollen are gorgeously cute—some are spherical, some spiked, some ovular, some shaped like potato gnocchi or triangular stars, some are textured, and others smooth as peach skin. Some are bigger, some smaller, and they come in fantastic shades of purple, blue, orange, green, yellow, pink, gray, and more, even multicolor. You can view wondrous images of them online. These adorable little packages are full of nutritional elements, each slightly different from the others.

Plant Pollen

Some plant pollens are toxic to humans, so it's best not to eat anything unless you are 100 percent sure it is okay to eat. In general, the pollen of an edible plant is edible too, but if you suffer from respiratory allergic reactions to a certain type of plant pollen, don't eat it.

Pine pollen is considered by some to be a superfood with antiaging properties. It contains plant-based hormones that are believed to be especially useful to both male and female athletes and body builders. Its other possible benefits include aiding in arthritis relief, helping alleviate skin problems, and supporting the immune system. It is full of amino acids, antioxidants, anti-inflammatories, flavonoids, vitamins, and minerals.

To collect pine pollen, in the spring place a paper bag over a flowering male branch and shake the branch. Repeat over several branches. You don't need pounds of pollen—a few teaspoons will go a long way.

Saffron is considered a spice, and it's actually the pollen of the spring-flowering *Crocus sativus*. It is used in recipes to impart a delicately sweet, earthy, and uniquely pronounced flavor and a lively yellow color. It is renowned for being quite costly: a tiny vial containing just a few red threads can cost five or six dollars per gram (less than half a teaspoon).

The red saffron threads are the pollen-coated stigmas of the wild crocus flower. Each flower produces only three stigmas and they must be carefully harvested by hand.

Saffron is the traditional spice used in Spanish paella, Milanese risotto, Welsh saffron bread, and in Moroccan chicken stew, and it has been successfully incorporated into newer creative recipes especially with fish, chicken, and rice. Because saffron is so expensive, it is sometimes substituted with turmeric, which will give a dish the same lively color but will not give the distinctive flavor of saffron.

Saffron has such a unique flavor and scent, due to the natural chemicals picrocrocin and safranal, that it is also widely employed in perfume formulations. It is often used in oud- or leather-reminiscent perfumes for its mysterious and unique Arabian-like notes.

Nutritionally, similar to other pollens, saffron contains high amounts of potassium, vitamin C, vitamin B_6, magnesium, calcium, and protein. Of course, you would eat such a miniscule amount of this spice that the nutritional benefits might not matter.

Saffron also contains healthy antioxidants and is believed to help alleviate depression and help improve sexual libido, but, again, unless you are regularly taking a supplement, the addition of a pinch of saffron to a recipe every now and then will mainly just add to your pleasurable eating experience.

Years ago, when I was first laying out my extensive herb gardens, I put a couple of fennel plants in a sunny spot. These have self-seeded and spread every year, so I have quite a large patch of fennel flowers in early summer. The flowers are yellow umbellifers, and each tiny blossom on each umbellifer produces a bit of pollen. When the flowers are ready, one can be snipped off its stem and the fresh pollen rubbed out over whatever I want it on—potato salad, deviled eggs, fresh garden vegetables, fish, and even ice cream. Its flavor is similar to fennel bulb or frond but more intense and citrus-like. Fennel pollen's flavor comes from the natural chemical compound anethole.

Dill pollen, harvested just like fennel pollen, has a stronger flavor than the dill fronds traditionally used in pickles and the dill seeds in potato salads. The pollen's flavor is also more flowery and sweet. This comes from phellandrene, cymene, and terpinene.

Hemp pollen can be gathered from the male plants using a small paper bag, the same way you'd gather pine pollen. It can also be purchased. It can be sprinkled on salads, fresh garden vegetables, yogurts, and more.

All pollens should be added to cooked dishes just at the very end of cooking. They should never undergo the cooking process.

Whole Edible Flowers Containing Pollen

If a flower is edible, its pollen is too. Many edible flowers are tiny, and collecting even a pinch of pollen would be tricky, time-consuming work. Just make certain that you are not allergic to a particular flower's pollen before eating it.

Anytime you eat a whole flower blossom, you are eating its pollen as well. Zucchini blossom fritters are made from the male flowers of the plants (which will not produce a fruit). Cut these off the vine just before they bloom, dip them into a light egg batter, and then fry in hot oil—they are a tasty treat, full of pollen. Some people remove the stamens before using them, saying they are bitter, but I have not found this to be so.

Tiny whole violets, pansies, and blue borage flowers tossed into a fresh green salad add not only magic and color but also a little bit of pollen.

Years ago, I read that unopened wild daylily flowers were a good forager's substitute for green beans, and I ate these raw, not considering at the time that I was eating their pollen. Unopened daylily blossoms can be prepared and fried the same way as zucchini fritters.

Nasturtiums, both the leaves and flowers, make a slightly peppery and gorgeous addition to salads, and of course the bright red, yellow, and orange flowers come complete with pollen.

Lavender flowers, lovely little purple blossoms on stalks, are delicious when added to cool summer drinks as well as to roast chicken, potatoes (where you might also add some rosemary flowers), and even cold chicken salads.

When you make a cup of chamomile tea, if the tea has been properly gathered and is only made from the whole flowers, you are reaping some of the benefits of the flowers' pollen.

In the spring, let some of your chives make buds, and just as they flower, cut the flowers to float on potato soup, or chop them up and stir them into mayonnaise.

Elderberry flowers can be made into fragrant fritters, as can the white flowering racemes of black locust flowers in May.

Chopped whole passionflowers mixed with a little sugar, port, honey, lemon, and orange juice can be left a few hours to macerate and then spooned over vanilla ice cream for a refreshing summer dessert.

Try biting the tiny flowers off a spire of blooming mint for a pleasantly delicate breath freshener.

Dandelions can, of course, be processed to make wine, but you can also put the whole flowers, chopped up, into omelettes or crepes. Just be certain you do not use dandelions picked from a lawn that has been sprayed with toxic chemicals or dirtied by traffic dust.

Other Uses for Pollen

There are many more uses for edible flowers, including in vinegars, liqueurs, and baked goods, and often an herb plant produces pretty and tasty flowers that you may as well use!

Pollen can also be used in beauty products. Because of its high vitamin, mineral, and protein contents, it is believed to be beneficial to the skin, keeping it smooth and rejuvenated, and removing any free radical pollutants you may be exposed to. Prepared beauty products such as facial masks, creams, and soaps containing pollen can be purchased, but you may get better results by simply adding some of your locally produced bee pollen to your regular bought or homemade mask, scrub, or night cream!

Herbal Remedies for Better Sleep

⤙ Mireille Blacke, RD, CD-N ⤚

I've suffered from chronic insomnia and disordered sleep patterns all my adult life and can share from the perspective of a patient as well as a healthcare provider. Most of us know that sleep deprivation, whether acute or chronic, or recurrent bouts of insomnia can lead to significant disruption in our overall health and well-being. In my experience as a registered dietitian and addiction counselor, issues with sleep dysregulation often emerge when I'm addressing behavioral health nutrition considerations with clients. Sometimes the treatment can be as troubling as the underlying condition.

For example, I, along with many of my clients, have been prescribed

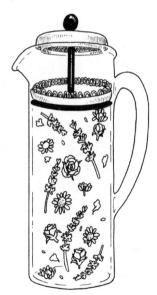

Ambien (zolpidem) for sleep. This prescription medication works for sleep, but there might be unexpected side effects, which may or may not be known to you. There is evidence that some individuals taking Ambien fall asleep initially but later eat during the night, with little to no memory of their eating behaviors during the nocturnal episodes. Obviously, this can lead to baffling weight gain and other issues that must be addressed. In addition to sleep eating, there are other reported nighttime behaviors that may occur without recollection, from the benign (watching movies) to the dangerous ("waking up" behind the wheel).

In my case, I emailed close friends, with no recollection of doing so, in a language barely resembling English. Frankly, until I put the facts together, I thought my email account was hacked. I also "creatively cooked" while taking Ambien, meaning the concoctions I made didn't consist of actual food. I stored these uneaten "dishes" in the closet, laundry room, or other parts of the house—we're talking inedible creations regardless. I was rather lucky, though; friends and clients have sustained falls, fractures, and various at-home accidents while under the influence of Ambien or other prescribed sleep medications.

It's clear that while appropriate for some, Ambien, Lunesta, and other prescription sleep aids are not well-suited for everyone. It's reasonable that some people seek out alternative remedies for sleep, including herbal options.

Always consult with your healthcare provider or pharmacist before taking any herbs or herbal supplements. They'll inform you of the latest safety and risk information. If you're under eighteen or over sixty-five years of age, pregnant, lactating, or within two weeks of having surgery, it's best to avoid herbal supplements.

To determine if herbal remedies for sleep might work for you, it's important to know a bit more about the mechanics of sleep. Like most issues humans deal with, sleep is multifactorial and complex. The inability to sleep will not usually just come down to late-night caffeine intake or a snoring spouse. There are a number of possible underlying medical reasons for disrupted sleep, such as obstructive sleep apnea, gastroesophageal reflux disease, restless legs syndrome, and anxiety. (A sleep study can investigate some of these.) Otherwise, making some nutrition and behavioral changes may help.

There are certain foods that interfere with sleep, and these should be avoided or adjusted in your daily intake. Stimulants such as caffeine should be limited in quantity and to earlier times of the day. Caffeine's diuretic effect can lead to nighttime waking for urination, which doesn't facilitate a good night's rest. Eating your larger meals earlier in the day is recommended, as a heavier meal before bed can lead to problems sleeping due to indigestion. Similarly, moving spicier meals to earlier in the day is preferred to avoid stomach distress that can keep you awake. It's important to assess food additives like monosodium glutamate (MSG), prevalent in Chinese food, which may lead to bloating, and your intake of other gas-forming foods. Similar discomfort may come from allergies to corn, wheat, chocolate, or lactose. One of the most important sleep disrupters in food is tyramine, found in aged cheeses, red wine, cured meats, smoked fish, and some beers, as it triggers the release of the brain-stimulating neurotransmitter norepinephrine.

In terms of food sources to include, our focus must shift to certain micronutrients and tryptophan, melatonin, and gamma-aminobutyric acid (GABA).

The essential amino acid tryptophan is the building block for serotonin, the neurotransmitter that regulates sleep. Think about turkey overload at the Thanksgiving holiday and the subsequent sleepiness that follows for the effect of tryptophan, as turkey is a high-protein source of it. An essential amino acid is one that humans don't produce naturally and must come from the diet. However, some food sources (like milk) that are high in tryptophan also contain compounds that will compete with tryptophan for absorption and entry into the brain. Therefore, it's possible to influence natural tryptophan levels for longer and better quality sleep by eating a light, high-carbohydrate, low-protein snack one to two hours before bedtime. See the baked apple and savory cilantro dip with baked tortilla chips recipes in the related recipes section for examples.

Drinking tart cherry juice an hour before bedtime may improve sleep, because it contains melatonin and helps increase tryptophan levels.

Melatonin is a hormone secreted by the pineal gland in the brain to regulate the sleep-wake cycle, when triggered by darkness. When melatonin levels drop, an individual may experience difficulty falling or staying asleep. Unfortunately, natural melatonin levels decrease as we age. Melatonin is found naturally in cardamom and purslane, as well as goji berries, milk, and pistachios.

GABA is a neurotransmitter that facilitates sleep by inhibiting stress and anxiety. Examples of herbs that impact GABA activity include chamomile, hops, lemon balm, passionflower, and valerian root.

Certain micronutrients are vital to healthy sleep cycles. B vitamin deficiencies in particular derail healthy sleep patterns, notably B_1, B_6, B_{12}, and folic acid. B_6 specifically is critical for normal serotonin production. Calcium and magnesium are minerals that work in tandem to relax and contract muscles, stimulate nerves, and assist in deep-sleep eye movements. Low magnesium leads to low melatonin, resulting in wakeful nights, inability to fall asleep, and irritability. Low copper and iron intake also impact sleep negatively, leading to more night-time awakenings, restlessness, and longer latency to sleep. For guidance on finding food sources containing B vitamins, magnesium, calcium, copper, and iron, please see the online guide recommendations and resources sections at the end of this article.

Herbs and Spices

Some herbs and spices can promote better sleep directly by increasing tryptophan, melatonin, and GABA levels or by helping replace micronutrient (e.g., magnesium) deficiencies linked to impaired sleep. Others may have an indirect effect by calming the digestive system, dulling inflammatory pain (like arthritis), or relieving anxiety. Many of the following herbs may be brewed as a "sleepy tea" to drink an hour before bedtime.

Banana

Active Compounds: Potassium, magnesium, vitamin B_6
Mechanism: Micronutrient source
Side Effects: In excess, nausea, vomiting, upset stomach, high potassium levels

Cardamom

Active Compounds: Melatonin, alpha-terpineol, limonene
Mechanism: Alpha-terpineol increases sleep duration; limonene decreases restlessness at night.
Use: Tea, milk, lentils, curries, chicken, rice, bread
Side Effects: Contact dermatitis; in excess, gallstones, diarrhea

Chamomile

Active Compound: Apigenin
Mechanism: Apigenin binds to GABA receptors; decreases anxiety and stress.
Use: See turmeric chamomile milk recipe.
Side Effects: Nausea, vomiting. Don't take with blood thinners, birth control pills, or alcohol; allergic cross-reaction to pollen.

Cinnamon

Active Compound: Cinnamaldehyde
Mechanism: Anti-inflammatory and calming properties in cinnamon reduce stress and indirectly promote sleep.
Use: Try warm milk and cinnamon with a dash of vanilla thirty minutes before bed.
Side Effects: In excess, mouth sores, dizziness, digestive problems, respiratory problems

Garlic
Active Compounds: Zinc, potassium, allicin
Mechanism: Micronutrient source; allicin is a natural relaxant.
Use: Eat with last meal of the day, in moderation.
Side Effects: In excess, bloating, nausea, heartburn, diarrhea

Ginger
Active Compound: 6-gingerol
Mechanism: Relieves indigestion and nausea, indirectly making falling asleep and staying asleep easier.
Note: May interact with blood thinner warfarin (Coumadin).
Side Effects: Should be avoided in persons with gallstones, as it stimulates bile production. Avoid the "ginger jitters" (central nervous system excitation) by keeping intake to less than two grams of ginger per kilogram (1 kg = 2.2 lbs.) of body weight.

Hops
Active Compounds: Humulene, lupulin
Mechanism: GABA increase in the brain, which promotes relaxation and sleep.
Use: For tea, pair with valerian and passionflower for best effect.
Side Effects: Dizziness; allergic cross-reaction to birch pollen.

Lavender
Active Compounds: Calcium, iron, limonene
Mechanism: Stress and anxiety reduction, facilitating sleep.
Use: For tea, add 2 teaspoons dried lavender flowers to 8-ounce cup of boiling water. Sweeten with 1 teaspoon of organic honey. Alternatively, place 4 teaspoons of

fresh lavender buds into a tea ball after boiling 8 ounces of water. Add the tea ball to the water, and steep for 10 minutes.

Side Effects: Women who are pregnant or breastfeeding should avoid using lavender oil or ingesting the plant. If mint affects you negatively, you may also experience negative side effects (headaches, constipation, increased appetite) from the lavender plant.

Lemon Balm

Active Compound: Rosmarinic acid

Mechanism: Combined with valerian root, hops, and chamomile, helps reduce anxiety and restlessness to promote sleep.

Interactions/Side Effects: Avoid with glaucoma or antiretroviral medications.

Mustard Seed

Active Compounds: Omega-3 fatty acids, tryptophan

Mechanism: Tryptophan promotes serotonin production, benefiting sleep.

Use: Add to mashed potatoes or roasted cauliflower.

Side Effects: In excess, abdominal pain and diarrhea

Nutmeg

Active Compound: Myristicin

Mechanism: A moderate amount can relieve anxiety, soothe muscle/joint ailments, and promote healthier digestion, leading to better sleep.

Use: Add a pinch of nutmeg to warm milk to act as a calming agent.

Side Effects: Use in moderation only; in excess, nausea and hallucinations.

Passionflower

Active Compound: Apigenin
Mechanism: Increases GABA, promoting relaxation and sleep.
Side Effects: Dizziness, confusion

Purslane

Active Compounds: Melatonin, omega-3 fatty acids, B vitamins, calcium, magnesium, iron
Mechanism: Increases melatonin; micronutrient source, decreases nightmares (indirect).
Use: Tea; as a lettuce or spinach substitute
Side Effects: Kidney stones with overconsumption

Turmeric

Active Compounds: Iron, vitamin B_6, potassium, omega-3 fatty acids, curcumin
Mechanism: Micronutrient source; indirectly benefits sleep as anti-inflammatory and digestive aid.
Use: See turmeric chamomile milk recipe on page 156.
Side Effects: Excess may lead to stomach distress.
Note: Curcumin needs piperine in black pepper for best absorption. Toss in some black pepper when you use turmeric in recipes.

Valerian Root

Active Compound: Valerenic acid
Mechanism: Increases GABA
Side Effects: Unpleasant taste, vivid dreams/nightmares, stomach upset, headache. Overdoses of valerian can cause blurred vision, changes in heartbeat, and excitability.

Tips for Incorporating Herbals for Better Sleep

1. Before taking any herbs or herbal supplements, ask your healthcare provider's opinion about safety, risks, and interaction potential with medications. If you have the herbal container or label, review it with your provider(s).

2. Avoid alcohol and caffeine, particularly in the evening. Set a caffeine cut-off point (e.g., noon) if necessary.

3. Moderate meal plans based on potential sleep interference: meal sizes, spiciness, additives (e.g., MSG), gas-forming foods, allergens, and foods containing tyramine.

4. Incorporate food sources that provide optimal levels of B vitamins, calcium, magnesium, copper, and iron into your daily intake. (See the recommended online guides section for resources.)

5. Select herbs and plant-based food sources that boost tryptophan, melatonin, and GABA levels to enhance sleep.

6. Consume a light, carbohydrate-rich, low-protein snack one to two hours before bedtime. See the related recipes section.

7. Practice moderation. Too much of a good thing might be harmful, and herbals are no exception. For example, stomach distress is common with large quantities of ginger, nutmeg, and turmeric.

8. Chronic sleep disturbances can be frustrating as well as exhausting. But before throwing in the towel, please discuss your individual situation with a licensed healthcare provider (sleep medicine is a specialty) to discuss potential causes and solutions.

So, do herbal remedies ultimately improve sleep quality? The answer is: it's complicated. If you struggle with occasional insomnia, it's very likely one of these herbal suggestions will work for you and promote better sleep. But if you've struggled with a diagnosed sleep disorder for most of your adult life, it's probably unrealistic to expect an herbal tea or simple lifestyle modification to improve your sleep quality after one night. It's more likely that you'll need to work with a sleep medicine specialist or a multidisciplinary team to further investigate your individual situation.

Speaking as someone who has been on both sides of the sleep study, I encourage you to communicate openly about your concerns, because support is out there. Just wait until morning to send any emails.

Related Recipes

⤳ *Savory Dip with Baked Tortilla Chips*

This tasty recipe has been adapted from *The Food and Mood Cookbook*. Because I'm not a fan of cilantro, I exclude it when I make this outstanding dish, and it's just as good. Regardless of your personal preferences, be sure to give yourself enough time to refrigerate the dip and prepare the tortilla chips when you make it!

You will need:

  1 8-ounce container fat-free or low-fat sour cream
   (Choose a firm brand of sour cream to avoid a runny dip.)

  ¼ cup nonfat mayonnaise

  ½ cup fresh chopped cilantro

  1 tablespoon honey

  ½ teaspoon cumin

  ¼ teaspoon red pepper flakes

2 tablespoons fresh lime juice

½ cup premade salsa

12 corn tortillas

Salt, cayenne, or garlic powder

To make the dip, in a medium bowl, combine sour cream, mayonnaise, cilantro, honey, cumin, red pepper flakes, and lime juice. Mix well. Cover the bowl and refrigerate for 1–2 hours.

Prior to serving, pour ½ cup salsa over the dip. Serve with chips.

To make the chips, preheat your oven to 375°F. Stack corn tortillas. First, cut them in half, then into thirds. Place the wedges on ungreased cookie sheets and sprinkle with salt, cayenne, or garlic powder, to your preferred taste. Bake about 10 minutes, or until wedges are crisp but not burned.

Makes about 6 dozen chips (about 8 servings).

⇗ Turmeric Chamomile Moon Milk

Try the following recipe, adapted from the *Plant and Soul* blog, for a single serving of soothing sleep assistance prior to bedtime.

You will need:

8 ounces whole milk (Substitute with plant-based milk if you prefer.)

4 ounces water

1 heaping tablespoon dried chamomile flowers

½ teaspoon ground turmeric

¼ teaspoon freshly cracked black pepper

1 teaspoon maple syrup, or to taste (optional, for sweetness)

Add the listed ingredients to a small saucepan on the stove. Heat to just before a full boil, then reduce the heat to low and cover the saucepan.

Steep the covered saucepan on low heat for 10 minutes. Strain all ingredients through a mesh sieve into a mug.

Serve within an hour of bedtime.

⇜ Baked Apples

This recipe, adapted from *The Food and Mood Cookbook*, is an example of a light, high-carbohydrate, low-protein snack ideally for eating one to two hours before bedtime to elevate tryptophan levels and provide better quality sleep. Please note that for this recipe cooking times may vary with apple and oven types.

You will need:

6 medium red cooking apples

½ cup raisins and / or dried cranberries

¼ cup brown sugar

½ teaspoon cinnamon

½ teaspoon nutmeg

Pinch of cardamom

2 tablespoons (6 teaspoons) reduced-fat margarine

½ cup apple juice concentrate

½ cup water

Preheat oven to 350°F.

Core and peel the top half of each apple. Set aside.

Combine and stir raisins (and / or cranberries), brown sugar, cinnamon, nutmeg, and cardamom. Evenly spoon the raisin-cranberry mixture into opening of each apple.

After placing apples into a baking dish, top each apple with 1 teaspoon margarine.

Mix apple juice concentrate with water. Pour this mixture over the apples and cover.

Bake in the oven for 50 minutes or until apples are tender. Baste occasionally.

The apples may be served warm or cooled. Makes 6 servings. For snack-size pieces, let the apples cool and cut into 1-inch slices.

Recommended Online Guides

Choose MyPlate: myplate.gov

National Center for Complementary and Integrative Health (NCCIH). Herbs at a Glance: nccih.nih.gov/health/herbsataglance.htm

NIH MedlinePlus Database of Herbs and Supplements: medlineplus .gov/druginfo/herb_All.html

Resources

Jillian. "Turmeric Chamomile Moon Milk Recipe." *Plant and Soul* (blog), January 7, 2021. https://plantandsoul.com/turmeric-and-chamomile-moon-milk/.

Somer, Elizabeth. *The Food and Mood Cookbook: Recipes for Eating Well and Feeling Your Best.* New York: Holt, 2004.

Antivirals

⤡ Charlie Rainbow Wolf ⤡

My late parents dealt with viral infections in very different ways, but both with homemade remedies. My mother's consisted of honey, lemon, and ginger; my father's of garlic, black pepper, and apricots. Mum's concoction went into a wee dram of scotch, while Dad's was boiled in grog (half water, half navy rum), then strained, and the liquid taken by the tablespoon in a mug of hot water. Both of them swore their concoction worked, and to this day every time I smell a hot toddy (water, whisky, honey, and lemon) my olfactory takes me right back to my childhood.

There's more than just folklore when it comes to some of these old-timer's remedies, though, and the recent pandemic has caused many people to reevaluate their diets, their lifestyles, and their use of herbs as more than just seasonings. Now, I never want to encourage anyone to avoid seeking medical attention when it is necessary: many aspects of herbal remedies may be used *in conjunction with* modern treatments. Always seek the advice of your primary caregiver before trying anything new.

Eat Your Greens

I grew up being told by my mum to eat my greens, and there's a reason for that. Green leafy vegetables are high in a phytochemical called sulforaphane, which in addition to having anticancer properties also looks to inhibit the replication of SARS-CoV-2.[1] Sulforaphane is found largely in cruciferous veggies such as broccoli, brussels sprouts, and leafy greens like kale, cabbage, and spinach.

Of course, foods with antiviral properties are not limited to just a few green veggies! Fruits like Daddy's apricots also help fight off viral infections, as do nuts, seeds, other fruits, seafood, and fungi. In short, plant-based foods and those found in the wild have more antiviral properties, as opposed to processed foods.[2]

Spice Things Up

Enter Mum's ginger. Ginger and other spices have a history of being effective when it comes to viral infections because they help inhibit the buildup of plaque in the airways. According to the National Library of Medicine, it has to be fresh ginger, rather than dried.[3] I have to admit that once I started using fresh ginger root in cooking and baking rather than dried, the difference in the taste was so profound that I now only use dried ginger in anything as a last resort.

Dad's garlic has a role to play here too. According to Mountain Rose Herbs, the use of garlic goes back centuries—five thousand years, in fact—and has been in use for so long that it is hard to determine exactly where its popularity started.[4] It has a history in folklore as well as healing properties. Medicinally, it is an antiviral; it boosts the immune system; it may help with the prevention of high blood pressure, cancer, and high cholesterol; it's said to improve athletic performance; and because it helps the body detox itself, it may even help prevent the onset of dementia and Alzheimer's disease.

Top It Off with Fruit

Fresh fruit assists the body in fighting off viruses. Citrus fruits are high in vitamin C, which helps attack pathogens and also promotes the removal of old immune cells from infected areas. Other beneficial fruits are berries such as strawberries and black currants and fruiting veggies like capsicum (peppers) and tomatoes. Once again, it is best to take these fruits and fruiting vegetables fresh, rather than in supplement form.[5]

Fresh fruit—and most vegetables, for that matter—not only help fight off infections, but they help keep the microbiome in the gut healthy. Many battles against disease are won or lost in the gut, no matter where the actual symptoms are manifesting. There are helpful bacteria, viruses, and fungi in the gut, and when they are weakened or out of balance, it is easy for unwanted bacteria and pathogens to invade. The beneficial organisms in the gut produce short chain fatty acids by digesting fiber, and fresh fruits and vegetables are a great source for getting fiber into the diet. The gut microbiome is also linked to mental health via the nervous system and to the immune system and how well the body responds to infection.[6]

The Antiviral Menu

Wheef! That was a lot of heavy stuff, but hopefully it brings some insight as to how important it is to consume antivirals in the diet, every day. It's easy to grow many of these important foods and spices in the garden.

We start every week by planning out a menu that consists of a lot of G-BOMBS. What are G-BOMBS? This is the term that Dr. Joel Fuhrman uses to describe important inclusions on the diet to help optimize the gut microbiome and improve the immune system. G-BOMBS stands for greens, beans, onions, mushrooms, berries, and seeds.[7] There's nothing exotic there, so it's all quite easy to either purchase or grow. Here at the Keep we grow cabbage, brussels sprouts, kale, green and wax beans, raspberries, gooseberries, and serviceberries (and I'll throw rose hips into that too), and in the past we have had blueberries and salad onions. Even for those living in an apartment, it's possible to get a mushroom kit and grow mushrooms or get a seed sprouting kit and grow supergreens by eating the shoots of the sprouted seeds.

The more I learn about modern farming methods, the pickier I become about my food source and the more I want to grow my own food. Even foods marked non-GMO are often sprayed with glyphosate to make them ripen faster. I recently read a very disturbing report on this, and it has changed the way I shop—particularly for grains and bread flour. Glyphosate is sprayed onto the non-GMO crop before harvest to hurry up the ripening. It does not have time to break down before the grain is harvested![8] I thought I was doing the right thing buying non-GMO flour, but I was still consuming glyphosate.

Antiviral Herbs

To me, this is where things get interesting. I was battling an illness in the early months of 2022 and couldn't get the medical community to listen to me. They kept trying to diagnose me and push their pills onto me without doing any testing, which only exacerbated the issue. Fed up, I started to look for alternatives. I went to a Chinese herbal medicine doctor, and within six weeks of following his guidelines and taking his herbs, I was much improved. I'm convinced he saved my life.

There are as many herbal remedies as there are conditions that plague us in twenty-first-century Western society, but sadly many of the traditional herbal treatments are either overlooked or treated as bogus. Don't get me wrong—Western medicine has its place, and just because something is folk medicine doesn't mean that it is a cure-all. Modern medicine has saved a lot of lives! For me, it's a case of "Don't throw the baby out with the bathwater." Even my Chinese herbal medicine doc looks at lab results.

My top six antiviral herbs are ones that I can grow here as well as ones easily obtainable either fresh or dried through greengrocers, supermarkets, health food shops, and gardener's suppliers.

Sage

Many people wax lyrical about the properties of the white sage (*Salvia apiana*), but I'm talking about plain ol' garden sage, *Salvia officinalis*. I grow it in multiple places in the yarden (yard + garden = yarden). It is easy to use fresh, is easy to dry at home, and can be included in many herbal preparations, from turkey stuffing to tea to infused oils and vinegars, and even shower steamers!

Sage is easy to grow, either in the yarden or on a patio or windowsill. It's a perennial (although I have found that it's best to prune it hard and split it now and then to keep it vigorous), and it's a member of the mint (Lamiaceae) family and very hardy. It's been used for centuries both as a medicinal treatment and in folklore; sage is said to ward off evil. It's one of the four herbs included in four thieves vinegar, which reputedly protected against the plague. More recently (well, within the last century), it was made famous in Simon and Garfunkel's version of "Scarborough Fair," recorded in 1968 on the soundtrack of the film *The Graduate*.

As a medicine, sage can be taken internally or applied topically. It's got quite a good track record as being an antiviral, and recent studies have shown that even as little as a tea bag full of sage could have a very positive influence.[9] I like to cook with sage, making sage and onion stuffing, adding it to soups and stews, and making sage and rice barmcakes.

Here at the Keep, when we start to feel puny, we reach for the sage. I'll throw it in mint and ginger tea, but the main way we use it is aromatically, at least at the start. I have sage in homemade hemp oil soaps, which make a fragrant lather in the shower, and I put it in homemade shower steamers. Many people forget that inhaling the smells from essential oils or even hot herbal infusions is a good way of getting the healing elements of herbs into their system. Remember the mentholated vapor rubs mothers slathered onto their children's chests in days gone by? Yes, that!

Rosemary

Rosemary is second on my go-to list for healing herbs. Again, it is easy to grow and easy to obtain either as a plant, dried leaves, or essential oil. It's also a member of the *Salvia* genus (which makes it a member of the Lamiaceae family too). It relates it to sage in many ways, and like sage, its story goes back many centuries. We grow rosemary here but have yet to have it establish itself as a perennial; our winters are too harsh for the varieties we have been trying to cultivate. This year I'm going to try bringing it indoors during the worst of the winter, and see what happens—fingers crossed!

Traditionally, rosemary was used as a seasoning and a preservative; medicinally, it was used as an antibiotic, anti-inflammatory, and antiviral. In folklore, rosemary is considered to be a sign of remembrance (it's reputed to improve memory), and it was worn to ward off evil energies and to attract good ones.

I use rosemary with juniper in one of my most popular incense blends. The aroma seems to lift the energies and restore the balance of the area when I've burned it. In cooking, rosemary and potato is one of our favorite bread recipes. It's another herb that I add to shower steamers and soaps; it's cleansing, invigorating, and it seems to lift and rejuvenate the energy when used in the shower at the end of a long and trying day.

Oregano

Yet another easy to grow and easy to obtain herb containing many helpful qualities is the pungent oregano. I stumbled across this quite accidentally a couple of decades ago when I was looking for a remedy for a toenail infection. None of the over-the-counter methods worked, and someone suggested I try oregano oil. Success! Me being me, that sent me down the rabbit hole to discover what else oregano could do. I was not disappointed!

Origanum vulgare is yet another member of the mint family. We grow it as an annual. It has a small mauve flower that should be pinched back to encourage the leaves to grow. We plant it well away from the roses as in the past we've seen aphid activity around the oregano (we now plant marigolds near the oregano to deter the aphids).

In folklore oregano is a symbol of joy and love. In cooking it is one of the ingredients in an Italian spice mix, and I often add it to soups, stews, and salad dressings. Medicinally, oregano is used to settle the stomach and soothe the nerves. It contains natural antihistamines, which makes it a valuable tea; hot it can be sipped and cold it can be applied to rashes or other minor skin irritations. Added to a carrier, it is useful as a massage oil. I applied oregano oil directly to my infected toe, and I can vouch for its success as an antifungal. It's also got a strong reputation as an antiviral, an antibacterial, an antioxidant, and an anti-inflammatory.

Lemon Balm

We have a lot of lemon balm in the yarden! It's a lemon-scented and lemon-flavored member of the mint family, and it grows and spreads just like you'd expect from mint. We gave up trying to discipline it; we let it come up in the lawn and when we mow, we get the benefit of the wonderful aroma released by the leaves. It's just as happy in a pot on the patio or windowsill, provided the leaves are pinched back regularly and it is repotted when it gets too big.

Lemon balm (*Melissa officinalis*, often shortened to melissa) is such a prolific and versatile herb that I don't think I'd ever want to be without it. In the garden the small white flowers attract pollinators. The leaves can be candied in sugar for culinary decorations. It makes a wonderful-tasting tea with mild sedative properties. *Culpeper's Herbal* (first published in 1653 and still used today) describes lemon balm as useful for settling stomachs and lifting the spirits.[10]

Recent research has shown that lemon balm acts as an antioxidant and has the capability to assist with lessening stress, reducing inflammation, and improving conditions related to diabetes, Parkinson's disease, and cardiovascular function.[11] It's also indicated that lemon balm is another herb containing antiviral, antibacterial, and antifungal properties.

Elderberry

What's not to like about the elderberry bush? It's steeped in folklore and tradition, its beautiful white flowers smell divine in early summer, and the deep purple berries are full of flavor and health benefits. We grow four different kinds here at the Keep: 'Adams', 'Johns', 'Black Lace', and 'Black Tower'—the latter two having purple leaves, pink flowers, and smaller berries (they are new additions, so we're still waiting on fruit from them).

In summer I make marmalade from tea containing elder flowers and orange peel. It looks and feels like sunshine, and we always save half a pint to open at Yule, to welcome back the sun. The elder flowers are fragrant with a sweet neutral taste, but it is the berries that pack the punch.

Elderberries are very high in antioxidants and vitamins, giving a huge boost to the immune system. Because of this, elderberry is reputed to help the immune system fight off infections and viruses. If I can get to the berries before the birds do, I make an elderberry cordial with elderberries and simple sugar syrup that can be taken hot or cold. My late aunties used to make elderberry vinegar with honey and malt vinegar, which they used as a "sipping vinegar" whenever they felt a bit under the weather.

Rose

We had a very tired hedge that needed replacing, and last year we did just that, planting several *Rosa rugosa* roses. I've had a love affair with the beach rose ever since I lived on the Lincolnshire farm. The flowers are large and fragrant, and the hips have so many uses.

Rose hips are high in vitamin C and E. In fact, rose hips—the fruit of the rose after it has flowered—have more vitamin C than oranges! Keeping up the vitamin C levels is crucial to fighting off infections from bacteria and viruses. Inflammation often accompanies illness, and rose hips are also believed to be anti-inflammatory.

In the past (because our hedge is not yet mature enough to produce a large harvest) I have made jam, jelly, vinegar, cordial, and even wine from the rose hips. They are very versatile and extremely beneficial, and the beautiful colors on the bushes in the autumn are easy on the eye too. If it's not practical to grow a rugosa rose, the hips and products made from the hips are readily obtainable online and in high street apothecaries and health food shops.

Conclusion

These are just my six go-to plants, and I'll admit I use them for just about anything! The list of antiviral herbs is extensive, though, and also includes—but is not limited to—basil, fennel, peppermint, echinacea, garlic, ginger, ginseng, the humble dandelion, and more. While these are *not* a substitution for seeking medical assistance, it is useful to know that there are plant helpers that are easy to find and easy to grow.

Also remember that plants, like you, have their own energy signature and personality. What works for one person might not work for another because of the unique differences from plant to plant and from person to person. Just like you might like some people more than others, you're going to benefit from some plants more than others too. It's just part of your individuality!

Whether you plant a huge garden or have a pot on your kitchen windowsill, whether you work with live plants making your own teas and tinctures, or whether you purchase dried herbs or essential oils, focus on quality and on what feels right *to you*. We only have a postage stamp of land here at the Keep, but we try to fill it full of plants and make it coefficient, helping the plants that in turn will help us, either by feeding us or keeping us healthy. In this world of uncertainty, where new pollutants and diseases seem to be just around the corner, I find it comforting to be able to reach back in time and pull from history the knowledge that has kept us as a species going all these years.

Endnotes

1. Alvaro Ordonez, et al., "Sulforaphane Exhibits Antiviral Activity against Pandemic SARS-COV-2 and Seasonal HCoV-OC43 Coronaviruses in Vitro and in Mice," *Communications Biology* 5, no. 1 (2022): 242, doi:https://www.nature.com/articles/s42003-022-03189-z.

2. Ahmad Alkhatib, "Antiviral Functional Foods and Exercise Lifestyle Prevention of Coronavirus," *Nutrients* 12, no. 9 (2020): 2633, doi:10.3390/nu12092633.

3. Jun San Chang, Kuo Chih Wang, Chia Feng Yeh, Den En Shieh, and Lien Chai Chiang, "Fresh Ginger (*Zingiber officinale*) Has Antiviral Activity against Human Respiratory Syncytial Virus in Human Respiratory Tract Cell Lines," *Journal of Ethnopharmacology* 145, no. 1 (2013): 146–51, doi:10.1016/j.jep.2012.10.043.

4. "Garlic Powder," Mountain Rose Herbs, accessed August 3, 2022, https://mountainroseherbs.com/garlic-powder.

5. "Vitamin C," Medline Plus Encyclopedia, US National Library of Medicine, accessed August 3, 2022, https://medlineplus.gov/ency/article/002404.htm.

6. Ruairi Robertson, "Why the Gut Microbiome Is Crucial for Your Health," Healthline, June 27, 2017, https://www.healthline.com/nutrition/gut-microbiome-and-health.

7. Joel Fuhrman, *Super Immunity: The Essential Nutrition Guide for Boosting Our Body's Defenses to Live Longer, Stronger, and Disease Free* (New York: HarperOne, 2012), 83.

8. Sarah West, "Are You Eating Glyphosate? How Organic Farming Can Help," Nature's Path, January 23, 2018, https://www.naturespath.com/en-us/blog/are-you-eating-glyphosate-organic-farming-can-help/.

9. Sally Robertson, "Sage and Perilla Herbal Teas Could Help to Prevent or Treat COVID-19," News-Medical.net, November 22, 2022, https://www.news-medical.net/news/20201122/Sage-and-perilla-herbal-teas-could-help-to-prevent-or-treat-COVID-19.aspx.

10. Nicholas Culpeper, *Culpeper's Complete Herbal* (New York: Sterling, 2019), 140.
11. Sepide Miraj, Rafieian-Kopaei, and Sara Kiani, *"Melissa officinalis L: A Review Study With an Antioxidant Prospective,"* *Journal of Evidence-Based Complementary & Alternative Medicine* 22, no. 3 (2016): 385–94, doi:10.1177/2156587216663433.

DIY
and
Crafts

Herbal Drying Racks and Techniques

⇜ Rachael Witt ⇝

With the arrival of spring comes the reemergence of the growing season, which also means the beginning of the harvest season. Vibrant green shoots are rising, leaves are unfurling, and roots are swelling with nutrients underground. It's time to collect and process, making space for the new and capturing the freshness of the year's seasonal offerings.

I often find myself caught off guard at this time of year. Though my body yearns for the return of the plants and the vibrancy of spring, it is still waking from the winter slumber. Sometimes, I am not quite ready to clean out the herb kitchen and jump into the effort of gathering and processing. Nonetheless, the plants are springing back to life, and so my energy is too.

Spring lends itself as a teacher to gatherers learning the ways of harvesting, processing, and storing plants. Finding the right time to forage in between breaks in the weather is one teaching. Drying and processing the plants is another. The intermittent coldness and dampness of the season can serve as a challenge in dehydrating and storing herbs to preserve their potency.

Living in the Pacific Northwest has taught me the ways of rain, moisture, and cool temperatures. As an herbalist, this is important for knowing how to work with plants based on their growing season, usable and harvestable parts, and preservation techniques. The wet environment has informed how I dry plants—requirements of drying, methods of drying, and techniques of drying and storing.

The Art of Drying Herbs

Did you know that the sunlight can depreciate the quality of the herb by its searing intensity? And ovens can trap the moisture of plants, causing them to bake instead of dry? And drying plants on a solid surface can create mold? And stripping the fresh leaves off of a stalk to dry can cause bruising and discoloration?

While there are many methods to drying herbs, there are certain requirements to preserve their color, taste, smell, and vitality.

The art of drying herbs requires warmth, airflow, dryness, minimal light, and clean space. Herbs are best dried in consistent warm temperature, ideally between 80 and 110 degrees Fahrenheit depending on the plant parts being dehydrated. There needs to be good airflow and minimal to no humidity—

this limits a moldy environment. There should be no direct sunlight. The plant's pigments are sensitive to solar rays, and any direct contact can encourage the plant to compost instead of dehydrate. From flowers to ripe fruit and seeds, plants attract all sorts of beings. Make sure to flick off as many insects as possible prior to drying and also to dry your herbs in a space that is rodent and insect free.

The art of drying herbs requires warmth, airflow,
dryness, minimal light, and clean space.

It's ideal to dry plant material the same day that it is harvested. Preferably the harvest takes place on a dry day when the plant does not contain any dew or moisture. The aerial parts of plants do not need to be washed before they are dried. Roots are the only plant part that I wash prior to drying. Depending on the size of root, I will chop or slice the root into smaller pieces because it is easier to process when the root is fresh as opposed to hard and dry. This processing technique can also be applied to fruit. When drying the aerial parts of a plant, including the flowers and seeds, I try to keep the plant whole to extend its shelf life.

The amount of time to dry an herb depends on the part of the plant being harvested. Most roots and fruits need higher temperature or longer time to fully dehydrate, whereas most leaves and flowers need low heat and a shorter time period—unless they are mucilaginous.

Drying Methods

Methods for drying herbs are dependent on the local environment, the space available, and the season. For instance, I know an herb farmer in Davis, California, who lays her tulsi on a screen supported by two saw horses in a covered outdoor space. The tulsi dries in a day or two. Because I live east of Seattle, Washington, that wouldn't be possible for me until late July (if that!), and the moisture in the air might further prevent the herb from fully drying. Instead, I use a dehydrator for my tulsi harvest. We make do with what we have and where we are.

Here are some different drying methods to try out and learn what works best for your work or home space and environment.

Hang Drying

This method of drying herbs is truly beautiful. To see the plants hanging upside down in bundles brings their beauty and vibrancy from the outside to indoors. The colors, the textures, and the smells bring joy and uplift the spirit.

Hang drying allows versatility in where the herbs can be dried—ideally a warm, dark room with airflow. I have seen strands of herbs hanging across living rooms, kitchens, pantries, and more. Depending on your commitment to this drying method, there are different ways of hang drying. The easiest way to hang dry herbs is to set up a clothesline with space above for the bundled stems to extend and an area below for the plant material to hang. One idea is to mount a curtain rod to a beam or the ceiling of a room. In this way, herb bundles can be hung from S-hooks, curtain clamps, or string. I've used a shower curtain rod in between a door frame and clipped the loops of the tied herb bundles onto the shower curtain hooks. This technique worked until I needed to go back and forth between the rooms. If you are willing to commit to a hang dry space, hammer nails or screw in hooks about six inches apart from a beam that drops below the ceiling. These more permanent hooks can function for other uses throughout various times of the year.

When hanging herbs to dry, make small bundles and use rubber bands, twist ties, or string to hold the herbs together. It is important to make the bundles small as well as space the bundles apart, allowing air flow in between them. This reduces the development of mold.

Hang drying herbs is most successful when working with the aerial parts of a plant. This includes the leaves, stems, and flowers. Fruits can be strung in strands with space in between to gradually dry out over time. I love making rose hip garlands as a way to dry these small fruits and enjoy their beauty. Note that when plants are hang drying, they are affected by the changing temperature and humidity in the room. If the moisture content changes, the herbs can begin to rehydrate, which will depreciate their medicinal strength. It's this reason why I do not hang dry herbs in the PNW until midsummer. And as soon as the moisture returns in autumn, I have to quickly take my herbs down or place a dehumidifier in the room.

Herbs will shrink when they lose their moisture content. It is not uncommon for the hanging bundles to fall down when they're dehydrated. In this case, be mindful of the ground below the bundles and its cleanliness. Twist ties can easily be tightened around the stems if they are shrinking—it's just a matter of catching this in time before the bundles fall. Parts of the plants, such as small flowers, might also drop from the bundles. To prevent this from happening and to catch the floral parts before they fall, cover the bundles with small paper bags, tying the opening of the bag around the bundle. In this way, the bag will catch any of the loose material. If the herbs aren't falling from above you, then maybe they've been strung along for more time than they need to dry out. In scenarios where herb bundles are left strung for long periods of time, they can serve as dust collectors and space holders for cobwebs. Be sure to move your dried herbs into proper storage space once they have fully dried out.

Stripping, cutting, and garbling are best left for after the herb is dried. Any processing prior can damage the plant, causing discoloration and loss of luster.

Screen Drying

Drying herbs on a screen is one step closer to the concept of an electric dehydrator. Screens take up more space yet can hold finer plant material or bulky root material. They can also be stacked, creating a vertical drying area. This drying method calls upon creativity in finding or making functional screens as well as a supportive frame that allows for airflow above and below.

Like screens, baskets are interwoven fibers that can hold a variety of plant material based on the weave. Baskets can be used alternatively to screens. I recommend using baskets that lie flat with a lot of surface area and a semi-tight weave. Since the herbs are lying horizontally, it is important to place the plant material in a single layer. Ideally, the plants are spaced apart on the screen or basket. Again, the more air flow, the better.

This method of drying can be used for all parts of plants: the roots, aerial parts, flowers, fruits, and seeds. I prefer screens when I am harvesting large quantities and loose plant material such as flowers. Chamomile, calendula, rose petals, and poppies are some of my favorite herbs to dry using the screen method. A tightly woven screen is well-suited for drying seeds, especially those that I am saving to plant for the next grow season.

Make a Screen Drying Rack

Screens or baskets can be stacked on clothes drying racks or shelving frames that do not have solid shelves. When making drying screens, it is important to avoid using metal wire for mesh, as the metal can react with certain fresh plants, changing their properties.

Here is my method of making screens for a simple wooden X-frame drying rack. The supplies listed will make three screens for the three shelves on the drying rack.

You will need:

Wood X-frame drying rack approximately 29 inches long × 14 inches wide × 42 inches high (see steps 1 and 2)

6 18-inch × ⁵⁄₁₆-inch × 1½-inch wood laths

6 28-inch × ⁵⁄₁₆-inch × 1½-inch wood laths

Saw

Scissors

Mesh screen: BPA-free silicone or food-grade nylon (84 inches long × 18 inches wide)

Heavy duty staple gun with ¼-inch staples

8 ½-inch screws

Drill

1. Purchase a foldable clothes drying rack. Ideally, this would be a wood frame; however, there are many options with steel or alloy metals as a frame. These collapsible drying racks have three shelves, so we will make three drying screens to be placed on top.

2. Measure the length and width of the outside frame to confirm dimensions. A standard foldable clothes drying rack is about 29 inches long × 14 inches wide × 42 inches high, so the screens will be built for this standard measurement, but you can adjust accordingly to the one you've purchased.

3. Cut the mesh screen to have 3 pieces that are 18 × 28 inches.

4. Line up the shorter end of the mesh screen on top of one of the 18-inch wood laths. Staple the mesh onto the wood below, keeping the screen taut. Do the same technique for the opposite side.

5. Keeping the 18-inch wood pieces below the screen mesh, spread the two ends apart to make the mesh taut. Take one of the 28-inch-long pieces of wood and line it up with the edge of the taut screen mesh, squaring the corners with the two 18-inch side pieces. Using a ½-inch screw, drill the 28-inch piece to the 18-inch pieces at the corners, sandwiching the mesh in between the wood. Repeat with the opposite side.

6. Gently flip the drying frame upside down to staple the screen mesh edging to the two 28-inch-long sides of the drying screen.

7. Repeat steps 4 through 6 to complete all three screens.

One benefit to this screen method is that it is collapsible. This can be set up temporarily when you have a lot of herbs to dry and taken down when there's less. I used to use this type of drying method in a laundry room with a dehumidifier and fan. The drying rack served two main purposes: to dry large amounts of herbs in the spring through early autumn and wet clothes in the winter. Plus, having portable screens makes it easier to move the dried herbs into the kitchen for garbling and storing.

The Dehydrator

A homemade dehydrator can be purchased as a DIY kit or from a local maker. There's also the option to buy an electric dehydrator for both food and herbs. This type of dehydrator is smaller yet can be used for anything from meat to fruit leather to herbs. I recommend having different screens for these various uses—especially keeping the meat screens separate from the herb screens. If you choose this method for drying plants, make sure that the temperature is on a lower setting (80–110°F). I also like to remind folks to have their dehydrator out in a location where they will use it. I have found many dehydrators tucked underneath cabinets or stored in the garage—out of sight and out of use. When a dehydrator is available, it's much more likely that you will fill it and process what's in front of you.

Processing and Storing Dried Herbs

Make sure to move the herbs forward after they have fully dried. Flowers become brittle upon touch, leaves crunch, and roots and seeds harden. If left unattended, there's opportunity for the herbs to rehydrate, gather dust and cobwebs, and lose medicinal potency. Stripping, cutting, and garbling should be left until after drying the herb to avoid damaging the plant and therefore causing discoloration and loss of luster.

Store dried plant material in an air-tight container. Amber glass jars are ideal. Due to my limited storage space, I keep my dried herbs in reusable plastic bags or mylar bags. If you are looking for a more eco-friendly option, silicon bags, kraft bags, and rice paper bags are biodegradable. However, these bags might not be as air-tight and protective against sunlight or moisture.

Even when the dried herbs are stored in an airtight container, it is still ideal for the container to be in a cool and dry environment. Dried herbs should be stored away from direct light and any heat source.

And don't forget to use your herbs! As with the dehydrator, if herbs are out of sight, they are less likely to be used. Dried herbs are best if used within one year. Roots and seeds have a longer shelf life than herbaceous plant parts. However, I like to use my herbs on an annual basis. In that way, I can meet the start of the spring with excitement and inspiration—for the new year's harvest season is just beginning and I can reconnect with my herbal allies again.

Resources
Gladstar, Rosemary. *Rosemary Gladstar's Medicinal Herbs: A Beginner's Guide*. North Adams, MA: Storey Publishing, 2012.

Green, James. *Herbal Medicine-Maker's Handbook: A Home Manual*. Berkeley, CA: Ten Speed Press, 2000.

Herbal Business Tips and Strategies

ᨑ Holly Bellebuono ᨑ

You love plants and are obsessed with potted green things, bottles, jars, scents, and flowers. In fact, you run a business based on plants: you're an herbalist, a gardener, a landscaper, a shopkeeper, a boutique owner, an aromatherapist, a forager, an edible plant chef, or one of a myriad other small business owners seeking to combine passion with profit. Whether you set up a farmer's market stand in season, run a brick-and-mortar store, sell online, or a combination of these, here are tips and tricks I've learned in the twenty-six years since I opened my first little apothecary, Sweet Cicely Herbs, in 1996.

Since I first dipped my toes into the world of sole proprietorship, I've

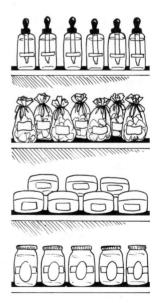

run a larger apothecary, Vineyard Herbs, and become an author (with books such as Llewellyn's *An Herbalist's Guide to Formulary*), as well as leading an international herbal medicine certification school. To be sure, while there is a lot to enjoy by running these enterprises, they are certainly one thing: a business. You must build your business acumen to make it successful. With each company, I've learned lessons that stewarded me personally and professionally toward a better version of myself and a stronger blend of passion, purpose, and profit. I hope the following tips help you enhance your business strategies.

Financial Tips

Most business owners are familiar with the 80-20 rule, which can help ensure a balance of efforts and costs in your business.

Profits

Eighty percent of your business should be profit-making, while 20 percent should be donation, community service, volunteering, and community goodwill. In other words, spend the bulk of your time conducting business activities that will earn a profit, but about one-fifth of your time and effort should be expansive, community-enhancing, offering on-the-spot discounts, or not focused on earnings. This is not only the right thing to do, but it will build your social capital and enhance the networks upon which your business is built.

Pricing

Eighty percent of your customers should feel comfortable with the price of your products, while 20 percent feel your product or service is too expensive. In this pricing strategy, four out of five potential customers will make a purchase—

even if it is at the top of their budget. One out of five will decline. In this way, you know you've struck the proper balance of cost, ensuring your products and services are neither too expensive nor too cheap. Experiment with pricing after a market or weekend. Did more people pick up your products and put them back on the shelf rather than purchasing them? Or—the opposite—did you sell out completely? Each of these scenarios tells you that your pricing strategy needs work.

Subsidizing Products

If you find that you're investing far more time into your business than you are recouping in sales, you may need to identify one product to subsidize your others. Twenty percent of your products can subsidize other products. For example, I created and sold a fantastic first aid ointment that was incredibly time-consuming to make (growing, harvesting or wildcrafting dozens of types of plants, purchasing oils and beeswax and containers, and making batch after batch). However, in the market, it would only bear a maximum $16.95 purchase price, when really it cost me far more to produce it. To counter this and allow my business to continue offering this needed and popular product at a reasonable price, I crafted and sold a much simpler and more cost-effective face cream that required much less input and sold at a more expensive price because people expect to pay more for face creams. In this way, the face cream "subsidized" the first aid ointment, evening out costs. Note that this is not a long-term strategy, and if you find your revenues are consistently not meeting the cost of paying yourself or your staff for their time, other interventions are needed.

Severance

Maintain business-specific bank accounts and credits cards, keeping them completely separate from your personal finances. Also, if you invest an initial amount of personal funds into your business to start it, consider this a loan and be sure to pay yourself back. Develop strict separate financial habits so that going forward your business can run independently of you. When you're ready, you'll be able to sell the business without the headache of prying business costs and funds apart from your personal costs. Keep it clean.

Partnership

Consider a partnership. Establishing your business with a business partner and forming an LLC or a Sub-S corporation may be helpful; it diffuses risk across the business and also creates a sense of identity and accountability. Visit SCORE.org to work with a retired business executive. These volunteers have chapters across the country and provide valuable free business guidance for small business owners.

Supply Chain

When considering inventory, don't neglect the complexity of the supply chain. It's currently a mess, and there is no guarantee that bottles, jars, labels, beeswax, oils, and other ingredients or packaging items that make up your brand will be available. Stick with inventory that is relatively easy to purchase and avoid making those experimental international purchases that require a customs journey. Cheap packaging from other countries can be appealing, but sticking with somewhat pricier options with a more stable supply may be worth it.

In addition to packaging, consider the herbs themselves. Do you grow them? Wildharvest them? If your business requires using more herbs than you can grow or harvest yourself, consider the following:

Hire

Hire out that part of your business to a local grower. This payment will be listed as a business expense on your Schedule C for tax purposes. Identify a reputable grower and draw up a written contract for goods provided (herbs), specifying quantity of herbs, timeline for delivery, batch number, harvest date, and whether the grower possesses an organic certificate. This is an investment in your own business and will help ensure a reliable supply of fresh herb ingredients for your products.

Barter

In lieu of a monetary contract, barter your products, skills, or other farm products for the herbs you need. Be aware that this is not as reliable as hiring with a contract, but it provides for innovation and flexibility.

Partner

Is there a college or university near you with whom you can partner? A 4-H club or a gardening club that may be willing to grow a crop for you, perhaps in exchange for a donation? Seek out those partnerships that can fill the gaps in your business and in which a quid-pro-quo arrangement will help both of you.

Purchase

Finally, for herbs you can't find locally, research the nationally available wholesale distributors that supply dried herbs from around the world. When you purchase, be sure to request a

Certificate of Analysis, which will include a batch number for your record keeping. The largest wholesalers will have documents to certify an herb's provenance and whether or not it is certified organic, ethically wildcrafted, fair-trade / fair-wage sourced, and free of contamination. Establish a filing system in your office to keep these records when you use these ingredients in your products.

Personal Tips

Competition

Determine how you—and your community—feel about competition. In some places, fellow herbalists are territorial and the competition is fierce. In others, herb vendors work together seamlessly, as sisters, helping each other's businesses thrive. For instance, when I set up my farmer's market booth (for eleven years in the Martha's Vineyard summers), two other herbalists and a variety of crafters also vended. Heather raised bees, collected her own beeswax and honey, and made incredible products, so I avoided making similar things. Likewise, I blended teas, and Heather avoided selling tea blends. Another crafter focused on making soap, which I never did. We allowed ourselves to complement each other, competing in a market in such a way that each business flourished.

Children

If you have young children, don't feel bound to bring them to your market or shop, especially if they're fussy and don't want to be there. I made that mistake, thinking I would introduce my kids to a lovely environment and instill a sense of entrepreneurship in them, but when they were miserable, my business suffered. Get childcare and allow your products to shine.

Full-Time?

Don't feel pressured to make your business your sole money-making endeavor. There are many herbalists who work full-time elsewhere, as a nurse, counselor, clerk, teacher, or engineer, whose herbal businesses flourish on the side. As long as you enjoy it and it is a worthwhile contribution to your community, grow your business as small or as large as you wish.

Other Business Tips

Decision-Making

When deciding on a course of action for yourself or your business, consider the SMART guidelines: specific, measurable, attainable, realistic, and time-bound. These are logical fundamentals upon which to build a plan of any sort. However, I also suggest what I call the WISE guidelines. Be sure your decisions are . . .

Wholistic: They address you wholistically, taking into consideration your business needs as well as your personal, social, and spiritual desires.

Imaginative: Don't limit yourself or your decisions based on the SMART guidelines. Instead, brainstorm, think outside the box (or the glass jar), and let imagination have a seat at your decision-making table.

Sustainable: Is your decision something that will last for a long time? Will it sustain you economically, or is it a short-term fix? Is it sustainable for the environment? Is it a decision you'll be proud of making ten years from now, or is it one you might regret?

Energetic: Does this decision light you up? Does it make you happy and energized? Does it feed your passion? Again, this is where the 80-20 rule can appear, because perhaps the right decision makes you mostly energized and excited, but there's also some trepidation or fear. This is normal and shows a mature balance in the process.

Wholesale or Retail?

These are two separate animals, and determining early which business strategy you will pursue will make a huge difference to your bottom line. I did both and it was a mistake, and I wasted a lot of time preparing my products to sell in other people's stores when the most lucrative type of sale was in my own shop. Don't get sucked into the big-name stores with promises of "going regional" unless you absolutely know it's the right thing for you. I entered into a wholesale agreement with one of the largest natural foods chains and ended up traveling at my expense, providing sample products at my expense, handing out tasters and trial products, and even producing signage for the store, all for a measly per-product purchase price and no contract for going further. Even local stores can be a time sink when your real revenue comes from selling directly to your own customers. Determine which animal you will be—a wholesale company or a retail company—and move in that sole direction 100 percent. (And if you decide to be a wholesale company, hire a distributor.)

Marketing

Film it. If you're young, you probably consume and engage with a fair amount of video content each day. I grew up in the Dark Ages (I'm in my early fifties), and the thought of filming my work process rarely occurs to me. Hundreds of times I've completed a gorgeous day of product-making, gardening, or crafting with colorful products and labels ready to sell, and I box everything away for market, only to realize I never took a single picture or video. Today, video is what will bring customers through your door, because they'll find you on Instagram, Facebook, TikTok, and YouTube. I find that, in addition to videos about a process or a beautiful garden, I'm often intrigued when I find videos of an herbalist being interviewed or sharing thoughts for the camera. Making it personal is key; many customers seek companies whose mission and personality aligns with theirs, and getting to know you online will eventually bring them to your cash register.

<hr/>

I worked as a sole proprietor for decades, successfully sold my apothecary to another herbalist, sunsetted my herb school due to COVID-19, and am now the executive director of an education nonprofit. I truly enjoyed my time as a retail business owner, but for now, I value the lessons I learned because they are applicable in any career. I hope you find these business tips useful as you pursue what makes you happy.

Simple Floral Arranging

Annie Burdick

If your goal is to find a fast, simple way to add vibrance and life to your space, there's nothing I'd recommend more highly than simply putting out fresh floral and foliage arrangements as often as you can. Bringing a pop of life, greenery, and color into your home in one easy step is a no-brainer, but if you find the cost of purchasing a weekly premade arrangement from a florist or market is unreasonable for your budget, I don't blame you—it gets pricey!

Instead, follow some simple tips and techniques to create your own stunning floral arrangements from scratch, and you'll probably love them even more. Building your own arrangements allows you to save money

(especially if you're able to use foliage and flowers from your own garden or your friends') and become more connected to the process, so every time you walk past that stunning bouquet on the table, you can take pride in making something so lovely to adorn your space. Plus, you can include elements that may be more unusual and unique—like your favorite herbs and other bits and pieces from your own garden. This way, you have one more way to enjoy and cherish your herbal bounty and hard work in the garden.

Planning and Structuring an Arrangement

Any eye-catching arrangement will incorporate variety and diversity. This means utilizing a mix of different heights, textures, and elements in each, so the result is an arrangement that you'll never tire of looking at. Anyone can throw a handful of roses in a vase (and that's a lovely thing to do for a quick floral piece!), but arranging flowers can be quite the art form if you let it, granting you some truly lovely results.

You may choose your arrangement elements based on what's seasonal, what you're growing yourself, what you forage or have available, or what you purchase and is in budget. You might lean toward flowers based on your preference toward them, or because of their size, color, or fragrance. You might prefer a low and wide arrangement or a tall, reaching one. But for any arrangement, you can try to include some or all of these types of elements:

Something for Height: Even if the overall piece is shorter, you generally want to include one or two elements that reach a bit higher. Varying heights adds visual interest and playfulness. In a standard-height or tall arrangement, some items should still reach above others.

A Feature Element: The most eye-catching or interesting component of the arrangement, perhaps your feature element is one massive and stunning central flower, or even something more unique, like a piece of fruit.

Filler Elements: For filler, you're looking for flowers or other foliage that fills in gaps and takes up space between the larger statement elements. While flowers can be a part of filler, this is definitely the place to get greenery in. Make use of herbs, whether they've flowered or not.

Accents and Other Unique Elements: Here you're looking for those small elements that add a last bit of visual excitement and even a hint of surprise. It might be some branches, berries, or even some non-plant options.

All About the Flowers

For any arrangement, you have three main options for your flowers and foliage: grow, forage, or shop. There's no wrong option, as long as you never take flowers grown by and for someone else. Foraging might look like trimming a few wildflowers at the park or asking to trim some flowers from your friend's garden—perhaps in exchange for something from your own garden. It's a great way to share a bounty.

If you're lucky enough to have outdoor space and the ability to grow and garden flowers of your own, you have an incredible bounty for homemade arrangements. It is a lovely thing to be able to grow your own flowers, cut your favorites, and give them a second life inside the home for décor and mood-boosting.

Here are some top flowers that are fairly simple to grow and fit well in arrangements:

- Aster

- Dahlia

- Daisy

- Daylily

- Peony

- Russian sage

- Snapdragon

- Sunflower

- Sweet pea

Of course, ultimately, your picks are fairly unlimited, and should be chosen based on your climate, available space, and preferences. Planting native options is always your best bet, both for gardening success and for the environment. And perhaps you're blessed with lots of existing flowering bushes and trees that you can utilize!

If you're cutting fresh flowers yourself and want to make them last as long as possible, there are a few steps you can take. First, cut stems with a sharp knife rather than scissors. This leaves the stems able to intake water. Strip off the lower leaves. Right away, place the stems into a bowl of room-temperature, clean water for at least a few hours, if not longer, so they can acclimate. And before and after arranging, keep the flowers cool if possible. Your home refrigerator likely won't successfully imitate the conditions of a florist's commercial fridge, but setting them in a shaded or dim area is better than directly in sunlight.

Adding Herbs and Other Greenery

Including flowers in an arrangement is usually a given, but the extra components are where you can make things unique and interesting. Herbaceous elements can be excellent in an arrangement. They can simultaneously act as filler material, add beautiful greenery and visual interest, offer bright fragrance, and even add cost-free floral components as well. When removing blooms from your herbs to preserve the flavor of the leaves, use them in a bouquet first instead of tossing them directly into the compost pile.

Here are some great herbs to include in an arrangement:

- Basil
- Bay laurel
- Chamomile
- Chervil
- Dill
- Lavender
- Lemon balm
- Lemongrass
- Mint (any variety)
- Rosemary
- Sage
- Thyme

Naturally, you can choose the herbs you want based on the scent profile you're looking for, the type of arrangement you're building, or what you have growing in excess. If your garden has an abundance of sage, it may find its way into more arrangements, for example.

Aim to cut herb stems at a 45-degree angle; this lets them take in the most water while in the arrangement. As with flowers, remove any leaves that are lower on the stem and will be submerged in water once arranged.

If you want foliage options besides herbs, try these:

- Bells of Ireland
- Dusty miller
- Eucalyptus (any variety)
- Fern, many varieties
- Honeywort
- Houseplant clippings, like monstera
- Ivy
- Lemon leaf
- Myrtle
- Plumosa

Selecting by Season

Most who garden probably know by now how beneficial and essential it is to grow seasonally. Expecting a fall plant to bloom in spring is futile and won't lead to any of the joys of gardening you're looking for. Like gardening native plants, gardening seasonal plants is the best way to get the most out of your garden. And this applies just as much to floral arrangements: you can gain inspiration for your arrangements based on what is blooming and thriving at the current season.

Flowers and Herbs by Growing Season

Spring: Tulip, hyacinth, lilac, peony, magnolia, bloodroot, snapdragon, rose, basil, cardamom

Summer: Daisy, daylily, coneflower, dahlia, Russian sage, cosmos, begonia, allium, bee balm, lavender

Fall: Chrysanthemum, rose, goldenrod, viola, canna, cyclamen, rosemary, marjoram, lemon balm

Winter: Snowdrop, winterberry, English primrose, camellia, winter honeysuckle, glory of the snow, bluebell, mint, sage

Other Essential Supplies

Before building your arrangements, stock up on these beneficial supplies. A few are fully optional but may just give you the opportunity to diversify or fancify your arrangements.

Gardening Gloves: If you're cutting your own flowers and foliage, wear gloves!

Pruning Shears or a Sharp Knife: Use pruning shears or a sharp knife to cut fresh flowers and herbs.

Clippers or Scissors: Use these rather than a knife to trim off leaves or cut floral tape or wire, as needed.

Various Vases and Bowls: You can use any container that provides a shape and structure you like to fill.

Floral Foam: This is a piece of foam you can place at the bottom of your container to push stems directly into, giving you more control over exactly where your flowers and elements sit.

Flower Frog: In some wide or shallow dishes, there isn't enough support from the container walls, and in those cases a tiny tool like this, inserted into the bottom of the container, uses a series of pointed spikes to hold stems in place.

Floral Wire Netting: You can place a small piece of netting across the opening of your container and use the various gaps to more easily space your components.

Floral Tape or Floral Wire: Green floral tape and wire can help you secure elements to each other, creating structure and stability.

The container you choose will have a great effect on the type of arrangement you can create. A more traditional tall and narrow vase will limit how much you can fit, but it will support the stems so less supplies or intervention are needed. Other people will prefer wider and shorter containers, more dish-like than vase-like. In these, you'll likely trim stems much shorter, and then use wire netting, a flower frog, or foam at the bottom of the container to hold some of the elements in place, since there won't be much support from the container walls. If you want to still get solid height on a shorter container, this is especially helpful.

Building the Arrangement

Now to get down to the real business of it: putting together your arrangement. Once you've cut your flowers and herbs and chosen your container, you can start building. Remember, this is a relaxed, creative process. You can experiment, move things around, and make changes. Nothing is set in stone. If you don't like your first attempt, just disassemble and try again, or try it a different way next time.

Start by placing in some of your filler plants, like herbaceous foliage and other greenery. In a vase with high sides, you can rest the stems at a slight angle against the edges and start filling in more and more from there. These should be the elements that take up a lot of space and spread out in all directions. Starting with this lets you add other pieces in the spaces left open.

Take your tall elements and add these in wherever the filler seems to need a boost of something with extra height. From there, you can move on to your accent flowers. These aren't the star item or the focal point but the other flowering elements that are going to add color and fill space.

If possible, place your centerpiece element last. Once you've adjusted and fluffed the filler and accents, you can see what space naturally calls for a big, bold element to fill it in. Place your showstopper flower, the one that will tie it all together. Of course, this is just one way to tackle an arrangement. You might want several "feature" elements or none—perhaps you prefer a very cohesive and routine look. Or you might try for a pattern or layered look, with one color in a ring around the outside and then smaller and smaller rings of other items moving inward. There are endless ways to do a floral arrangement right.

Once all the elements are in the vase, move and tweak to your heart's content. If something looks too busy or out of place, remove it or trim it so it looks exactly how you like best.

Upkeep and Parting Ways

Once you've perfected an arrangement you're thrilled with, you want it to last as long as possible and stay fresh and bright too. You can help make this possible by . . .

- Using tepid or room-temperature water, not cold, as well as distilled water, if available
- Changing out the water daily

- Trimming the ends of the flowers and plants every three days and giving the fresh ends a rinse when you do

- Keeping them in a cooler room away from direct sunlight

Once your arrangement meets its natural end, as all will eventually, you can choose how you prefer to part ways with it. The easiest method, of course, is to add all the plant matter to your compost pile or bin and let it turn into nutritious soil to add to your plants and continue on the cycle of healthy gardening for more and more arrangements to come. But if you want to be creative, there are other things you can do with dead and dying flowers:

- Press the flowers to use in crafts like cards and wall art.
- Make potpourri.
- Add dried petals to homemade candles.
- Use dried petals as natural confetti at an event or in a gift.
- Dry bundles of herbs and use them as décor.

Once you start loving the craft of floral arrangement, you don't have to limit your skills and knowledge just to brightening your own home. Use your bounty to make gorgeous arrangements for special events, to gift to friends and family (for a birthday, for a baby shower, or during a hard time), or to gift to a senior living home or somewhere similar that may appreciate some natural beauty as well.

Ultimately, when it comes to making natural arrangements, there are very few steps and even fewer rules. As long as you select elements that make you happy and spend a little time putting together a piece, you're sure to love how it turns out—as will anyone else who gets to stop by and enjoy it.

Sew an Apron

⚜ Raechel Henderson ⚜

Aprons come in a variety of styles. The "bib" apron covers the torso and waist, secured by ties at the waist and neck. Some bib aprons have shoulder straps that attach to the waist rather than tie around the neck. Some even have crossover straps that hold the apron in place without a waist tie.

Half aprons cover only from the waist down. The most familiar of these are the lace trimmed, frilly varieties worn by the stereotypical 1950s American housewife. Decorative aprons were not limited to that time period (in fact they predate it by several centuries), but that particular apron version of the waist apron symbolized a kind of female servitude that 1960s feminists rebelled against.

Aprons have even acted as clothing themselves, ostensibly performing as protective outerwear as well as being a wardrobe item. Examples include the apron dresses of ancient Nordic culture and the pinafore dresses of the nineteenth and twentieth centuries. Both of these dresses are worn over underdresses, but they are meant for everyday wear outside of the apron's usual domains: the kitchen, workshop, and fields.

All this history shows us how versatile the apron is. From bits of worn-out or scrap cloth used to protect more valuable garments, to the "Kiss the Cook" novelty aprons that are gifted and then forgotten, the apron is a piece of clothing with a varied history.

The modern apron seems to have been relegated to the kitchen. Its most familiar iteration is the chef's apron or those worn by servers in restaurants. Aprons are in use in a variety of jobs, again most of them related to food production, like meat packing. And while it does serve a useful function in those environments, aprons have and can be used for so much more than just protecting one's clothes from grease splatter.

Pocketed aprons serve as a second set of hands for crafting and working. Specialty aprons, crocheted or knitted, can be used to gather eggs, nestling each one in its own individual pocket to avoid breakage. Gathering aprons have strings along the bottom that can turn the apron into a basket for fruits and vegetables from the garden. Double aprons can be used in foraging to protect clothes and the body from branches and thorns.

With all the uses in mind, you can make up any of these types of aprons to your size easily with the instructions that follow. An apron is a beginner-level project that even the most novice of sewists can make. While a sewing machine makes construction faster, an apron can be hand sewn. If hand sewing, make sure to keep your stitches small and even.

Fabric Choices

While early aprons were made from scraps, we have access to a wide variety of fabric choices these days. What fabric you use for your apron will depend on what the apron's function is. Beyond the fabric material, there are a plethora of options when it comes to color and patterns. My advice is to take a bit of time thinking about these choices before you buy your fabric. Pick one you enjoy not only the look of but also the feel of, even its smell and the way it sounds when it moves. You are more likely to regularly use your apron if it brings you delight.

Cotton

Cotton is often the go-to for aprons. It is an absorbent and strong material that can put up with a lot of wear and tear. It can also be gotten fairly cheap. Broadcloth is a tightly woven, often solid color fabric that won't break the bank to buy. There are other, heavier-weight cotton fabrics that are also suitable for aprons. For aprons that will be worn outdoors for gardening and foraging purposes, you might want to consider a denim or duck cloth, both of which are heavier weight and can withstand a lot of work. You can look into quilting cotton, which is a medium-weight cloth that comes in many different patterns. Some, like batiks, will hide cooking stains well. Or you could wear your love of baking in a novelty muffin print. Cotton cloth will also get softer and more absorbent as you use and wash it.

Linen

Linen is the other fabric often used in aprons and kitchen towels. It is much more expensive than cotton but often comes in a weight that falls somewhere between the light weight of broadcloth and the heavier weight of denim. Like cotton, it will get much softer and more absorbent as it is used. You may find linen-polyester blends in the store that are cheaper than 100 percent linen. I don't recommend those for aprons, as the two different materials will react to heavy use differently, eventually leading to the fabric puckering and fraying. Linen comes in fewer colorways and patterns than cotton, so you might have to spend a little more time searching the internet for that perfect fabric.

Wool, Blends, and More

While cotton and linen tend to be the two main fabrics used in making aprons, you shouldn't feel limited to just those. Tightly woven wool is waterproof, and polyester blends come in a variety of styles that just might suit what you are looking for. While lightweight and sheer fabrics might not be suitable for going through the underbrush looking for berries, they could be used as decorative bits for a kitchen apron or even made into a purely ornamental apron. Take your time in finding fabric you love.

Wash Your Fabric

Fabric is often treated with chemicals to keep it from wrinkling when it is being shipped and sold. Most fabric can also shrink up to 5 percent or more when washed and dried for the first time. Because of this you want to wash and dry your fabric before you start cutting and sewing. If you don't, your finished garment can shrink, pucker, and warp the first time you launder it. Wash your fabric according to the manufacturer's instructions. Then iron it, if needed, to get rid of any wrinkles.

Making Your Apron

The amount of fabric you need will be determined by your measurements. Using the measurements described on page 210, get a piece of fabric that is equal to (your B measurement + 2 inches) × (your D measurement + 2 inches).

You will need:

Fabric

Thread that matches your fabric

Sewing machine or hand sewing needle

Scissors

2 or more packages of extra-wide double-fold bias binding (or you can make your own from excess fabric using the technique below)

Steam iron and ironing board

How to Make Your Own Extra-Wide Double-Fold Bias Binding

Bias binding is made from fabric that has been cut at a 45-degree angle to the selvage. This gives the binding lots of stretch, making it good for binding curves.

To make bias binding, cut 2-inch strips of fabric. Fold the edges in ½ inch down the length of the strip to the wrong side of the fabric and press with an iron. Fold the strip in half down the length of the strip, with the raw edges on the inside, and press again.

If you need longer lengths, take two strips of fabric and lay one on top of the other, right sides together, at a 90-degree angle. Stitch a diagonal line from outer corner to outer corner. Trim off the excess and open up the strip. Press the seam open.

Measurements

You will need four measurements for your apron:

A Measurement: Across your chest from your armpit to your armpit.

B Measurement: Length from mid-chest to your waist.

C Measurement: Length from mid-chest to where you want the apron to fall (knee length, for example).

D Measurement: Your waist.

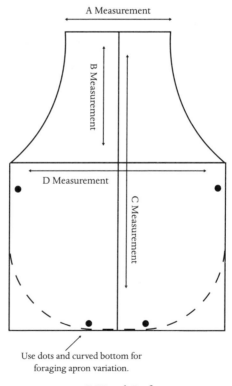

Use dots and curved bottom for
foraging apron variation.

Pattern

You can make a pattern on paper beforehand or draw it directly onto the fabric. In either case fold your paper or fabric in half lengthwise.

1. At the top of the paper or fabric, mark a point out that is ½ your A measurement from the fold. Draw a line from the fold to the point to make the top of the apron. This is the A line.

2. Measure down from the A line your B measurement and then out from the fold to mark a point that is half of your D measurement. This is the B point.

3. Measure down from the A line your C measurement and then out from the fold to mark a point that is half of your D measurement. Draw a line from the fold to that point to make the bottom of the apron.

4. Draw a curved line from the end of your A line to the B point.

5. Draw a line from the B point to the end of the bottom line.

Construction

1. Cut out your apron.

2. Hem the top of the apron: Fold the top edge of the apron to the wrong side (back side) ½ inch and press with an iron. Then fold it in again another ½ inch. Press. Top stitch this hem close to the first fold.

3. Hem the bottom of the apron: Fold the bottom edge to the wrong side ½ inch and press. Then fold it in again another ½ inch. Press. Top stitch close to the first fold.

4. Hem the straight sides of the apron: Fold the raw edges to the wrong side ½ inch and press. Then fold it in again another ½ inch. Press. Top stitch close to the first fold.

5. To make the neck and waist ties, cut 2 pieces of bias tape that measure 18 inches + the length of the curved side line + ¼ your D measurement (minimum 8 inches). These ties will be attached along the curved sides in lieu of hemming them.

6. Open up the ends of the bias tape and fold them inside ¼ inch. Press and then close up the tape again.

7. Mark 18 inches down from one end of each piece of bias tape. Align the marking to the top edge of the apron. Baste or pin the bias tape around the curve, enclosing the raw edge in the bias tape.

8. Stitch the opening of the bias tape from one end to the other, stitching through all layers of fabric when you get to the curved side of the apron. Repeat on the other side.

Variations

You can customize your apron in a variety of ways to suit your purposes.

Pocketed Apron

For a kitchen apron, add a button to the front at the waist to hang a hand towel to dry your hands on. Or you can add deep pockets for cooking utensils by cutting out a rectangle that measures 14 × 9 inches. Hem the two sides and bottom of the pocket by folding the raw edges to the wrong side ½ inch, pressing, and then basting close to the fold. Fold the top edge in ½ inch and then another ½ inch. Press and then top stitch close to the second fold.

Center the pocket in the middle of your apron with the top edge even with the waist and pin. Sew around the sides and bottom of the pocket, near the folded edge, making sure to back stitch a couple times at the start and finish to reinforce the corner openings. You can segment the pocket by stitching another line through it and the apron at the center of the pocket, making two rather than one long one.

Foraging Apron

To make an apron with a skirt that can be gathered into a basket, make the skirt rounded and create a drawstring channel with extra-wide bias binding around the sides and bottom of the apron. You'll need cording in addition to the material for making the basic apron.

1. Begin by making your pattern just as for the standard apron, but give the bottom corners a gentle curve.
2. Cut out the apron and hem the top as per the construction instructions in step 2 on page 211.
3. Take a piece of extra-wide double-fold bias binding the length of the skirt's bottom and side edges. Open out the bias binding and match one long edge to the edge of the skirt with the right side (front or printed side) of the bias binding to the wrong side (back side) of the skirt. Sew the bias binding to the skirt with a ¼-inch seam.
4. Press the bias binding out away from the skirt with the seam edge pressed in toward the apron.
5. Make four dots on the right side of the bias binding (see figure on page 210): 2 marks 7 inches from each end of the bias binding, and then 2 marks on either side of the center of the skirt's bottom edge.
6. Sew eyelets or ¼-inch button holes at the dots and open them up. These are where you will thread the cording through.

7. Fold the bias binding over the right side of the apron skirt. Make sure the unsewn edge of the bias tape is folded in. Press.

8. Sew along the folded edge of the bias binding to make the drawstring channel. Make sure not to sew through the button holes or eyelets.

9. Using a bodkin, loop turner, or small safety pin, thread your cording in one side buttonhole or eyelet and out one bottom buttonhole or eyelet. Leave a good 5–6 inches of cording on either side of the channel openings. Tie knots or add beads to the ends of the cording to keep them from pulling back into the channel. Repeat on the other side.

10. Continue with steps 5–8 of the basic apron instructions to finish the apron.

To gather the apron for foraging, pull on each end of the cording to gather the fabric between them. Tie the ends together. Repeat on the other side so that the skirt forms a basket.

If you have even basic sewing skills, an apron can take an hour or two to complete. It is such a useful piece of clothing that you might even consider making a couple of different ones, perhaps even for gifts. Make a gathering apron and add in a few seed packets and a gardening book for a friend who is interested in getting started gardening. Or perhaps for a loved one who enjoys cooking, make a pocketed apron with a favorite recipe written on a card and the spices needed to make it tucked into the pocket.

Plant
Profiles

Plant Profiles

This section features spotlights on individual herbs, high-lighting their cultivation, history, and culinary, crafting, and medicinal uses. Refer to the key below for each plant's sun and water needs, listed in a helpful at-a-glance table.

Key to Plant Needs	
Sun	
Shade	—
Partial shade	☀
Partial sun	☀ ☀
Full sun	☀ ☀ ☀
Water	
Water sparingly	💧
	💧 💧
Water frequently	💧 💧 💧

USDA Hardiness Zones

The United States is organized into zones according to the average lowest annual winter temperature, indicating a threshold for cold tolerance in the area. This USDA Plant Hardiness Zone Map uses the latest available data. For best results, plant herbs that can withstand the climate of their hardiness zone(s) and bring less hardy plants indoors during colder weather. Seek additional resources for high summer temperatures, as these can vary within zones.

It is helpful to keep track of temperatures and frost dates in your neighborhood or check with a local gardening center or university extension for the most up-to-date record. Climate change and local topography will also affect your growing space, so compensate accordingly.

USDA Plant Hardiness Zone Map

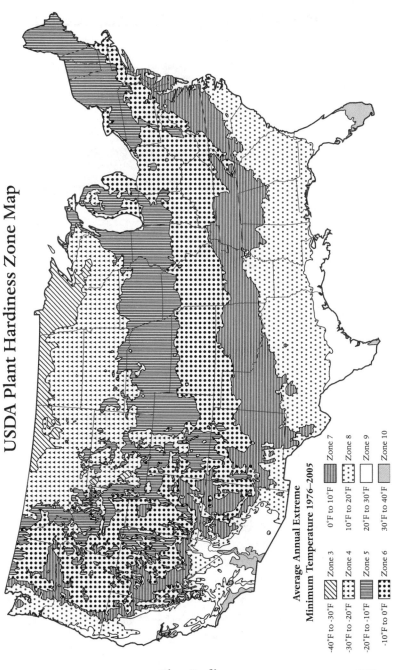

**Average Annual Extreme
Minimum Temperature 1976–2005**

-40°F to -30°F Zone 3	0°F to 10°F Zone 7
-30°F to -20°F Zone 4	10°F to 20°F Zone 8
-20°F to -10°F Zone 5	20°F to 30°F Zone 9
-10°F to 0°F Zone 6	30°F to 40°F Zone 10

USDA Plant Hardiness Zone Map (Cont.)

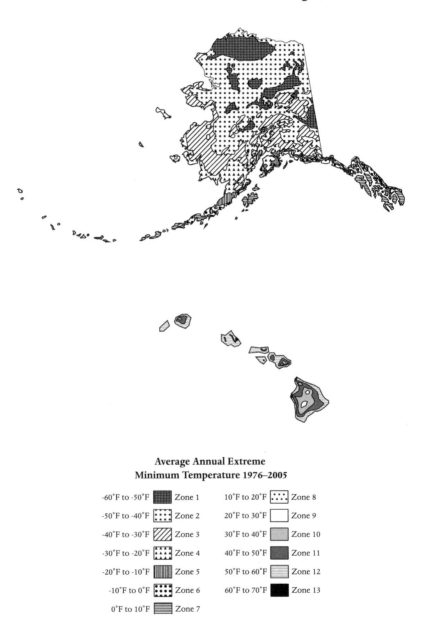

**Average Annual Extreme
Minimum Temperature 1976–2005**

-60°F to -50°F	Zone 1	10°F to 20°F	Zone 8
-50°F to -40°F	Zone 2	20°F to 30°F	Zone 9
-40°F to -30°F	Zone 3	30°F to 40°F	Zone 10
-30°F to -20°F	Zone 4	40°F to 50°F	Zone 11
-20°F to -10°F	Zone 5	50°F to 60°F	Zone 12
-10°F to 0°F	Zone 6	60°F to 70°F	Zone 13
0°F to 10°F	Zone 7		

Zucchini

≫ Anne Sala ≪

If you are new to gardening and are unsure if you will be good at it, then plant zucchini. They are notoriously easy to grow, but just keep in mind—a happy zucchini plant will give you a bumper crop. While fun, it can be overwhelming if you don't have a plan.

Native to the Americas but embraced by the rest of the world, zucchini is a mild-flavored member of the summer squash family, *Cucurbita pepo*, and is botanically classified as a fruit. It is related to winter squash, cucumbers, and melons.

Explorers brought seeds back to Europe and, according to an article from the Library of Congress website, got the name *squash* "from the

Zucchini	
Species	*Cucurbita pepo*
Zone	3–9
Needs	☀☀☀ 💧💧💧
Soil pH	6–7.5
Size	3–4', out and up

Narragansett Native American word *askutasquash*, which means 'eaten raw or uncooked.'" All manner of squash have been an important food staple throughout the Americas for thousands of years and became a symbol of fertility, wealth, and status.

In the American Southwest, a popular item of jewelry made by Navajo, Pueblo, and Zuni jewelers is the squash blossom necklace. It often incorporates sacred turquoise stones in silver settings and a horseshoe-shaped crescent that looks like a stylized squash blossom. Young unmarried Hopi women wore their hair in a magnificent style called the "squash blossom whorl"—it is thought Princess Leia's iconic hairstyle in *A New Hope* was inspired by it.

Zucchini's cultivation history is rather brief. Shared in research presented by Teresa Lust and Harry Paris in the "Annals of Botany," zucchini may be the newest of the eight identified summer squash species: crookneck, straight neck, pumpkin, acorn, vegetable marrow, cocozelle, and scalloped (a.k.a. pattypan). Mention of it first appeared in cookbooks from the region around Milan, Italy, in the 1800s, where it is thought to have received its name. *Zucca* is the Italian word for squash, and so they gave this newcomer the diminutive ending of the word for its name, most likely in reference to it being picked young. The same thing happened in France, where it is called a *courgette*, the diminutive of their word for squash, *courge*.

The phrase "food is medicine" is very appropriate for zucchini. It has a high water content and contains both soluble and insoluble fiber. The flesh is rich in a long list of vitamins and minerals, including vitamin A, vitamin C, manganese, magnesium, and potassium. And the skin is full of antioxidants such as lutein and zeaxanthin.

If you have a compost pile, hydrate it with the
liquid you squeeze out of shredded zucchini.

These attributes make zucchini beneficial in combating cancer, constipation, eye ailments, and gastrointestinal disorders. Its fiber content can help control blood sugar levels, and it has only three grams of carbohydrates per serving, making it a good food for diabetics.

Growing and Harvesting Zucchini

Zucchini grows vigorously in a creeping manner with large, deeply lobed leaves, which are dark green with silver speckles. The sturdy pentagonal stems and leaves are covered with small, prickly hairs. Soon after the leaves are established, clusters of flower buds appear. In a few days, the buds open into brilliant yellow, five-petalled flowers. In my experience, male flowers appear first and grow on slender stems. The female flowers form at the tip of a miniature zucchini. As the bud swells, so does the size of the fruit. The flowers open early in the morning and wilt by noon.

Zucchini ripen quickly in hot weather, and depending on the cultivar, its soft rind can be dark green, green and white striped, or even speckled with yellow. Its shape can be long and cylindrical, ridged (so slices look like stars), or even round, like a ball or teardrop.

Generally speaking, zucchini should be picked "young," which means when they are about six to eight inches long.

At this size, the seeds are small and soft. I have to admit that letting a zucchini stay on the vine simply to watch it grow is entertaining, but then you have to ask yourself what to do with the behemoth.

Growing zucchini requires little preparation. They do well in nearly all temperate climates in nutrient-rich soil with full sun. I once read that four zucchini plants is three too many, so plan your garden accordingly. If this is your first time, I recommend starting with two. This will ensure that they can cross pollinate and provide a more manageable number of zucchini.

Zucchini can be planted in a traditional three sisters grouping of squash, beans, and corn, which is a considerate way to honor its ancestral American roots.

When planting the three sisters, do so over the course of about three weeks. Once the danger of frost is past, start by planting the corn so it can grow a couple inches before the other sisters emerge. Plant the beans next, and as soon as they have a few leaves, set the zucchini seeds in the ground. Its big leaves will discourage weeds from growing and will create shade, which will help the soil retain moisture.

If planting zucchini on its own, the main consideration is space. Ensure a couple feet between plants so they won't crowd each other. Most zucchini do not send out tendrils or vines; rather, the main stem grows longer as it produces new nodes of flowers and leaves. Picking the zucchini while small will encourage the plant to continue growing.

All squash plants need copious amounts of water. During dry spells, water the soil daily at the base of the stem under the leaves. On especially hot days, you may see the leaves wilt. This is not usually a cause for alarm and is merely because more moisture is evaporating from the leaves than the roots can replenish. Once the sun starts to go down, the leaves should return to their customary shape. (I was actually glad for this daily leaf wilt because I did not space my garden well this year, and it meant my marigolds and basil got some sun.)

Zucchini can be susceptible to a number of garden pests, such as squash vine borers and aphids. The best way to protect your plants is to keep the garden weed free, plant flowers to encourage visits from beneficial insects, and remove the pests by hand. Powdery mildew can also cause damage. Cut off affected leaves and dispose of them—do not compost. An application of neem oil, which is safe for food-bearing plants, can kill the fungus. Be vigilant and continue to check and treat throughout the season. There are also specific zucchini varieties bred to withstand some of these afflictions.

Cooking with Zucchini

The beauty of zucchini is its mild flavor; it complements nearly every cuisine. And with its ease of growing, home cooks can become fearless in their use of it in recipes since they will probably discover four more in the garden tomorrow. It can be pickled, turned into relish, or marinated. My family enjoys eating thick planks of zucchini dressed in olive oil and charred on the grill, or sliced into disks, sauteed, and sprinkled with parmesan cheese.

Zucchini is a wonderful vehicle for strong flavors, and that's why it is often paired with garlic, basil, and tomato. It is an important component of the classic French recipe ratatouille. But don't stop your experimenting with zucchini's classic uses! If you shred zucchini and toss with Old Bay Seasoning, it makes a convincing stand-in for crab in crab cakes.

Sliced in half moons and mixed with sugar, cinnamon and nutmeg, zucchini can be used to make mock apple pie.

Zucchini can also be eaten raw. I once sat down to a raw food meal of "pasta and sauce" at a vegan restaurant in Minneapolis, where thinly shaved strips of zucchini served as the pasta and strawberries and cashews were the sauce (this was before the spiral vegetable slicer, a.k.a. "spiralizer," was invented). I thought this was an earth-shaking idea and marveled over the construction of the dish.

Another welcome feature of zucchini is its ability to melt into a recipe. This is a boon to parents of picky eaters and why zucchini bread is so popular. Shredded zucchini can also be added to soup, sauces, meatloaf, and meatballs.

One need not wait for the zucchini to grow before appreciating the plant. Small young leaves can be cooked like spinach, and the flowers are edible.

✍ Zucchini Blossom Fritters

I have written for *Llewellyn's Herbal Almanac* for a long time. Incorporating the subject plant into my garden and seeing where the experience takes me is part of my summertime tradition. This year, when I selected zucchini, I knew it would be a way for me to honor my father-in-law, Joseph Ardolino, who passed away at the end of May 2022. He was born on the side of Mount Vesuvius in Musciabuono, Italy, and moved to the United States as a boy. He worked many jobs throughout his life, including restaurateur. Making food was one of his greatest joys, and I am glad to share his legacy in these pages.

As my zucchini plants started to flourish, I watched for the first flowers to appear. My husband remembered his father making zucchini blossom fritters, and he asked me to recreate the recipe. We had nothing to go by other than my husband and his mother's taste memory. We knew it was a pancake, not simply a blossom fried in batter. It took a while to get the right consistency, but luckily, my zucchini plants kept sending up more flowers, so I could keep experimenting.

If you pick a blossom and it starts buzzing, don't be alarmed!
A bee is trapped and needs your help. Hold the flower away
from you by its stem and give it a gentle shake.

Depending on the number of plants you have, this recipe may need some preplanning in order to get enough blossoms. You need at least twenty big flowers, but they will keep for three to four days in the refrigerator, so you can make a collection. My husband and I would pick the blossoms at about 11 a.m., when they were starting to close. Some recipes say to pick them when the flowers are fully open, but the bees were so active around them in the morning that I hated to remove this food source prematurely. We picked only the male blossoms and left the female blossoms attached to the mini zucchini. Once you have picked your day's worth of blossoms, store them with a paper towel sheet in a zip-top bag in the refrigerator.

This recipe is extremely adaptable, which is part of why it was so difficult for me to figure out how my father-in-law made his! As far as we knew, he just threw things together in a bowl and out popped the most tender fritters. So if you want to make the fritters but don't have twenty blossoms yet, make them anyway. Serve them plain, with a sprinkle of salt, or alongside marinara sauce, oil, and balsamic vinegar, or even eat them like bruschetta—piled with fresh toppings.

When using zucchini blossoms in a recipe, you want only the petals. Gently tear them off the anther and stem, making sure no green sepals are attached. Check for bugs and remove them. I don't recommend rinsing the flowers because the petals are so fragile. For this reason, be sure the flowers come from a garden that is away from the road and from plants that are not sprayed with pesticides.

You will need:

1½ cups flour

1 teaspoon baking powder

1 teaspoon salt

½ teaspoon black pepper

1 egg

1–2½ cups water

20–30 zucchini blossoms, torn into pieces or sliced into ribbons

Vegetable oil for pan frying

Combine the flour, baking powder, salt, and pepper in a medium-size bowl.

Crack the egg into a small bowl and add 1 cup water. Whisk with a fork to combine.

Add the egg mixture to the dry ingredients and mix. If the consistency is stiff, add more water. You are aiming for it to look like thick pancake batter.

Gently stir in the blossoms. Allow the batter to sit for at least 10 minutes.

Place a skillet over medium heat and add ¼ inch vegetable oil. You want the fritters to sit on the floor of the pan but have the oil come up the sides of the batter.

Once the oil is hot and a drop of batter immediately starts to bubble, spoon ¼ cup batter into the pan. Pour in more fritters, but do not crowd the pan. Let them cook for about 2 minutes, then carefully flip them (the oil can splatter).

Once the fritters are puffed and lightly browned on both sides, remove them and set them on a wire rack or on a paper towel-lined plate. Serve immediately with a shake of salt.

Freezing Zucchini

At some point you may look at all the zucchini stacked in your refrigerator and decide you want to make room for other things and don't want to prepare another zucchini-centric meal for a while. Freezing the bounty is a logical way to save it for another day. With its high water content, thawed zucchini does not act like fresh zucchini, so it is not good for all recipes, but it will work great when it needs to melt into the other ingredients.

You will need:

Colander

1 or more clean cloth tea towels

Knife

Cutting board

As many zucchini as you have, rinsed

Food processor with a grating disk installed or box grater

Large plate or bowl that will fit under the colander

1-cup measuring cup

Parchment paper

1 or more baking sheets that will fit in your freezer or
    silicone food storage molds

Zip-top freezer bags

Line the colander with the tea towel, allowing the ends to
drape over the sides.

Cut the zucchini into a manageable size for either the food
processor or box grater. Grate the zucchini in batches that
won't overwhelm the machine or your grater.

Transfer the shreds to the colander until it is about ¾ full.
Pull up the sides of the tea towel and squeeze the liquid out of
the zucchini. Discard the liquid—there will be a lot!

Use the measuring cup to portion out zucchini onto the
parchment-lined baking sheet, or pack the food storage molds.

Place the baking sheets or molds on a level surface in the
freezer for at least 4 hours or overnight.

Continue processing the rest of the zucchini in this
method.

When frozen all the way through, pop the zucchini into
zip-top freezer bags. Expel as much air as possible before sealing it, and be sure to write the date on the bag so you remember to use it up within 3–6 months.

———

Welcoming zucchini into your garden can feel a little like welcoming a child with a big personality into your life. It can be
overwhelming at times, but no matter the amount of work
you put in throughout the summer, winter will offer you time
to reflect on the good meals, and by spring you will find your-

self setting aside room in your garden for yet another season contending with this rewarding yet exasperatingly prolific crop.

Resources

"Everyday Mysteries: How Did the Squash Get Its Name?" Library of Congress. November 19, 2019. https://www.loc.gov/everyday -mysteries/agriculture/item/how-did-squash-get-its-name/.

Graff, Michele. "The History Behind . . . the Squash Blossom Necklace." National Jeweler. February 7, 2018. https://www.national jeweler.com/articles/9551-the-history-behind-the-squash -blossom-necklace.

Kafka, Barbara, and Christopher Styler. *Vegetable Love*. New York: Artisan Publishing, 2005.

Lust, Teresa, and Harry Paris. "Italian Horticultural and Culinary Records of Summer Squash (*Cucurbita pepo*, Cucurbitaceae) and Emergence of the Zucchini in 19th-Century Milan." *Annals of Botany* 118, no. 1 (2016): 53–69. https://doi.org/10.1093/aob /mcw080.

Peluso, Laura. "Mystery Monday: The Squash Blossom as a Symbol of Fertility." *On Pins and Needles* (blog), October 18, 2012. https:// pinsndls.com/2012/10/18/mystery-monday-the-squash-blossom -as-a-symbol-of-fertility/.

Garlic

⤞ Kathy Martin ⤝

Garlic is wonderful to grow in a home vegetable garden. It's simple to plant and easy to harvest. You can enjoy home-grown garlic year-round by storing the heads all winter, harvesting green garlic in spring, and picking garlic scapes in the summer. You can replant your own garlic that you save year after year, so you don't need to keep buying more seed garlic. Best of all, garlic is a delicious and super nutritious vegetable, herb, and spice that enhances many recipes. It's also one of the healthiest things you can add to your diet!

I've just finished harvesting my garlic. Some from my mother's yard, some from my backyard, and some

Garlic	
Species	*Allium sativum*
Zone	1–11
Needs	☼☼☼ 💧💧
Soil pH	6.0–7.0
Size	1–3' tall

from my community garden. I have too many gardens, but I could never have too much garlic. Right now, I am looking at two baskets that together contain at least three hundred heads of freshly pulled, aromatic, and neatly cleaned garlic.

What is garlic? A spice? An herb? A vegetable? Minced fresh and added as a flavoring to a red sauce, garlic can be considered an herb. When it's dehydrated and sprinkled as garlic powder on pizza or baked squash, we can call it a spice. But rather than calling it an herb or a spice, some people like to think of garlic as a vegetable that flavors other vegetables. When you eat a whole head of caramelized oven-roasted garlic, it seems to be a vegetable on its own. And when I add a full head of minced fresh homegrown garlic to a salsa or guacamole, it does seem like I am using garlic as a vegetable to flavor other vegetables.

Planting Garlic

Garlic is best planted in late fall. It's the last crop of the year to go into the garden and should be planted about two to four weeks before the ground freezes. Northernmost gardeners, in USDA zones 1 to 4, should plant in late August to September, gardeners in zones 5 to 8 should plant in mid-October through mid-November, and those in zones 9 to 10 should plant in late November to December. Garlic needs some degree of winter cold weather to form a bulb and in tropical areas can only be grown for its leaves. In zone 6, I plant my garlic around Halloween. Passersby at my community garden plot are surprised to see me in there in the cold dreary weather planting something so late in the year. To plant garlic, separate each clove from the head, leaving the wrappers on the clove. Plant each clove three inches deep and six inches apart, making sure the pointy end is up. Cover the bed with three to four inches of chopped leaves, hay, or straw mulch to protect the garlic from freeze-thaw cycles in the winter and from drying out in the summer.

If you forget to plant in the fall or find a few more cloves later that you want to plant, all is not lost. The bulbs will be a bit smaller, but you can still plant garlic in the spring. You can plant it indoors in pots three to four weeks before the time your soil usually becomes workable or plant it directly in the garden as soon as the soil can be worked. **Workable soil** means it is fully thawed and not muddy—so you could stick a shovel into it and turn over a clump. To start garlic in pots in the spring, I like to plant about ten cloves in a twelve-inch pot, with each clove about two inches apart. Transplant it to the garden as soon as you can or when the leaves are about six to eight inches tall. Gently separate each garlic plant, carefully teasing apart the roots, and plant them six inches apart with the clove three inches deep.

Garlic is a great companion plant for most garden vegetables because it repels pests.

And what about those sprouted cloves of supermarket garlic? Sure, you can plant them, but if you are hoping to get a garlic head, be sure to plant in late fall or early spring. If it's the middle of winter or in the summer, try planting the sprouted cloves in a pot indoors. They won't make a head, but you can cut and enjoy the fresh green garlic leaves like scallions.

Garlic's unique planting schedule is due to its growth cycle. Originating as a wild plant in Central Asia, garlic has a growth cycle evolved to allow it to survive harsh, hot, dry summers and severe winters. The fleshy underground head, or bulb, is garlic's secret to survival. The bulb is a storage organ that retains the plant's fuel reserves during periods of dormancy, which happen in the hot, dry summer and again in the cold winter. The garlic plant's life cycle begins (if any cycle can be said to have a beginning or end) when summer ends. Once fall arrives and conditions become favorable for growth, the garlic bulb breaks its dormancy and grows, forming a strong underground network of roots and sometimes a couple inches of above-ground leaves before winter arrives. During the cold of winter, the garlic plant again stops growing. When spring rains begin, the garlic plant now faces its big challenge: to grow as rapidly as it can and form leaves, a flower, and a bigger bulb before the heat of summer sets in and the garlic plant returns to its dormancy. It's a wonderful growth cycle not only because it allows the plant to survive, but also because it provides us with three times for harvesting—green spring garlic, garlic scapes, and best of all, the garlic bulb.

Saving Your Garlic Stock

One of the things I like best about garlic is that you can save your own heads to regrow year after year. Each year I select the biggest heads with the largest cloves from my harvest and save them as my planting stock. Large cloves will produce the largest heads the following year. Store the intact heads you select in a cool, dry location. Wait to separate the heads into individual cloves until planting time.

I usually grow about a hundred heads of garlic for my-self and forty or so for my mother. I plant 'Majestic', which only has four or five very large cloves per head. I also grow a smaller, purple-colored variety that has about ten cloves per head. For the variety with four or five cloves per head, I save about one-quarter to one-fifth for replanting. For the heads with ten cloves per head, I save and replant one-tenth to get my same harvest the following year.

Garlic Varieties

Phew, there are so many! Many hundreds of named varieties. These are grouped into two main groups: hardneck and soft-neck. The softnecks grow faster, tend to last longer in storage, and have a more pungent flavor. They are the type most often found in supermarkets, and they also grow well in a home garden. The neck of this garlic is soft and can be braided. The hardneck garlics are generally better adapted to growing in the north and have a wider range of flavors and colors. Seven groups of hardnecks include rocambole, purple stripe, tur-ban, porcelain, Asiatic, elephant, and creole. Garlic varieties with the best flavor are often considered to be the rocamboles and purple stripes.

Garlic flavor can range from rich and mild to sharp and pungent. If you are trying to decide what type to grow, select a couple and see which you like best. At my farm we occasion-ally hold garlic tastings. We select about five varieties (from the twenty or so that we grow) and prepare them the night be-fore tasting by mincing the cloves in olive oil and labeling them. The next day at the farm, we set out a small bowl of each vari-ety with crackers or bread to spread them on. This is the best way to compare raw garlic differences and see what you prefer. It is surprising how different varieties taste. In our tastings, we liked the flavor of the white porcelain variety 'Georgian Crystal' best. The very popular variety 'Music' came in a close second. At home, I grow 'Majestic' and I love its large heads. 'Korean Mountain' is a beautiful variety with deep purple stripes.

Enjoying Home-Grown Garlic Year-Round

There are several ways to harvest garlic. When the plant is young, it can be pulled and eaten raw like green onions or scallions. At this stage it is called **green garlic**, and the entire plant is edible. The flavor of green garlic is milder, fresher, and sweeter than garlic cloves, though it is spicier than scallions. It is delicious chopped and sprinkled on scrambled eggs.

A garlic braid can be made from homegrown softneck garlic and is a beautiful way to store your harvest.

Around the time of the summer solstice, hardneck garlic will send up a flower stalk called a **scape**. Typically, the garlic scape is cut off from the plant when it has curled around into a full loop so that energy from flower formation is redirected to the bulb. Garlic scapes are the second edible stage of the garlic plant. They are stronger in flavor than green garlic but milder and sweeter than garlic bulbs. Scapes are delicious in stir fries or pesto.

And finally, the most common way to eat garlic is to use the bulb, which is harvested by digging in midsummer. A well-stored garlic harvest will keep through April or May of the following year, a time when you can begin all over again to harvest spring green garlic.

Harvesting Garlic Bulbs

Once the garlic plant develops three dried leaves, it should be pulled. Each leaf of the garlic plant extends into the soil all the way down to the base of the bulb and forms a layer of wrappers on the head. If all the leaves were to dry up, there would be no wrappers left holding the cloves of the head together. The cloves would not be protected from drying out or rotting. The perfect timing for harvest is to wait until three leaves at the base of the plant have dried. This is when the bulb has reached its maximum size and will still hold together and have a long shelf life.

To harvest garlic heads, grab hold of the stalk and pull. Usually this works fine. However, if your garden soil is compacted or the garlic stems are small, you may risk breaking off the garlic head and losing it in the soil. Loosen the soil with a garden fork if the stems break.

After harvest, garlic should be cleaned and cured. Curing properly will increase the length of time the heads can be stored. To clean garlic plants, brush off dirt or pull off a few of the outermost green leaves right down to the base of the head. Most growers do not like to risk rinsing with water because the moisture can initiate rotting. Also, most growers do not risk cutting the stem before the plant has dried and fully cured. To cure garlic, hang the plants in bunches or spread them out on a table in a dry dark area with good circulation. Properly cured garlic of most varieties should last several months. The varieties I grow usually last until April or May of the following year (about nine months). After that, I make one trip to the grocery store for some California-grown softneck garlic before I harvest my bulbs again in July.

Nutritional Benefits of Garlic

Garlic has had many uses in different cultures over the centuries. It has been used since ancient times as a food, as an effective health remedy in traditional medicine, as a food preservative, for spiritual purposes, and as a spice and seasoning herb. When I read about the health benefits of garlic, I noticed that it was often used prior to the discovery of our modern medicines as an effective antiviral treatment. It reportedly saved many people during the plagues in Europe in the seventeenth and eighteenth centuries. Garlic was also an important nutritional additive in ancient Egypt, where slaves were given large quantities to keep them healthy on meager food rations. Today, garlic is one of the bestselling herbal dietary supplements in the United States. From hundreds of scientific studies, we know that it has significant healthful effects on a wide range of diseases, including viral diseases, cardiovascular health, cancer, diabetes, and the immune system. Garlic protects against these conditions through its antioxidant, anti-inflammatory, and lipid-lowering properties.

The main components of garlic that bring these health benefits seem to be a compound called **allicin** and the related compounds S-allyl cysteine and allyl disulfide. Allicin is a sulfur-containing molecule that gives garlic its pungent taste and smell. It is generated from another molecule, **alliin**, which is stable in the garlic bulb but has no taste or smell. Only after garlic has been crushed or cut is the alliin converted to allicin, which gives garlic its pungency. Allicin is a short-lasting chemical that is degraded fast in the bloodstream and is inactivated by heat. Because of this, it has been difficult for scientific research to understand and replicate some of the effects of garlic on health. In addition, as noted in a review of garlic by Reuter and colleagues in 1996, it is likely that the effects of garlic are due to a "complex mixture of active ingredients which probably act synergistically to produce a clinical effect."

Here is a list of some of the known health benefits garlic:

Antiviral and Antimicrobial Activity: Garlic has been proven to have antibacterial and antiviral activity. It can reduce the growth of salmonella and other pathogens in food preparations. It can also help some antibiotics work better, for example antibiotics used in treating tuberculosis.

Immune System Stimulation: Garlic can enhance the activity of immune cells in the blood that fight different types of infections.

Cardiovascular System Protection: Garlic is often recommended for cardiac health. It can improve cardiovascular health by reducing cholesterol. It has been used to treat high blood pressure and heart arrhythmias. It can also inhibit platelet aggregation. Garlic is an antioxidant, and this activity may account for these four important cardiac protective activities. See works in the resources list at the end of the article by Reuter and colleagues (1996), Schwingshackl and colleagues (2015), and Ansary and colleagues (2020), which review hundreds of cardiovascular studies with garlic.

Diabetes Protection: Garlic lowers blood glucose and can be beneficial in moderating glucose levels in those with a slight elevation.

Anticancer Activity: Garlic can also reduce the risk of some cancers. In some studies, it has been shown to reduce the risk of cancers, in particular stomach and colon cancers, in some groups of people.

The health benefits of garlic are mainly achieved when it is eaten raw. It can be minced, crushed, sliced, or chopped and should be eaten in combination with other foods. A study by Pentz and Seigers in 1996 found that one clove of garlic a day, about 0.1 to 0.2 ounces (3–5 grams), is the amount that is reported to give a health benefit. A clove a day keeps the doctor away.

Recipes

≽ *Garlic Scape Pesto with Basil*

Garlic scapes taste milder and sweeter than garlic bulbs, more like chives or scallions, and are a perfect vegetable to use for making pesto. I find that basil is a nice addition, but this recipe is also delicious without it. Serve scape pesto on fresh pasta or crusty bread. You can also spread it on sandwiches or add it to lamb or fish dishes. This recipe makes about 1 cup of pesto and is best made the day before serving to allow time for the flavors to meld.

You will need:

  1 cup coarsely chopped garlic scapes, flower buds removed

  ½ cup basil leaves

  ¼ cup pine nuts or walnuts

  ½ cup extra virgin olive oil

  ¼ cup grated parmesan cheese

  Salt to taste

Place the scapes in a food processor and pulse for 30 seconds. Add the basil and nuts and pulse 30 seconds, scraping down the sides as needed. Add olive oil and process on high for 15 seconds. Add the cheese and process until smooth. Let the pesto rest in the refrigerator overnight. When serving, add warm water reserved from boiling pasta to adjust the consistency of the pesto. Also add salt to taste.

To store the pesto, leave out the cheese and freeze in a plastic bag or ice cube tray. Thaw and add cheese, pasta water, and salt to taste when serving.

⚛ Roasted Garlic

Roasting garlic caramelizes its sugars and brings out its sweetness. I have found that the varieties that taste best roasted are often different than those that taste best fresh, so try out several different types. California softneck supermarket garlic roasts up great, as do my big heads of 'Majestic' garlic.

You will need your garlic heads and extra-virgin olive oil for this recipe.

Preheat your oven to 400°F. Slice off the top ¼ inch of the garlic heads, exposing the top of the garlic cloves, and remove most of the outer garlic skins. Wrap the heads in a small piece of aluminum foil and place cut-side up in muffin tins or on a baking sheet. Drizzle the tops of the garlic with a couple teaspoons of olive oil. Use your finger to make sure the oil coats the cut surfaces well. Pinch the foil closed over the head and bake for 30–45 minutes, or until the heads are browned and soft when pressed. Once roasted and cooled enough to handle, the roasted garlic can be removed from its wrappers with a small knife or spoon, or it can be squeezed out using your fingers. Enjoy it on crackers, crusty bread, baked potatoes, or pasta.

Resources

Ansary, Johura, et al. "Potential Health Benefit of Garlic Based on Human Intervention Studies: A Brief Overview." *Antioxidants* 9, no. 7 (2020):619. doi:10.3390/antiox9070619.

Cavallito, Chester J., Johannes S. Buck, and C. M. Suter. "Allicin, the Antibacterial Principle of *Allium sativum*. II. Determination of the chemical composition." *Journal of the American Chemical Society* 60, no. 11 (1994): 1952–58. https://doi.org/10.1021/ja01239a049.

Meredith, Ted Jordan. *The Complete Book of Garlic; A Guide for Gardeners, Growers, and Serious Cooks.* Portland, OR: Timber Press, 2008.

Pentz, R., and C. P. Siegers. "Garlic Preparations: Methods for Qualitative and Quantitative Assessment of Their Ingredients." In *Garlic: The Science and Therapeutic Application of* Allium sativum L. *and Related Species,* 109–34. 2nd ed. Edited by Heinrich P. Koch, Larry D. Lawson. Baltimore, MD: Williams and Wilkins, 1996.

Reuter, H. D., Heinrich P. Koch, and Larry D. Lawson. "Therapeutic Effects and Applications of Garlic and Its Preparations." In *Garlic: The Science and Therapeutic Application of* Allium sativum L. *and Related Species,* 135–212. 2nd ed. Edited by Heinrich P. Koch, Larry D. Lawson. Baltimore, MD: Williams and Wilkins, 1996.

Schwingshackl, Lukas, Benjamin Missbach, and Georg Hoffmann. "An Umbrella Review of Garlic Intake and Risk of Cardiovascular Disease." *Phytomedicine* 23, 11 (October 2016): 1127–33. doi:10.1016/j.phymed.2015.10.015.

Caraway

≫ Linda Raedisch ≪

If you could travel back five thousand summers or so and drop in on a Swiss lake dweller, you would find white caraway flowers blooming in the kitchen garden of his wattle-and-reed house. Early twentieth-century imaginings of such houses, and the villages they formed, inspired the "Lake-town" to which Bilbo and the dwarves float in *The Hobbit*, but back in the Neolithic Age, the ground on which the houses stood was more marsh than lake. Caraway, which closely resembles its fellow carrot family members anise, cumin, fennel, and dill, loves moisture. Because it has deep roots, it can hold out in dry weather too, so it shouldn't be overwatered. Caraway is especially happy in a raised bed.

Caraway	
Species	*Carum carvi*
Zone	4–10
Needs	☀☀☀ 💧💧
Soil pH	6.0–7.0
Size	Up to 3' tall

In warmer climates, caraway might flower the same year as it's planted, but in temperate lands, it should be covered with wood chips or garden cuttings over the winter so it can come back and flower the next year. To earn its keep the first year, caraway's tender young leaves can be eaten in soups and salads. Cut the second year's stalks as soon as the seeds turn brown and hang them upside down to dry. Leave a receptacle underneath the hanging bunches to catch the falling seeds. Caraway won't come back after the second year, so you can dig up the fennel-like root and roast it or add it to soups and stews.

The belief that a pouch of caraway seeds worn around the neck would keep the witches away probably didn't arise until the Middle Ages. In Germany's Thuringia, if you wanted the help of the little wood-folk (Germanic brownies), you had to be careful not to offer them any bread with caraway seeds in it; if you did, you'd never see the little helpers again. Caraway isn't used much for magical purposes nowadays, but a scattering of seeds added to foods that might cause flatulence, like cabbage and cheese, makes life more pleasant for everyone. Like the wood-folk, many humans are repelled by the caraway seed's sharp taste, which comes from a combination of bitter tannin and essential oils high in anethole, the same compound that gives anise, fennel, and licorice their strong through-the-nose flavors. A little caraway makes for smoother digestion, but too much can upset the stomach.

The English word *caraway* comes from the Arabic *karawaya*, after the ancient kingdom of Caria in what is now Turkey, where the plant was thought to have originated. The Sanskrit word *karavi,* which may be derived from Arabic, or the other way around, can also mean "fennel." I've found several mentions of the use of caraway in ancient Egyptian medicine, specifically the Ebers Papyrus, but Danish Egyptologist Lisa Manniche is strangely silent on the subject. Her definitive reference, *An Ancient Egyptian Herbal,* includes several examples of cumin, nigella ("black cumin"), fennel, and aniseed in ancient recipes and prescriptions and in tombs, but not caraway. Frequently, ancient names that have been translated into English as "caraway" originally denoted other species. To this day, several European languages have one word for both cumin and caraway. The German word *Kümmel* can mean caraway, cumin, or caraway-infused brandy, though Germans do sometimes make a distinction between "cross" *Kümmel* (cumin) and "real," "field," or "meadow" *Kümmel* (caraway).

Caraway as Condiment

Some say that the farther north caraway is grown, the better the seeds taste, so it makes sense that they pop up in a lot of northern European breads made with cold-hardy rye, the most familiar of which is Jewish rye bread. (One of Jewish rye bread's Yiddish names is *sissel,* which means "caraway.") Caraway seeds have long been served as a condiment too. Excavations of the lake dwellers' villages have turned up quantities of crab apples, fruits that are only palatable after cooking or roasting. It's tempting to think that the lake folk might have originated the practice of accompanying roasted apples with a side dish of caraway seeds, still a popular snack in Shakespeare's time. Caraway seeds also go nicely with semi-soft cheeses, either mixed in during the aging process, as with some varieties of the Danish havarti, or served on the side, as with munster géromé.

In Germany, caraway seeds are added to sauerkraut, to cut the gas as much as for the flavor. I like to add a little curry and onion powder to my store-bought sauerkraut too. Drain yours well and put a little olive oil in the bottom of the pot before cooking. A dash of white wine doesn't hurt, either.

Making my own sauerkraut from scratch is still on my list of things to do, but I have made my own kimchi and enjoyed it very much, both in the making and in the eating. Yes, kimchi is fermented cabbage, but don't let the "F" word scare you; making kimchi isn't all that different from making coleslaw. Even though I've made it many times, I still get a Christmas morning feeling when, after about twelve hours, I press down on the cabbage leaves and see the first bubbles rising up around them. In the days before refrigeration, burying kimchi in earthenware jars was the best way to keep it cool, but you can keep your kimchi in the refrigerator.

The following recipe is for "white kimchi," which was what all kimchi was before the red, new-world chili pepper arrived in Korea.

⤝ White Kimchi with Apple and Caraway

- 1 small head napa cabbage, cored and cut into slightly larger than bite-size pieces
- 2 Honeycrisp or other hard apple (not Macintosh), peeled and cut into large chunks
- ⅓ cup kosher salt
- 1–2-inch piece of ginger, peeled and minced
- 6 garlic cloves, minced
- 1 bunch chives cut into inch-long pieces (You can use scissors.)
- 4 tablespoons fish sauce

2 tablespoons sugar

2 tablespoons caraway seeds

Put the cabbage in a very large bowl or basin, fill it with enough water to cover, and sprinkle with salt, reserving some for the apples. Put the apples in another bowl and do the same, using up all the salt. Let both soak for 45 minutes, pushing them down every so often to keep them under the water.

While the cabbage and apples are soaking, combine the other ingredients in another bowl.

Drain and rinse the salted cabbage thoroughly in a colander. Squeeze it by the handful to get as much of the brine out as possible before returning it to the rinsed-out bowl. Drain and rinse the apples too, and add them to the cabbage. Add the other ingredients and mix thoroughly with your hands.

Spoon kimchi into a glass jar or jars, pushing it down to compact it as much as possible. Place the lid on loosely and let sit at room temperature for a day or two. The longer you let it ferment, the more sour it will be.

Screw the lid on before storing it in the refrigerator.

Eat cold with chicken, tofu, any kind of sausage, potatoes, or noodles.

Gandalf Tea Wednesday

Caraway entered the British Isles as an expensive import, but by the late 1500s, the English had gotten the hang of growing "caruwayes" themselves. By the late 1600s, even the working classes could afford to eat caraway seeds with their apples and cheese. They'd started baking them into cakes too. "But I don't mind some cake—seed-cake, if you have any," the dwarf

Balin says in response to Bilbo's reluctant offer of a cup of tea in the first chapter of *The Hobbit*. Balin wants his seed cake with beer, not tea. Seed cake, which farmers' wives used to serve at the end of the spring sowing, has always been a rustic cake, despite efforts by some gourmets to elevate it.

The most surprising thing I learned about seed cake was the fact that I'd baked it before. The recipe I'd followed the first time around, copied from a vintage Royal Baking Powder advertisement I'd seen in a museum, had called it "nun's cake," but the two are one and the same. My nun's cake, as I recall, was too dry, a problem I have sought to correct here. The following recipe is for a cake somewhat fancier, I imagine, than what Bilbo would have served but not nearly as fancy as the one eighteenth-century author Hannah Glasse included in *The Art of Cookery, Made Plain and Easy*. In addition to rose or orange flower water, Glasse suggests we liven up our seed cake with cinnamon and ambergris—the greasy gray, highly expensive mass that sperm whales poop out! My recipe does not include ambergris, but only because I couldn't find it in the baking aisle.

✎ Seed Cake

- ¼ cup plus 2 tablespoons (1¼ sticks) butter
- ¾ cup sugar
- 1½ tablespoons caraway seeds, whole
- 1 tablespoon candied orange peel, chopped fine, or zest of 1 small- to medium-size orange
- 3 eggs
- 1 tablespoon rosewater

1 cup flour

1 teaspoon baking powder

Cream the butter and sugar together. Add the caraway seeds and orange peel. Beat in the eggs and rosewater. In a separate bowl, mix the flour and baking powder. Add the dry ingredients to the wet to make an easily spreadable batter. Scoop the batter into a small greased and floured loaf pan or 8-inch layer cake pan. Bake at 350°F for 40 minutes or until golden and a knife inserted in the center comes out clean. (A round cake will bake faster than a loaf.) Cool your cake 10 minutes before turning it out of the pan and serving.

In the pantry of a not overly warm hobbit hole, seed cake will keep for several days.

Caraway Comes Clean

"Victoria and Albert's favorite soap!" I wrote on the labels of the brown Windsor soaps (not to be confused with brown Windsor *soup*) I made for my town's Historical Society Craft Fair a few years ago. Victoria and Albert weren't the only ones; Lewis and Clark took this caraway-heavy, distinctly masculine-scented soap with them when they went west, and rumor has it that Napoleon liked it too. Unfortunately, since the close of the nineteenth century, brown Windsor soap's star has fallen, and I only sold one bar.

I first heard of Windsor soap in Merilyn Mohr's invaluable little history and guidebook, *The Art of Soapmaking*. While I used Mohr's recipe as a springboard for the additives, hers is for a tallow (animal fat) soap, which I don't make. Because sassafras is now recognized as a carcinogen, I have replaced it with birch. In order to achieve a dark brown color without overpowering the bars with too much cinnamon, I made the lye solution with strong black tea instead of plain water. I left out Mohr's citrusy bergamot because not all Windsor soap recipes call for it and because bergamot essential oil is very expensive. You'll still get a little citrus scent from the grapefruit seed extract, which also helps the soap batter trace.

According to Mohr, the only really essential ingredient in Windsor soap, other than the fat and the lye, of course, is caraway. For a more abrasive soap, you can replace the caraway essential oil with half a cup of crushed caraway seeds added to the coconut oil as you heat it.

Because basic soap-making instructions are beyond the scope of this caraway profile, I have provided resources at the end. You can also use the instructions for basic tea soap in my article "Adventures in Tea Soap–Making" in *Llewellyn's 2020 Herbal Almanac*. One cannot be told often enough to use gloves and eye protection when handling lye and to work in an extremely well-ventilated space.

⁂ Brown Windsor Soap

2.2 ounces lye dissolved in 5 ounces very strong, cooled black tea (brewed with distilled water)

11 ounces olive oil

4 ounces coconut oil, melted

½ ounce castor oil

1 teaspoon grapefruit seed extract (GSE)

2 teaspoons caraway essential oil

2 teaspoons birch essential oil

1 teaspoon cinnamon

½ teaspoon ground cloves

1 teaspoon honey

The GSE is optional, but without it your soap will take longer to trace (thicken), especially if you are stirring it with a spoon, not a stick blender. Wait until the soap has traced before adding the essential oils, spices, and honey. Because the honey will heat the batter up, I don't recommend silicone molds for this recipe; the molds won't melt, but the soap might erupt out of them. Use plastic molds or a shoebox lined with freezer paper instead. When the soap has set and cooled (about 2 days), you can cut the loaf into 8 bars. They will be ready to use after 1 month (at least) of air drying.

Annotated Resources

Badertscher, Vera May. "Hannah Glasse and Seed Cake or Nun's Cake." *Ancestors in Aprons* (blog), March 7, 2018. https://ancestorsinaprons.com/2018/03/hannah-glass-seed-cake-nuns-cake/. *This post includes the Royal Baking Powder advertisement recipe for nun's cake in all its early-twentieth-century Gothic glory.*

Buttery, Neil. "To Make a Seed Cake." *British Food: A History* (blog), May 23, 2021. https://britishfoodhistory.com/2021/05/23/to-make-a-seed-cake/.

Faiola, Anne-Marie. *Pure Soapmaking: How to Create Nourishing Natural Skin Care Soaps*. North Adams, MA: Storey Publishing, 2016. *Faiola offers one of the prettiest guides to cold-process soapmaking there is.*

Glasse, Hannah. *The Art of Cookery, Made Plain and Easy*. London, 1774. Page 273.

Kamm, Minnie Watson. *Old Time Herbs for Northern Gardens*. New York: Dover, 1971.

Luludi. YouTube channel. https://www.youtube.com/channel/UC0cSNgu4XuwPfnaAgafarug. *Luludi makes soaps to sell, but the videos on this channel are all about soapmaking techniques, along with folklore and wildcrafting.*

Mohr, Merilyn. *The Art of Soapmaking*. Altona, Canada: Camden House Publishing, 1979. Page 90. *An oldie but goodie with lots of history and even information about naturally soapy herbs.*

O'Connell, John. *The Book of Spice*. New York: Pegasus, 2016.

Raedisch, Linda. "Adventures in Tea Soap–Making." In *Llewellyn's 2020 Herbal Almanac*, 133–38. Woodbury, MN: Llewellyn Publications, 2019.

Scherf, Gertrud. *Zauberpflanzen Hexenkräuter*. Munich, Germany: BLV, 2003.

Tolkien, J. R. R. *The Hobbit*. New York: Houghton Mifflin, 2001. Page 11.

Spinach

⤳ Susan Pesznecker ⤶

I'm of that generation that grew up hearing the theme song to a beloved cartoon in which the day was always saved by the swarthy sailor Popeye squeezing open a can of spinach, downing its contents, and popping out instantaneous muscles. We believed!

While true spinach (*Spinacia oleracea*) probably originated in Asia (sometimes credited to Africa or the Middle East), we should all be grateful that it and its cousins have become peripatetic: traveling the planet. Available in grocery stores year-round and easy to grow in regions with a bit of warm, sunny summer, spinach is accessible to people all over the globe and is known

Spinach	
Species	*Spinacia oleracea*
Zone	5–10
Needs	☀☀ 💧💧
Soil pH	6.5–7
Size	2–12"

to be an incredibly healthful and delicious food with herbal and medicinal applications.

The Details

True spinach—and yes, that's its actual name—is a member of the Amaranthaceae family. Most of the amaranths are perennial herbs, featuring stems and simple, rather broad leaves. True spinach, however, is an annual and must be replanted each year. Rarely, in some very warm climates, true spinach persists from one year to the next, perennial style, without replanting. A number of the Amaranthaceae family are eaten as vegetables or grains, including amaranth, beets and sugar beets, chard, lamb's quarters, and quinoa.

Most of what people in the United States buy at the store is true spinach. Two other common variants include New Zealand spinach (native to Australia and New Zealand) and Malabar or Ceylon spinach (native to India). New Zealand spinach is much like its "true" cousin but is somewhat easier to grow in a wider range of climes, while Malabar spinach is limited to warmer regions and is known for its larger, thicker, more succulent leaves.

Cultivating Spinach

Spinach in some form has been cultivated for at least two thousand years. True spinach is a cool-season crop that prefers well-aerated soil and plenty of full sun. It is best planted in spring after frost date has passed, and it matures slowly over the course of several weeks. Water regularly, but allow soil to dry between waterings. In the heat of summer, true spinach is quick to bolt and go to seed, launching a thick stem with small flowers. And that's not bad news, for these "bolts" are bee-friendly: your local pollinators will be grateful! Harvest spinach by cutting the entire clump at ground level. For a continuous crop, replant every three weeks or so throughout the growing season.

Spinach connoisseurs might obtain seeds for the other spinaches. New Zealand spinach (*Tetragonia tetragonioides*) is a perennial in areas with mild winters. As with true spinach, plant in spring after the last frost date has passed. Harvest by plucking off the tender top leaves and stems; new growth will follow. This plant is tolerant of heat and doesn't bolt quickly. It can also tolerate drought, to a point.

Malabar spinach (*Basella alba*) needs warm days and nights and cannot tolerate frost or even cool night temperatures. Sow the seeds in early summer after nights have warmed to the mid or upper 50s Fahrenheit, or grow the plant in a greenhouse. This spinach forms vines and can be trellis trained. Harvest the leaves individually.

Nutritional Qualities

Pound for pound, spinach is one of our most nutrient-dense vegetables. It contains high levels of calcium as well as magnesium and vitamin K; this combination strengthens bones and teeth. Magnesium and vitamin E are known to support a healthy immune system. The folate and B_6 in spinach are not only important for cell growth and metabolism but also essential to fetal development during pregnancy. The carotenoids vitamin A, lutein, and zeaxanthin are essential for eye health, while vitamin A is also a potent antioxidant and may reverse or prevent the cell damage that leads to inflammation and even to certain kinds of cancer. The vitamin C in spinach spurs the healing of tissue damage and wounds. Natural nitrates and glycoglycerolipids (naturally occurring plant-based fats) in the plant lubricate and protect the colon and support healthy digestion, while its water content helps maintain hydration. Spinach leaves also contain CoQ_{10}, an enzyme that helps create and repair tissues. All these wonders aside, spinach is perhaps best known for its high levels of iron, which helps maintain the body's iron stores and works to prevent anemia. It's easy to see how spinach acquired its well-deserved reputation as a superfood!

Many of spinach's medicinal uses are obtained by actually eating the vegetable. But it has traditional herbal preparations as well and may be used as a supplement for specific purposes, such as bone healing, gastric distress, and anemia.

The dried, powdered leaves may be put into capsules, allowing for specific dosage control and making it easier to take large doses if needed, such as if treating anemia.

A liquid extract may be made by cold-pressing or distilling the leaves. High in CoQ_{10}, spinach is valued for its anti-inflammatory actions. The extract is taken via drops added to water.

Cautions

For those taking certain anticoagulants, the high vitamin K levels in spinach may interfere with the anticoagulant actions, with a typical portion of spinach providing about four times of the recommended daily dose of vitamin K. Spinach also contains high levels of oxalic acid; in very large doses, this can, paradoxically, cause both kidney stones and low blood calcium levels. Any concern over these issues should be discussed with one's healthcare provider.

In recent years, spinach has been associated with *E. coli* contaminations, making it important to always wash the leaves before using and stay alert to any CDC breakout warnings.

Culinary Uses

Known as one of America's favorite vegetables, spinach has a wide range of culinary uses—and most importantly, it's so versatile that just about anyone can find a way to work it into their diet, even if they aren't a friend of all things green (sorry, Kermit). For anyone trying to follow a nutritious, natural, "whole" diet, spinach can't be beat. It's extremely low in calories, which may be of value to many. And for vegetarians and vegans, it's a great way to add iron to a plant-based diet.

To cook or not to cook? Many vegetables actually become more nutritious (their vitamins and minerals become more accessible or easier to digest) with heat—carrots are an excellent example. Some of spinach's water-soluble vitamins, such as vitamins B_6 and C, are reduced by heating. But its iron, magnesium, potassium, and calcium are actually easier to absorb when cooked.

Spinach may be eaten raw (in salads, juiced, blended into smoothies) or cooked (stir-fried, creamed, added to soups or dips). It's delicious however it's served, but for veggie skeptics, spinach is one of those vegetables that can easily be smuggled into various dishes, provided one can explain the green color. Some people may be sensitive to a gritty texture in the spinach when it's cooked; this is a result of the oxalic acid, and for those folks, the texture issue is much less of a problem when the leaves are eaten in raw form.

✎ Stir-Fried Spinach

One of my favorite ways to cook spinach is this stir-fried recipe; it's fast and easy and makes a wonderful side dish.

You will need:

Vegetable oil

¼ raw onion, thinly sliced

¼ cup pine nuts (more if desired)

1 clove garlic, chopped

¼ cup dried cranberries (more if desired)

6–10 ounces raw spinach, washed and drained (patting dry not needed)

Good olive oil

Heat a large skillet over medium-high heat. When hot, add 2 tablespoons vegetable oil.

Once the oil shimmers, add onions and cook for 2–3 minutes stirring constantly. Add the pine nuts and cook-stir for another minute. Add the garlic, and cook-stir for about 30 seconds.

Add the cranberries and the spinach all at once. Cook, stir, and rotate the greens until the spinach is partially wilted; this will take 2–3 more minutes. For this step, kitchen tongs work well to make sure all the contents are being continually mixed and not sitting on the pan bottom.

Pile the stir-fry onto a serving plate, drizzle with olive oil, and enjoy! Thanks to the pine nuts and cranberries, the dish is visually appealing and full of texture. It's a quick, delicious, nutritious, and good-looking dish that would serve 2 hungry people as a hearty side dish. It could also be a smaller side for up to 4 diners.

Beauty and Cosmetics

Spinach extract in strengths of 1 to 5 percent appears frequently in commercial facial masks and skin care products. In a more DIY approach, a poultice of spinach leaves pulverized with water may be used as an anti-inflammatory facial mask. Finely chop a couple handfuls of fresh spinach and mix with water to form a soft mass. Even better, puree spinach and a bit of water in a food processor, or grind them in a mortar and pestle. Apply the spinach mixture to the skin, leave in place for 15–20 minutes, and rinse off, being careful not to clog the drain with bits of spinach. In a pinch, frozen spinach can be used in place of fresh.

Other commercially available beauty products use spinach extracts in shampoos, conditioners, lotions, creams, and lip balms. Both extract and powdered dried spinach leaves can be added to similar homemade preparations, and it's easy to find recipes for these on the web. Here's a simple base recipe I've used before that works wonderfully with added spinach:

Simple Spinach Lotion

2 parts olive oil

1 part coconut oil

1 part grated beeswax

Several drops to ¼ teaspoon vitamin E oil

Several drops of your favorite essential oil (for scent)

Several drops of spinach extract or ¼–½ teaspoon powdered spinach

Place the olive oil, coconut oil, and beeswax in a large glass jar. Place the jar in a saucepan of very hot water over low heat. Heat until melted, then cool. Once cool, add the remaining oils and the spinach component (adjusting the amount as desired).

Store the lotion in a clean lidded jar, and keep it in the fridge if not using quickly. You can adjust the consistency of further batches by altering the amount of beeswax.

Gardening
Resources

Companion Planting Guide

Group together plants that complement each other by deterring certain pests, absorbing different amounts of nutrients from the soil, shading their neighbors, and enhancing friends' flavors. This table of herbs and common garden vegetables offers suggestions for plants to pair together and plants to keep separated.

Plant	Good Pairing	Poor Pairing
Anise	Coriander	Carrot, basil, rue
Asparagus	Tomato, parsley, basil, lovage, Asteraceae spp.	
Basil	Tomato, peppers, oregano, asparagus	Rue, sage, anise
Beans	Tomato, carrot, cucumber, cabbage, corn, cauliflower, potato	Gladiola, fennel, *Allium* spp.
Bee balm	Tomato, echinacea, yarrow, catnip	
Beet	Onions, cabbage, lettuce, mint, catnip, kohlrabi, lovage	Pole bean, field mustard
Bell pepper	Tomato, eggplant, coriander, basil	Kohlrabi
Borage	Tomato, squash, strawberry	
Broccoli	Aromatics, beans, celery, potato, onion, oregano, pennyroyal, dill, sage, beet	Tomato, pole bean, strawberry, peppers
Cabbage	Mint, sage, thyme, tomato, chamomile, hyssop, pennyroyal, dill, rosemary, sage	Strawberry, grape, tomato
Carrot	Peas, lettuce, chive, radish, leek, onion, sage, rosemary, tomato	Dill, anise, chamomile

Plant	Good Pairing	Poor Pairing
Catnip	Bee balm, cucumber, chamomile, mint	
Celery	Leek, tomato, bush bean, cabbage, cauliflower, carrot, garlic	Lovage
Chamomile	Peppermint, beans, peas, onion, cabbage, cucumber, catnip, dill, tomato, pumpkin, squash	
Chervil	Radish, lettuce, broccoli	
Chive	Carrot, *Brassica* spp., tomato, parsley	Bush bean, potato, peas, soybean
Coriander/cilantro	*Plant anywhere*	Fennel
Corn	Potato, beans, peas, melon, squash, pumpkin, sunflower, soybean, cucumber	Quack grass, wheat, straw, tomato
Cucumber	Beans, cabbage, radish, sunflower, lettuce, broccoli, squash, corn, peas, leek, nasturtium, onion	Aromatic herbs, sage, potato, rue
Dill	Cabbage, lettuce, onion, cucumber	Carrot, caraway, tomato
Echinacea	Bee balm	
Eggplant	Catnip, green beans, lettuce, kale, redroot pigweed	
Fennel	*Isolate; disliked by all garden plants*	
Garlic	Tomato, rose	Beans, peas
Hyssop	*Most plants*	Radish
Kohlrabi	Green bean, onion, beet, cucumber	Tomato, strawberry, pole bean
Lavender	*Plant anywhere*	
Leek	Onion, celery, carrot, celeriac	Bush bean, soy bean, pole bean, pea

Plant	Good Pairing	Poor Pairing
Lemon balm	*All vegetables*, particularly squash, pumpkin	
Lettuce	Strawberry, cucumber, carrot, radish, dill	Pole bean, tomato
Lovage	*Most plants*, especially cucumber, beans, beet, *Brassica* spp., onion, leek, potato, tomato	Celery
Marjoram	*Plant anywhere*	
Melon	Corn, peas, morning glory	Potato, gourd
Mint	Cabbage, tomato, nettle	Parsley, rue
Nasturtium	Cabbage, cucumber, potato, pumpkin, radish	
Onion	Beets, chamomile, carrot, lettuce, strawberry, tomato, kohlrabi, summer savory	Peas, beans, sage
Oregano	*Most plants*	
Parsley	Tomato, asparagus, carrot, onion, rose	Mint, *Allium* spp.
Parsnip	Peas	
Peas	Radish, carrot, corn, cucumbers, bean, tomato, spinach, turnip, aromatic herbs	*Allium* spp., gladiola
Potato	Beans, corn, peas, cabbage, eggplant, catnip, horseradish, watermelon, nasturtium, flax	Pumpkin, raspberry, sunflower, tomato, orach, black walnut, cucumber, squash
Pumpkin	Corn, lemon balm	Potato
Radish	Peas, lettuce, nasturtium, chervil, cucumber	Hyssop
Rose	Rue, tomato, garlic, parsley, tansy	*Any plant within 1 ft. radius*
Rosemary	Rue, sage	

Plant	Good Pairing	Poor Pairing
Sage	Rosemary	Rue, onion
Spinach	Strawberry, garlic	
Squash	Nasturtium, corn, mint, catnip, radish, borage, lemon balm	Potato
Strawberry	Borage, bush bean, spinach, rue, lettuce	*Brassica* spp., garlic, kohlrabi
Tarragon	*Plant anywhere*	
Thyme	*Plant anywhere*	
Tomato	Asparagus, parsley, chive, onion, carrot, marigold, nasturtium, bee balm, nettle, garlic, celery, borage	Black walnut, dill, fennel, potato, *Brassica* spp., corn
Turnip	Peas, beans, brussels sprout, leek	Potato, tomato
Yarrow	*Plant anywhere*, especially with medicinal herbs	

For more information on companion planting, you may wish to consult the following resources:

Mayer, Dale. *The Complete Guide to Companion Planting: Everything You Need to Know to Make Your Garden Successful*. Ocala, FL: Atlantic Publishing, 2010.

Philbrick, Helen. *Companion Plants and How to Use Them*. Edinburgh, UK: Floris Books, 2016.

Riotte, Louise. *Carrots Love Tomatoes: Secrets of Companion Planting for Successful Gardening*. Pownal, VT: Storey Books, 1988.

Cooking with Herbs and Spices

Elevate your cooking with herbs and spices. Remember, a little goes a long way!

Herb	Flavor Pairings	Health Benefits
Anise	Salads, slaws, roasted vegetables	Reduces nausea, gas, and bloating. May relieve infant colic. May help menstrual pain. Loosens sputum in respiratory illnesses.
Basil	Pesto and other pasta sauces, salads	Eases stomach cramps, nausea, indigestion, and colic. Mild sedative action.
Borage	Soups	Soothes respiratory congestion. Eases sore, inflamed skin. Mild diuretic properties.
Cayenne	Adds a spicy heat to soups, sauces, and main courses	Stimulates blood flow. Relieves joint and muscle pain. Treats gas and diarrhea.
Chamomile	Desserts, teas	Used for nausea, indigestion, gas pains, bloating, and colic. Relaxes tense muscles. Eases menstrual cramps. Promotes relaxation and sleep.
Chervil	Soups, salads, and sauces	Settles and supports digestion. Mild diuretic properties. Useful in treating minor skin irritations.
Chive	Salads, potato dishes, sauces	Rich in antioxidants. May benefit insomnia. Contributes to strong bones.
Coriander/cilantro	Soups, picante sauces, salsas	Treats mild digestive disorders. Counters nervous tensions. Sweetens breath.

Herb	Flavor Pairings	Health Benefits
Dill	Cold salads and fish dishes	Treats all types of digestive disorders, including colic. Sweetens breath. Mild diuretic.
Echinacea	Teas	Supports immune function. May treat or prevent infection.
Fennel	Salads, stir-fry, vegetable dishes	Settles stomach pain, relieves bloating, and stimulates appetite. May help treat kidney stones and bladder infections. Mild expectorant. Eye wash treats conjunctivitis.
Garlic	All types of meat and vegetable dishes as well as soup stocks and bone broths	Antiseptic: aids in wound healing. Treats and may prevent infections. Benefits the heart and circulatory system.
Ginger	Chicken, pork, stir-fry, gingerbread and ginger cookies	Treats all types of digestive disorders. Stimulates circulation. Soothes colds and flu.
Hyssop	Chicken, pasta sauces, light soups	Useful in treating respiratory problems and bronchitis. Expectorant. Soothes the digestive tract.
Jasmine	Chicken dishes, fruit desserts	Relieves tension and provides mild sedation. May be helpful in depression. Soothes dry or sensitive skin.
Lavender	Chicken, fruit dishes, ice cream	Soothes and calms the nerves. Relieves indigestion, gas, and colic. May relax airways in asthma.

Herb	Flavor Pairings	Health Benefits
Lemon balm	Soups, sauces, seafood dishes	Soothes and calms the nerves. Treats mild anxiety and depression. Helps heal wounds.
Lemongrass	Marinades, stir-fries, curries, spice rubs	Treats all types of digestive disorders. Reduces fever. May reduce pain.
Lemon verbena	Beverages, any recipe asking for lemon zest	Calms digestive problems and treats stomach pain. Gently sedative.
Lovage	Soups, lovage pesto, lentils	Acts as a digestive and respiratory tonic. Has diuretic and antimicrobial actions. Boosts circulation. Helps menstrual pain.
Marigold	Soups, salads, rice dishes	Effective treatment of minor wounds, insect bites, sunburn, acne, and other skin irritations. Benefits menstrual pain and excessive bleeding.
Marjoram	Vegetables, soups, tomato dishes, sausages	Calms the digestive system. Stimulates appetite.
Nasturtium	Nasturtium pesto, salad dressings, salads	Strong antibiotic properties. Treats wounds and respiratory infections.
Oregano	Chicken, tomato sauces and dishes	Strong antiseptic properties. Stimulates bile production. Eases flatulence.
Parsley	Soups, stocks, bone broths	Highly nutritious. Strong diuretic action and may help treat cystitis. Benefits gout, rheumatism, and arthritis.
Peppermint	Desserts, teas	Treats all types of digestive disorders. May help headaches.

Herb	Flavor Pairings	Health Benefits
Purslane	Salads	Treats digestive and bladder ailments. Mild antibiotic effects.
Rosemary	Roasted red meats, potato dishes, grilled foods	Stimulates circulation. May stimulate the adrenal glands. Elevates mood and may benefit depression.
Sage	Chicken, duck, and pork	Relieves pain in sore throats. May help treat menstrual and menopausal disorders.
Spinach	Sautéed, soups, salads, spinach pesto, stuffed in chicken, ravioli	Iron-rich; supports healthy blood and iron stores.
Summer savory	Mushrooms, vegetables, quiche	Treats digestive and respiratory issues.
Tarragon	Chicken, fish, vegetables, sauces—"classic French cooking"	Stimulates digestion. Promotes sleep—mildly sedative. Induces menstruation.
Thyme	Soups, stews, tomato-based sauces	May treat infections. Soothes sore throats and hay fever. Can help expel parasites. Relieves minor skin irritations.
Winter-green	Ice cream, candies, desserts	Strong anti-inflammatory and antiseptic properties. Treats arthritis and rheumatism. Relieves flatulence.
Winter savory	Beans, meats, vegetables	Treats digestive and respiratory issues. Antibacterial properties.
Yarrow	Salad dressings, infused oils	Helps heal minor wounds. Eases menstrual pain and heavy flow. Tonic properties.

Gardening Techniques

Gardeners are creative people who are always on the lookout for the most efficient, interesting, and beautiful ways to grow their favorite plants. Whether you need to save money, reduce your workload, or keep plants indoors, the following gardening techniques are just a sampling of the many ways to grow your very own bountiful garden.

Barrel

Lidless plastic food-grade barrels or drums are set on raised supports. Before the barrel is filled with soil, slits are cut into the sides of the barrel and shaped into pockets. A PVC pipe is perforated with holes and set into the center and out of the bottom of the barrel as a delivery tool for watering, draining, fertilizing, and feeding the optional worm farm.

Strengths
Initial cost is moderate. Retains moisture, warms quickly, drains well, takes up little space, maximizes growing area, and repels burrowing rodents. Little weeding or back-bending required.

Weaknesses
Not always attractive, initially labor intensive, requires special tools to modify. Not generally suited for crops that are deep-rooted, large vining, or traditionally grown in rows, such as corn.

Hügelkultur

These permanent raised beds utilize decomposing logs and woody brush that have been stacked into a pyramidal form on top of the soil's surface or in shallow trenches and then packed and covered with eight to ten inches of soil, compost, and well-rotted manure. The rotting wood encourages soil biota while holding and releasing moisture to plants, much like a sponge. English pronunciation: "hoogle-culture."

Strengths

Vertical form warms quickly, drains well, reduces watering needs, increases overall planting surface, and reduces bending chores. In time the rotting wood breaks down into humus-rich soil.

Weaknesses

Labor-intensive construction and mulch tends to slide down sides. Requires two to three years of nitrogen supplementation, repeated soaking, and filling sunken voids with soil. Voids can also be attractive to rodents and snakes in the first few years.

Hydroponic

Hydroponics is based on a closed (greenhouse) system relying on carefully timed circulation of nutrient-enriched water flowing through a soilless growing medium in which plants grow. Aerial parts are supported above the water by rafts and, at times, vertical supports. With the addition of fish tanks to the system, hydroponics becomes aquaponics.

Strengths

Customizable to any size. Versatile, efficient, productive, and weedless. Produce stays clean.

Weaknesses

Large systems are expensive and complicated to set up and maintain; require multiple inputs of heat, light, and nutrients; and are limited to certain crop types.

Lasagna

Based on sheet composting, lasagna gardens are built up in layers, starting with paper or cardboard that is placed on top of turf-covered or tilled ground to smother weeds and feed ground worm activity. This is then covered in repeating layers of peat moss, compost, leaves, wood chips, manure, and yard waste (green, brown, green), which eventually break down into rich, humusy soil.

Strengths

Excellent natural method to enrich poor soils, utilizes organic waste, supports soil biota, and improves drainage while reducing the need for fertilizers and excessive watering.

Weaknesses

Initially labor intensive and the proper breakdown of bed materials takes months, so is not suited to "quick" gardening. Requires ready and abundant sources of clean, unsprayed, organic materials.

Ruth Stout

This "no work" garden is based on deep, permanent layers of progressively rotting straw mulch, which simultaneously builds soil, feeds plants, blocks weeds, and reduces watering. Seeds and plants are placed into the lower decomposed layers. Fresh straw is added as plants grow and kept at a depth of eight or more inches.

Strengths
No tilling, few weeds, reduced watering and fertilizing. Warms quickly in the spring and prevents winter heaving. An excellent method for rocky, sandy, or clay soils.

Weaknesses
Requires an abundance of straw each season, which can be expensive and difficult to transport, move, and store. Deep mulch may encourage burrowing rodents and provide shelter for slugs, insect pests, and diseases.

Soil Bag

This simple method utilizes one or more twenty- to forty-pound bags of commercial potting soil or topsoil simply laid out flat on turf, mulch, or wood pallets. A rectangular hole is cut into the top and drainage holes are punched through the bottom. A light dusting of fertilizer is mixed in and plants and seeds are sown.

Strengths
Super easy, weed-free, no-till garden and a great way to start an in-ground garden. Fun for kids and those without a yard.

Weaknesses
Limited to shallow-rooted crops, needs consistent watering and fertilizing, and may flood in heavy rains. Cats may find this an attractive litter box.

Straw Bale

One or more square, string-bound straw bales are placed cut side up either directly on the ground or on top of a weed barrier and soaked with water for several days or even months and treated with nitrogen to help speed the decomposition of the straw. Alternatively, bales can be overwintered in place before using. Once ready, bales are parted down the center, filled with soil and compost, and planted with seeds or starts.

Strengths

Good on poor soils, even concrete. No tilling required, few weeds, handicap accessible, versatile, easy to configure, and renter-friendly. Spent bales make excellent mulch.

Weaknesses

Straw bales can be expensive, heavy, and difficult to transport. These gardens can initially be labor intensive, require frequent watering and fertilizing, and must be replaced every one or two seasons. Nitrogen from treated bales can leach into the local environment and affect the watershed.

Square Foot

This modern take on French Intensive gardening utilizes raised beds filled with a special soilless blend enclosed in a box frame that is further divided into twelve-by-twelve-inch squares, or one square foot. Each square is planted or seeded based on the correct spacing requirements of each plant. Large crops, like tomatoes, are planted one to a square, while small crops like radishes are planted sixteen to a square.

Strengths

Proper plant spacing utilizes space, increases yields, and reduces weeds. Adding trellises increases growing capacity. Raised beds drain well, warm quickly, hold mulch, look tidy, and are easy to mow around.

Weaknesses

Initial construction is expensive, labor intensive, and often impermanent. Requires frequent watering in dry spells, and not all crops are suitable. Grids can be tedious to use and do not remove the gardener's need to learn proper plant spacing.

Vertical

Vertical gardens make use of nontraditional gardening space in two ways. The first is by training vining and climbing plants onto trellises, arbors, or fences and growing in raised beds, pots, urns, or tubs. The second is by firmly securing containers, troughs, rain gutters, or vertical garden felt pockets onto permanent frames supported by fences, walls, or other sturdy vertical structures. These gardens are typically irrigated by automatic drip or hydroponic systems. Soilless options are available.

Strengths

Attractive and weed-free indoor-outdoor garden perfect for small yards, renters, and disabled persons. Helps hide ugly structures and views and defines outdoor spaces.

Weaknesses

Construction of large systems and very sturdy structures can be initially expensive or labor intensive. Not conducive to all garden crops and requires frequent and consistent applications of moisture and fertilizer.

2024 Themed Garden Plans

Spaghetti Sauce Garden

Since I've been making an effort to eat fewer processed foods and become more self-sufficient, I thought it would be fun to grow a spaghetti sauce garden. Tomato sauce has been a staple in my house not just for spaghetti and other pasta-based dishes, but also for soups, meatloaf, and even just to sop up with really good bread. This garden is laid out like a formal Italian Renaissance garden: four plum tomato plants serve as the central "fountain," and the angular geometric layout is filled in with fragrant herbs, onions, and garlic. Most Italian families have their own special, often passed-down, formulas to make tomato sauce. Feel free to substitute the plants I've included for ones that you use. *Mangia!*

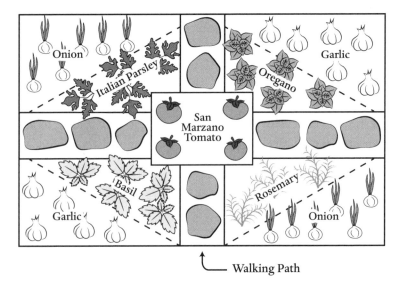

Walking Path

Dog Garden

If you've ever seen a dog grazing like a cow, he's probably eating grass to ease digestion. This garden features greens that are safe for dogs to eat. These plants (which you may like as well!) may also help address problems like tummy troubles and anxiety. This garden is laid out like a favorite dog treat—a bone! The bamboo should be planted in pots on each end of the rectangular garden plot. This will give the garden its shape and it will also contain the bamboo, which would otherwise spread rapidly (and even take over your space) once established. Dogs love greens—and some dogs will eat anything! Before you let your pooch graze in this (or any garden), check with your vet to make sure it's okay. And of course, avoid the use of chemical pesticides on plants that will be eaten.

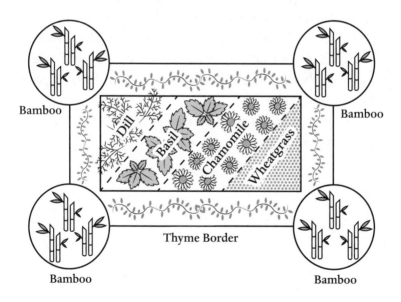

Hobbit Garden

Create a bit of J. R. R. Tolkien's Shire in your garden with plants that make appearances in his books and the films inspired by them. The Shire is divided into four sections, or "farthings," each represented by a garden bed. Plants of all kinds are found throughout the Shire, but each farthing has its own particular specialty.

Bilbo Baggins lives in the village of Hobbiton, located in the Westfarthing. Bag End's garden is always bright with flowers; we'll plant lilies and lobelia in this bed.

In the Northfarthing, plant a favorite hobbit vegetable, the cabbage!

Mushrooms are a bit of an obsession for hobbits; in the Eastfarthing, try growing some of the king oyster variety. When planning where to place your garden, situate it so that the Eastfarthing is in the shadiest available area.

The Southfarthing is famous for its wine, and Cabernet Sauvignon grapes are probably the closest to what might have been grown in the Shire. These are hardy, easy to grow grapes—give them a try!

This 6 × 6-foot bed is described in more detail in the article on pages 53–64.

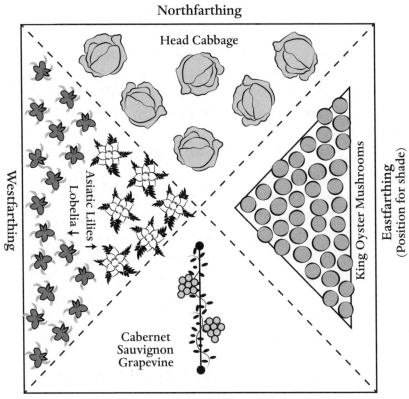

Northfarthing

Head Cabbage

Westfarthing

Asiatic Lilies ↑
Lobelia ←

Cabernet
Sauvignon
Grapevine

King Oyster Mushrooms

Eastfarthing
(Position for shade)

Southfarthing

Planning Your 2024 Garden

Prepare your soil by loosening and fertilizing. Use the grid on the right, enlarging on a photocopier if needed, to sketch your growing space and identify sunny and shady areas.

Plot Shade and Sun

For new beds, watch your yard or growing space for a day, checking at regular intervals (such as once an hour), and note the areas that receive sun and shade. This will shift over the course of your growing season. Plant accordingly.

Diagram Your Space

Consider each plant's spacing needs before planting. Vining plants, such as cucumbers, will sprawl out and require trellising or a greater growing area than root crops like carrots. Be sure to avoid pairing plants that naturally compete or harm each other (see the Companion Planting Guide on page 262).

Also consider if your annual plants need to be rotated. Some herbs will reseed, some can be planted in the same place year after year, and some may need to be moved after depleting the soil of certain nutrients during the previous growing season.

Determine Your Last Spring Frost Date

Using data from previous years, estimate the last spring frost date for your area and note what you'll need to plant before or after this date. Refer to seed packets, plant tags, and experts at your local garden center or university extension for the ideal planting time for each plant.

My estimated 2024 last spring frost date: _____

Growing Space Grid

☐ = _____ inches/feet

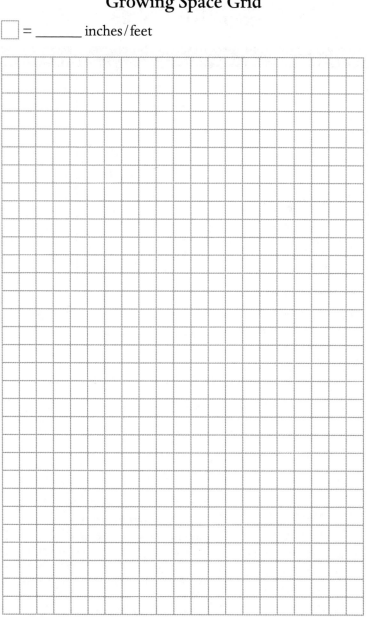

January

Task	Date

Notes:

_____

_____

_____

_____

_____

_____

_____

JANUARY

	1	2	◑	4	5	6
7	8	9	10	●	12	13
14	15	16	◐	18	19	20
21	22	23	24	○	26	27
28	29	30	31			

Take Inventory

Before you hit the seed catalogs or the garden center, do an inventory of any seed packets you have left over from last year. Many seeds will last for up to three years if they have been stored properly. Exceptions to this rule include alliums, many herbs, lettuces, parsnips, and celery.

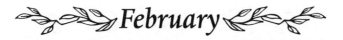

February

Task	Date

Notes:

_____

_____

_____

_____

_____

_____

_____

Roses

When it comes to pruning, hybrid teas, grandifloras, floribundas, and 'Knock Out' roses are pruned when the new growth buds begin to swell. For antique roses, heritage roses, and most climbing roses, it's best to wait until after the blooms have faded later in the season.

FEBRUARY

				1	◑	3
4	5	6	7	8	●	10
11	12	13	14	15	◐	17
18	19	20	21	22	23	○
25	26	27	28	29		

March

Task	Date

Notes:

_____

_____

_____

_____

_____

_____

_____

MARCH

					1	2
◑	4	5	6	7	8	9
●	11	12	13	14	15	16
◐	18	19	20	21	22	23
24	○	26	27	28	29	30
31

Plant Markers

As you set seeds in the garden, don't throw away the packet they came in. Carefully cover the entire packet with clear tape. Packing tape will last longest in the elements. Then tape or staple the packet to a tongue depressor stick and use it to mark the plant row.

April

Task	Date

Notes:

_____

_____

_____

_____

_____

_____

_____

Irrigation Setup

When it comes to irrigation, early installation is better than later. Whether you use drip irrigation or soaker hoses, positioning the watering system before the plants get very big or the temperatures soar is always easier than waiting until the last minute.

APRIL

◑	2	3	4	5	6
7	●	9	10	11	12	13
14	◐	16	17	18	19	20
21	22	○	24	25	26	27
28	29	30

May

Task	Date

Notes:

_____

_____

_____

_____

_____

_____

_____

MAY

			◑	2	3	4
5	6	●	8	9	10	11
12	13	14	◐	16	17	18
19	20	21	22	○	24	25
26	27	28	29	◐	31	

Attracting Hummingbirds

It's a mistake to rely only on red-flowering plants. These hungry flitters will visit anything with a tubular shape. Good candidates include agastache, hostas, lantanas, butterfly bushes, bee balm, salvias, penstemons, honeysuckle vines, and zinnias.

June

Task	Date

Notes:

_____

_____

_____

_____

_____

_____

_____

Vinegar as an Alternative Herbicide

A University of Maryland study reports it can work but comes with its own problems. The most effective vinegar is one with 20 percent acetic acid. This will kill any foliage it touches, corrode metal surfaces, and become toxic in the soil if overused. Apply with care.

JUNE

						1
2	3	4	5	●	7	8
9	10	11	12	13	◐	15
16	17	18	19	20	○	22
23	24	25	26	27	◑	29
30						

July

Task	Date

Notes:

_____

_____

_____

_____

_____

_____

_____

JULY

	1	2	3	4	●	6
7	8	9	10	11	12	◐
14	15	16	17	18	19	20
○	22	23	24	25	26	◑
28	29	30	31			

Summer Lawn Care

When the heat is on, it's okay not to mow, especially cool-season lawns. Cut back mowing to every other week and raise the mowing deck to a height of 4 inches. Never fertilize cool-season lawns in midsummer and, if possible, give 1 inch of watering each week.

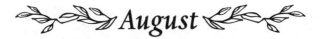

August

Task	Date

Notes:

_____

_____

_____

_____

_____

_____

_____

_____

Don't Wait to Repot Houseplants

If you've been putting off repotting your houseplants, don't wait any longer. Repotting now will give the plants time to recover from the shock of having their roots disturbed before the less-optimal conditions of winter set in, such as low light and low humidity.

AUGUST

				1	2	3
●	5	6	7	8	9	10
11	◑	13	14	15	16	17
18	○	20	21	22	23	24
25	◐	27	28	29	30	31

September

Task	Date

Notes:

_____

_____

_____

_____

_____

_____

_____

SEPTEMBER

1	●	3	4	5	6	7
8	9	10	◐	12	13	14
15	16	○	18	19	20	21
22	23	◑	25	26	27	28
29	30					

Outdoor Furniture Check-Up

Give furniture a once-over now and you'll be ahead of the game when it comes time to store the furniture for the winter. Repair or replace torn cushions. Give metal and plastic furniture a good cleaning. Stain or use wood sealant on wood furniture. Metal furniture can be painted now too.

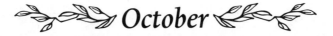

October

Task	Date

Notes:

_____

_____

_____

_____

_____

_____

_____

Dogwood Seed for Birds

As the dogwood trees set seed, gather some to share with the birds later this winter. Spread the berries on a cookie sheet and put them in the freezer until they are frozen solid. Package them up in a freezer bag and divvy them out this winter with your birdseed.

OCTOBER

		1	●	3	4	5
6	7	8	9	◐	11	12
13	14	15	16	○	18	19
20	21	22	23	◑	25	26
27	28	29	30	31		

November

Task	Date

Notes:

_____

_____

_____

_____

_____

_____

_____

NOVEMBER

					●	2
3	4	5	6	7	8	◐
10	11	12	13	14	○	16
17	18	19	20	21	◑	23
24	25	26	27	28	29	30

Planting Bulbs

How late is too late to plant bulbs? If you can put a shovel in the ground, you can plant bulbs. Now is still a good time to broadcast bone meal or bulb fertilizer on your existing bulb beds as well—if you can remember where they are!

December

Task	Date

Notes:

_____

_____

_____

_____

_____

_____

_____

Pruning Grapevines

Get a head start on next year's chores by pruning back grapevines now. Grape vines of all sorts can tolerate heavy pruning and still produce very well in the next season. Use the vines to create holiday wreaths for your home as well as gifting them to friends and family.

DECEMBER

●	2	3	4	5	6	7
◐	9	10	11	12	13	14
○	16	17	18	19	20	21
◑	23	24	25	26	27	28
29	●	31				

Gardening by the Moon

It is believed that the moon's gravitational pull extends beyond Earth's oceans, affecting the moisture in the soil, seeds, and plants. Some gardeners utilize this timing to strategically plan various gardening activities. Here's how:

Gardening by Moon Phase

During the waxing moon (from new moon to full moon), plant annuals, crops that need to be seeded anew each year, and those that produce their yield above the ground. During the waning moon (from full moon to new moon), plant biennials, perennials, and bulb and root plants. As a rule, these are plants that produce below the ground.

These are not hard-and-fast divisions. If you can't plant during the first quarter, plant during the second, and vice versa. There are many plants that seem to do equally well planted in either quarter, such as watermelon, hay, and cereals and grains.

First Quarter (Waxing): The first quarter begins with the new moon. Plant annuals that produce their yield above the ground and are generally of the leafy kind that produce their seed outside their fruit. Examples are asparagus, broccoli, brussels sprouts, cabbage, cauliflower, celery, cress, endive, kohlrabi, lettuce, parsley, and spinach. Cucumbers are an exception, as they do best in the first quarter rather than the second, even though the seeds are inside the fruit. Also in the first quarter, plant cereals and grains.

Second Quarter (Waxing): Plant annuals that produce their yield above ground and are generally the viney types that produce their seed inside the fruit. Examples include beans, eggplant, melons, peas, peppers, pumpkins, squash, and tomatoes.

Third Quarter (Waning): The third quarter begins with the full moon. Plant biennials, perennials, and bulb and root plants. Also plant trees, shrubs, berries, beets, carrots, onions, parsnips, peanuts, potatoes, radishes, rhubarb, rutabagas, strawberries, turnips, winter wheat, and grapes.

Fourth Quarter (Waning): This is the best time to cultivate, turn sod, pull weeds, and destroy pests of all kinds, especially when the moon is in the barren signs of Aries, Leo, Virgo, Gemini, Aquarius, and Sagittarius.

Gardening by Moon Sign

Some gardeners include the influence of the twelve astrological signs in their lunar gardening as well. The moon changes sign roughly every two and a half days.

Moon in Aries: Barren and dry. Used for destroying noxious growth, weeds, pests, and so on, and for cultivating.

Moon in Taurus: Productive and moist. Used for planting many crops, particularly potatoes and root crops, and when hardiness is important. Also used for lettuce, cabbage, and similar leafy vegetables.

Moon in Gemini: Barren and dry. Used for destroying noxious growths, weeds, and pests, and for cultivation.

Moon in Cancer: Very fruitful and moist. This is the most productive sign, used extensively for planting and irrigation.

Moon in Leo: Barren and dry. This is the most barren sign, used only for killing weeds and for cultivation.

Moon in Virgo: Barren and moist. Good for cultivation and destroying weeds and pests.

Moon in Libra: Semi-fruitful and moist. Used for planting many crops and producing good pulp growth and roots. A very good sign for flowers and vines. Also used for seeding hay, corn fodder, etc.

Moon in Scorpio: Very fruitful and moist. Nearly as productive as Cancer; used for the same purposes. Especially good for vine growth and sturdiness.

Moon in Sagittarius: Barren and dry. Used for planting onions, for seeding hay, and for cultivation.

Moon in Capricorn: Productive and dry. Used for planting potatoes, tubers, etc.

Moon in Aquarius: Barren and dry. Used for cultivation and destroying noxious growths, weeds, and pests.

Moon in Pisces: Very fruitful and moist. Used along with Cancer and Scorpio, and especially good for root growth.

Planting Guide for Moon Phase and Sign

The following table shows how to combine the moon's quarters and signs to choose the best planting dates for crops, flowers, and trees.

Plant	Quarter	Sign
Annuals	1st or 2nd	*See specific entry*
Apple trees	2nd or 3rd	Cancer, Pisces, Taurus
Asparagus	1st	Cancer, Scorpio, Pisces
Barley	1st or 2nd	Cancer, Pisces, Libra, Capricorn
Beans	2nd	Cancer, Pisces, Libra, Taurus
Beets	3rd	Cancer, Pisces, Libra, Capricorn
Berries	2nd	Cancer, Scorpio, Pisces
Biennials	3rd or 4th	*See specific entry*
Broccoli	1st	Cancer, Scorpio, Pisces, Libra
Brussels sprouts	1st	Cancer, Scorpio, Pisces, Libra

Plant	Quarter	Sign
Buckwheat	1st or 2nd	Capricorn
Bulbs	3rd	Cancer, Scorpio, Pisces
Bulbs for seed	2nd or 3rd	*See specific entry*
Cabbage	1st	Cancer, Scorpio, Pisces, Taurus
Cantaloupes	1st or 2nd	Cancer, Scorpio, Pisces, Taurus
Carrots	3rd	Cancer, Scorpio, Pisces, Libra
Cauliflower	1st	Cancer, Scorpio, Pisces, Libra
Celery	1st	Cancer, Scorpio, Pisces
Cereals	1st or 2nd	Cancer, Scorpio, Pisces, Libra
Chard	1st or 2nd	Cancer, Scorpio, Pisces
Chicory	2nd or 3rd	Cancer, Scorpio, Pisces
Clover	1st or 2nd	Cancer, Scorpio, Pisces
Corn	1st	Cancer, Scorpio, Pisces
Corn for fodder	1st or 2nd	Libra
Cress	1st	Cancer, Scorpio, Pisces
Cucumbers	1st	Cancer, Scorpio, Pisces
Deciduous trees	2nd or 3rd	Cancer, Scorpio, Pisces, Virgo
Eggplant	2nd	Cancer, Scorpio, Pisces, Libra
Endive	1st	Cancer, Scorpio, Pisces, Libra
Flowers	1st	Taurus, Virgo, Cancer, Scorpio, Pisces, Libra
Garlic	3rd	Libra, Taurus, Pisces
Gourds	1st or 2nd	Cancer, Scorpio, Pisces, Libra
Melons	2nd	Cancer, Scorpio, Pisces
Onion seeds	2nd	Scorpio, Cancer, Sagittarius
Onion sets	3rd or 4th	Libra, Taurus, Pisces, Cancer
Parsley	1st	Cancer, Scorpio, Pisces, Libra
Parsnips	3rd	Cancer, Scorpio, Pisces, Taurus
Peach trees	2nd or 3rd	Taurus, Libra, Virgo

Plant	Quarter	Sign
Peanuts	3rd	Cancer, Scorpio, Pisces
Pear trees	2nd or 3rd	Taurus, Libra, Virgo
Perennials	3rd	*See specific entry*
Plum trees	2nd or 3rd	Taurus, Libra, Virgo
Pole beans	1st or 2nd	Scorpio
Potatoes	3rd	Cancer, Scorpio, Taurus, Libra
Pumpkins	2nd	Cancer, Scorpio, Pisces, Libra
Quinces	1st or 2nd	Capricorn
Radishes	3rd	Libra, Taurus, Pisces, Capricorn
Rice	1st or 2nd	Scorpio
Roses	1st or 2nd	Cancer
Rutabagas	3rd	Cancer, Scorpio, Pisces, Taurus
Sage	3rd	Cancer, Scorpio, Pisces
Salsify	1st or 2nd	Cancer, Scorpio, Pisces
Spinach	1st	Cancer, Scorpio, Pisces
Squash	2nd	Cancer, Scorpio, Taurus, Libra
Strawberries	3rd	Cancer, Scorpio, Pisces
String beans	1st or 2nd	Taurus
Sunflowers	2nd, 3rd, 4th	Cancer, Libra
Tomatoes	2nd	Cancer, Scorpio, Pisces, Capricorn
Tulips	1st or 2nd	Libra, Virgo
Turnips	3rd	Cancer, Scorpio, Pisces, Taurus
Watermelon	1st or 2nd	Cancer, Scorpio, Pisces, Libra

2024 Moon Signs and Phases

Cross-reference the following month-by-month tables with the planting guide for moon phase and sign to determine the recommended planting times for 2024. Gray rows indicate the day of a phase change. All times are in Eastern Standard and Eastern Daylight Time, so be sure to adjust for your time zone.

January 2024

Date	Sign	Phase
1 Mon	Virgo	3rd
2 Tue 7:47 pm	Libra	3rd
3 Wed	Libra	4th 10:30 pm
4 Thu	Libra	4th
5 Fri 7:39 am	Scorpio	4th
6 Sat	Scorpio	4th
7 Sun 4:08 pm	Sagittarius	4th
8 Mon	Sagittarius	4th
9 Tue 8:33 pm	Capricorn	4th
10 Wed	Capricorn	4th
11 Thu 10:01 pm	Aquarius	New 6:57 am
12 Fri	Aquarius	1st
13 Sat 10:29 pm	Pisces	1st
14 Sun	Pisces	1st
15 Mon 11:49 pm	Aries	1st
16 Tue	Aries	1st
17 Wed	Aries	2nd 10:53 pm
18 Thu 3:12 am	Taurus	2nd
19 Fri	Taurus	2nd
20 Sat 8:58 am	Gemini	2nd
21 Sun	Gemini	2nd
22 Mon 4:51 pm	Cancer	2nd
23 Tue	Cancer	2nd
24 Wed	Cancer	2nd
25 Thu 2:37 am	Leo	Full 12:54 pm
26 Fri	Leo	3rd
27 Sat 2:11 pm	Virgo	3rd
28 Sun	Virgo	3rd
29 Mon	Virgo	3rd
30 Tue 3:04 am	Libra	3rd
31 Wed	Libra	3rd

February 2024

Date	Sign	Phase
1 Thu 3:37 pm	Scorpio	3rd
2 Fri	Scorpio	4th 6:18 pm
3 Sat	Scorpio	4th
4 Sun 1:28 am	Sagittarius	4th
5 Mon	Sagittarius	4th
6 Tue 7:08 am	Capricorn	4th
7 Wed	Capricorn	4th
8 Thu 8:59 am	Aquarius	4th
9 Fri	Aquarius	New 5:59 pm
10 Sat 8:42 am	Pisces	1st
11 Sun	Pisces	1st
12 Mon 8:26 am	Aries	1st
13 Tue	Aries	1st
14 Wed 10:02 am	Taurus	1st
15 Thu	Taurus	1st
16 Fri 2:39 pm	Gemini	2nd 10:01 am
17 Sat	Gemini	2nd
18 Sun 10:25 pm	Cancer	2nd
19 Mon	Cancer	2nd
20 Tue	Cancer	2nd
21 Wed 8:40 am	Leo	2nd
22 Thu	Leo	2nd
23 Fri 8:38 pm	Virgo	2nd
24 Sat	Virgo	Full 7:30 am
25 Sun	Virgo	3rd
26 Mon 9:29 am	Libra	3rd
27 Tue	Libra	3rd
28 Wed 10:09 pm	Scorpio	3rd
29 Thu	Scorpio	3rd

March 2024

Date	Sign	Phase
1 Fri	Scorpio	3rd
2 Sat 8:56 am	Sagittarius	3rd
3 Sun	Sagittarius	4th 10:23 am
4 Mon 4:15 pm	Capricorn	4th
5 Tue	Capricorn	4th
6 Wed 7:38 pm	Aquarius	4th
7 Thu	Aquarius	4th
8 Fri 8:03 pm	Pisces	4th
9 Sat	Pisces	4th
10 Sun 8:19 pm	Aries	New 5:00 am
11 Mon	Aries	1st
12 Tue 8:28 pm	Taurus	1st
13 Wed	Taurus	1st
14 Thu 11:16 pm	Gemini	1st
15 Fri	Gemini	1st
16 Sat	Gemini	1st
17 Sun 5:40 am	Cancer	2nd 12:11 am
18 Mon	Cancer	2nd
19 Tue 3:33 pm	Leo	2nd
20 Wed	Leo	2nd
21 Thu	Leo	2nd
22 Fri 3:42 am	Virgo	2nd
23 Sat	Virgo	2nd
24 Sun 4:37 pm	Libra	2nd
25 Mon	Libra	Full 3:00 am
26 Tue	Libra	3rd
27 Wed 5:03 am	Scorpio	3rd
28 Thu	Scorpio	3rd
29 Fri 3:52 pm	Sagittarius	3rd
30 Sat	Sagittarius	3rd
31 Sun	Sagittarius	3rd

April 2024

Date	Sign	Phase
1 Mon 12:05 am	Capricorn	4th 11:15 pm
2 Tue	Capricorn	4th
3 Wed 5:08 am	Aquarius	4th
4 Thu	Aquarius	4th
5 Fri 7:13 am	Pisces	4th
6 Sat	Pisces	4th
7 Sun 7:25 am	Aries	4th
8 Mon	Aries	New 2:21 pm
9 Tue 7:23 am	Taurus	1st
10 Wed	Taurus	1st
11 Thu 8:59 am	Gemini	1st
12 Fri	Gemini	1st
13 Sat 1:45 pm	Cancer	1st
14 Sun	Cancer	1st
15 Mon 10:24 pm	Leo	2nd 3:13 pm
16 Tue	Leo	2nd
17 Wed	Leo	2nd
18 Thu 10:10 am	Virgo	2nd
19 Fri	Virgo	2nd
20 Sat 11:08 pm	Libra	2nd
21 Sun	Libra	2nd
22 Mon	Libra	2nd
23 Tue 11:20 am	Scorpio	Full 7:49 pm
24 Wed	Scorpio	3rd
25 Thu 9:37 pm	Sagittarius	3rd
26 Fri	Sagittarius	3rd
27 Sat	Sagittarius	3rd
28 Sun 5:37 am	Capricorn	3rd
29 Mon	Capricorn	3rd
30 Tue 11:20 am	Aquarius	3rd

May 2024

Date	Sign	Phase
1 Wed	Aquarius	4th 7:27 am
2 Thu 2:52 pm	Pisces	4th
3 Fri	Pisces	4th
4 Sat 4:41 pm	Aries	4th
5 Sun	Aries	4th
6 Mon 5:42 pm	Taurus	4th
7 Tue	Taurus	New 11:22 pm
8 Wed 7:20 pm	Gemini	1st
9 Thu	Gemini	1st
10 Fri 11:13 pm	Cancer	1st
11 Sat	Cancer	1st
12 Sun	Cancer	1st
13 Mon 6:36 am	Leo	1st
14 Tue	Leo	1st
15 Wed 5:33 pm	Virgo	2nd 7:48 am
16 Thu	Virgo	2nd
17 Fri	Virgo	2nd
18 Sat 6:23 am	Libra	2nd
19 Sun	Libra	2nd
20 Mon 6:34 pm	Scorpio	2nd
21 Tue	Scorpio	2nd
22 Wed	Scorpio	2nd
23 Thu 4:24 am	Sagittarius	Full 9:53 am
24 Fri	Sagittarius	3rd
25 Sat 11:36 am	Capricorn	3rd
26 Sun	Capricorn	3rd
27 Mon 4:45 pm	Aquarius	3rd
28 Tue	Aquarius	3rd
29 Wed 8:33 pm	Pisces	3rd
30 Thu	Pisces	4th 1:13 pm
31 Fri 11:28 pm	Aries	4th

June 2024

Date	Sign	Phase
1 Sat	Aries	4th
2 Sun	Aries	4th
3 Mon 1:55 am	Taurus	4th
4 Tue	Taurus	4th
5 Wed 4:36 am	Gemini	4th
6 Thu	Gemini	New 8:38 am
7 Fri 8:41 am	Cancer	1st
8 Sat	Cancer	1st
9 Sun 3:29 pm	Leo	1st
10 Mon	Leo	1st
11 Tue	Leo	1st
12 Wed 1:39 am	Virgo	1st
13 Thu	Virgo	1st
14 Fri 2:12 pm	Libra	2nd 1:18 am
15 Sat	Libra	2nd
16 Sun	Libra	2nd
17 Mon 2:38 am	Scorpio	2nd
18 Tue	Scorpio	2nd
19 Wed 12:32 pm	Sagittarius	2nd
20 Thu	Sagittarius	2nd
21 Fri 7:08 pm	Capricorn	Full 9:08 pm
22 Sat	Capricorn	3rd
23 Sun 11:14 pm	Aquarius	3rd
24 Mon	Aquarius	3rd
25 Tue	Aquarius	3rd
26 Wed 2:08 am	Pisces	3rd
27 Thu	Pisces	3rd
28 Fri 4:52 am	Aries	4th 5:53 pm
29 Sat	Aries	4th
30 Sun 8:00 am	Taurus	4th

July 2024

Date	Sign	Phase
1 Mon	Taurus	4th
2 Tue 11:50 am	Gemini	4th
3 Wed	Gemini	4th
4 Thu 4:51 pm	Cancer	4th
5 Fri	Cancer	New 6:57 pm
6 Sat 11:56 pm	Leo	1st
7 Sun	Leo	1st
8 Mon	Leo	1st
9 Tue 9:48 am	Virgo	1st
10 Wed	Virgo	1st
11 Thu 10:06 pm	Libra	1st
12 Fri	Libra	1st
13 Sat	Libra	2nd 6:49 pm
14 Sun 10:53 am	Scorpio	2nd
15 Mon	Scorpio	2nd
16 Tue 9:25 pm	Sagittarius	2nd
17 Wed	Sagittarius	2nd
18 Thu	Sagittarius	2nd
19 Fri 4:14 am	Capricorn	2nd
20 Sat	Capricorn	2nd
21 Sun 7:43 am	Aquarius	Full 6:17 am
22 Mon	Aquarius	3rd
23 Tue 9:23 am	Pisces	3rd
24 Wed	Pisces	3rd
25 Thu 10:52 am	Aries	3rd
26 Fri	Aries	3rd
27 Sat 1:23 pm	Taurus	4th 10:52 pm
28 Sun	Taurus	4th
29 Mon 5:28 pm	Gemini	4th
30 Tue	Gemini	4th
31 Wed 11:19 pm	Cancer	4th

August 2024

1 Thu	Cancer	4th
2 Fri	Cancer	4th
3 Sat 7:10 am	Leo	4th
4 Sun	Leo	New 7:13 am
5 Mon 5:17 pm	Virgo	1st
6 Tue	Virgo	1st
7 Wed	Virgo	1st
8 Thu 5:31 am	Libra	1st
9 Fri	Libra	1st
10 Sat 6:34 pm	Scorpio	1st
11 Sun	Scorpio	1st
12 Mon	Scorpio	2nd 11:19 am
13 Tue 6:01 am	Sagittarius	2nd
14 Wed	Sagittarius	2nd
15 Thu 1:51 pm	Capricorn	2nd
16 Fri	Capricorn	2nd
17 Sat 5:45 pm	Aquarius	2nd
18 Sun	Aquarius	2nd
19 Mon 6:52 pm	Pisces	Full 2:26 pm
20 Tue	Pisces	3rd
21 Wed 7:02 pm	Aries	3rd
22 Thu	Aries	3rd
23 Fri 8:00 pm	Taurus	3rd
24 Sat	Taurus	3rd
25 Sun 11:04 pm	Gemini	3rd
26 Mon	Gemini	4th 5:26 am
27 Tue	Gemini	4th
28 Wed 4:47 am	Cancer	4th
29 Thu	Cancer	4th
30 Fri 1:09 pm	Leo	4th
31 Sat	Leo	4th

September 2024

Date	Sign	Phase
1 Sun 11:48 pm	Virgo	4th
2 Mon	Virgo	New 9:56 pm
3 Tue	Virgo	1st
4 Wed 12:12 pm	Libra	1st
5 Thu	Libra	1st
6 Fri	Libra	1st
7 Sat 1:18 am	Scorpio	1st
8 Sun	Scorpio	1st
9 Mon 1:26 pm	Sagittarius	1st
10 Tue	Sagittarius	1st
11 Wed 10:38 pm	Capricorn	2nd 2:06 am
12 Thu	Capricorn	2nd
13 Fri	Capricorn	2nd
14 Sat 3:53 am	Aquarius	2nd
15 Sun	Aquarius	2nd
16 Mon 5:39 am	Pisces	2nd
17 Tue	Pisces	Full 10:34 pm
18 Wed 5:24 am	Aries	3rd
19 Thu	Aries	3rd
20 Fri 5:03 am	Taurus	3rd
21 Sat	Taurus	3rd
22 Sun 6:24 am	Gemini	3rd
23 Mon	Gemini	3rd
24 Tue 10:50 am	Cancer	4th 2:50 pm
25 Wed	Cancer	4th
26 Thu 6:47 pm	Leo	4th
27 Fri	Leo	4th
28 Sat	Leo	4th
29 Sun 5:42 am	Virgo	4th
30 Mon	Virgo	4th

October 2024

Date	Sign	Phase
1 Tue 6:20 pm	Libra	4th
2 Wed	Libra	New 2:49 pm
3 Thu	Libra	1st
4 Fri 7:22 am	Scorpio	1st
5 Sat	Scorpio	1st
6 Sun 7:34 pm	Sagittarius	1st
7 Mon	Sagittarius	1st
8 Tue	Sagittarius	1st
9 Wed 5:38 am	Capricorn	1st
10 Thu	Capricorn	2nd 2:55 pm
11 Fri 12:31 pm	Aquarius	2nd
12 Sat	Aquarius	2nd
13 Sun 3:55 pm	Pisces	2nd
14 Mon	Pisces	2nd
15 Tue 4:34 pm	Aries	2nd
16 Wed	Aries	2nd
17 Thu 4:00 pm	Taurus	Full 7:26 am
18 Fri	Taurus	3rd
19 Sat 4:07 pm	Gemini	3rd
20 Sun	Gemini	3rd
21 Mon 6:50 pm	Cancer	3rd
22 Tue	Cancer	3rd
23 Wed	Cancer	3rd
24 Thu 1:24 am	Leo	4th 4:03 am
25 Fri	Leo	4th
26 Sat 11:47 am	Virgo	4th
27 Sun	Virgo	4th
28 Mon	Virgo	4th
29 Tue 12:30 am	Libra	4th
30 Wed	Libra	4th
31 Thu 1:29 pm	Scorpio	4th

November 2024

Date	Sign	Phase
1 Fri	Scorpio	New 8:47 am
2 Sat	Scorpio	1st
3 Sun 1:19 am	Sagittarius	1st
4 Mon	Sagittarius	1st
5 Tue 10:17 am	Capricorn	1st
6 Wed	Capricorn	1st
7 Thu 5:58 pm	Aquarius	1st
8 Fri	Aquarius	1st
9 Sat 11:00 pm	Pisces	2nd 12:55 am
10 Sun	Pisces	2nd
11 Mon	Pisces	2nd
12 Tue 1:26 am	Aries	2nd
13 Wed	Aries	2nd
14 Thu 1:59 am	Taurus	2nd
15 Fri	Taurus	Full 4:28 pm
16 Sat 2:09 am	Gemini	3rd
17 Sun	Gemini	3rd
18 Mon 3:50 am	Cancer	3rd
19 Tue	Cancer	3rd
20 Wed 8:51 am	Leo	3rd
21 Thu	Leo	3rd
22 Fri 6:01 pm	Virgo	4th 8:28 pm
23 Sat	Virgo	4th
24 Sun	Virgo	4th
25 Mon 6:20 am	Libra	4th
26 Tue	Libra	4th
27 Wed 7:21 pm	Scorpio	4th
28 Thu	Scorpio	4th
29 Fri	Scorpio	4th
30 Sat 6:53 am	Sagittarius	4th

December 2024

Date	Sign	Phase
1 Sun	Sagittarius	New 1:21 am
2 Mon 4:09 pm	Capricorn	1st
3 Tue	Capricorn	1st
4 Wed 11:21 pm	Aquarius	1st
5 Thu	Aquarius	1st
6 Fri	Aquarius	1st
7 Sat 4:49 am	Pisces	1st
8 Sun	Pisces	2nd 10:27 am
9 Mon 8:38 am	Aries	2nd
10 Tue	Aries	2nd
11 Wed 10:55 am	Taurus	2nd
12 Thu	Taurus	2nd
13 Fri 12:22 pm	Gemini	2nd
14 Sat	Gemini	2nd
15 Sun 2:21 pm	Cancer	Full 4:02 am
16 Mon	Cancer	3rd
17 Tue 6:39 pm	Leo	3rd
18 Wed	Leo	3rd
19 Thu	Leo	3rd
20 Fri 2:37 am	Virgo	3rd
21 Sat	Virgo	3rd
22 Sun 2:08 pm	Libra	4th 5:18 pm
23 Mon	Libra	4th
24 Tue	Libra	4th
25 Wed 3:06 am	Scorpio	4th
26 Thu	Scorpio	4th
27 Fri 2:46 pm	Sagittarius	4th
28 Sat	Sagittarius	4th
29 Sun 11:37 pm	Capricorn	4th
30 Mon	Capricorn	New 5:27 pm
31 Sat 12:08 pm	Taurus	2nd

Contributors

Anne Sala is a freelance writer located in Minnesota. She writes, gardens, and cooks alongside her two children and husband, who are usually eager to help. She has been a regular contributor to Llewellyn's annuals for more than fifteen years.

Annie Burdick is a writer and editor living in Portland, Oregon. She has written for numerous websites, magazines, and anthologies on wildly varied topics. She is also the author of *Unconscious Bias*, *Bring the Wild Into Your Garden*, and *Gardening for Mind, Body, and Soul*, published by an imprint of Hachette UK. She spends most of her spare time reading, playing with her rescue dogs, and having adventures around the Pacific Northwest. Find her at annieburdickfreelance.com.

Charlie Rainbow Wolf is happiest when she is creating something, especially if it's made from items that others have discarded. A recorded singer-songwriter and published author, she champions holistic living and lives in the Midwest with her husband and special-needs Great Danes. Astrology reports, smoke cleansing blends, and more are available through her website at charlierainbow.com.

Dawn Ritchie is an author, journalist, multimedia content provider, and TV writer/producer. Her work has appeared on all major networks, and her articles on design, cuisine, health, business, and entertainment have been published in dozens of national newspapers and publications. A regular contributor to the *Herbal Almanac*, Dawn is also an avid organic gardener, forager, cook, passionate beekeeper, and author of *The Emotional House* (New Harbinger Publications).

Diana Rajchel left her heart in San Francisco but moved most of her stuff to southwestern Michigan at the behest of her partner and dog. She is author of such titles as *Urban Magick* and *Hex Twisting*. She has begun the slow process of turning her home into an urban farm.

Elizabeth Barrette lives in central Illinois and enjoys magical crafts, historic religions, and gardening for wildlife. She has written columns on Pagan practice, speculative fiction, gender studies, and social and environmental issues. Her book *Composing Magic* explains how to combine writing and spirituality. Visit her blog at ysabetwordsmith.dreamwidth.org.

Holly Bellebuono is an internationally known herbalist, speaker, and author. She is best-known for her award-winning documentary *Women Healers of the World* and for her lectures on entrepreneurship, neurodiseases, and herbal medicine. Having founded, run, and sold various herbal businesses for twenty-six years, Holly has also spent years in the nonprofit world, serving as program director at an environmental advocacy organization and currently as executive director at an education nonprofit.

James Kambos is a writer, artist, and herbalist. He's written many articles on folk magic and herbs. He raises herbs and wildflowers in his southern Ohio garden.

JD Walker is an avid student of herbalism and gardening. She has written a regular garden column for thirty years. She is an award-winning author, journalist, and magazine editor and a frequent contributor to the Llewellyn annuals. Her first book, *A Witch's Guide to Wildcrafting*, published by Llewellyn Publications, was released in spring 2021. Her new book, *Under the Sacred Canopy*, was released in April 2023.

Jill Henderson is a backwoods herbalist, author, artist, and world traveler with a penchant for wild edible and medicinal plants, culinary herbs, and nature ecology. She is a longtime contributor to *Llewellyn's Herbal Almanac* and *Acres USA* magazine and is the author of *The Healing Power of Kitchen Herbs, A Journey of Seasons*, and *The Garden Seed Saving Guide*. Visit Jill's blog at ShowMeOz.wordpress.com.

Jordan Charbonneau is a homesteader, hiker, animal lover, and forager. She attended Sterling College (Vermont), where she double majored in ecology and environmental humanities. Today, Jordan lives in a little off-grid cabin she and her husband, Scott, built in the hills of West Virginia. Together they grow organic vegetables and care for tons of animals. You can find more of her writing at rabbitridgefarmwv.com.

Kathy Martin is a founder and farmer at Aurelia's Garden, a two-acre all-volunteer farm that donates thousands of pounds of vegetables each year to local food pantries. She is a Master Gardener and longtime author of the blog *Skippy's Vegetable Garden*, a journal of her vegetable gardens. The blog has won awards including *Horticulture Magazine*'s Best Gardening Blog. A retired biochemist, Kathy lives near Boston with her family, dogs, chickens, and honeybees. She strives to grow all of her family's vegetables herself using sustainable organic methods.

Linda Raedisch is the author of *Night of the Witches, The Old Magic of Christmas*, and *The Lore of Old Elfland*. Lately, she's been writing more about food history than the supernatural, but the witches always seem to find a way in. Linda lives in northern New Jersey, where she occasionally meets fellow Llewellyn author Natalie Zaman for tea and seed cake. Follow

Linda on Instagram at @lindaraedisch to see what she's baking, making, and reading.

Lupa is a naturalist Pagan author and artist in the Pacific Northwest. She is the author of several books on nature-based Paganism, including *Nature Spirituality From the Ground Up* and *The Tarot of Bones* deck and book. More about Lupa and her works may be found at thegreenwolf.com.

Marilyn I. Bellemore, a teacher and author, lives in an old Victorian house surrounded by vegetable and flower gardens in the seaside town of Wickford, Rhode Island. Her late grandfather, Anthony F. Matrumalo, was a registered architect who came to the United States from Italy when he was three years old. Marilyn loved whiling away the hours in her grandparent's vegetable garden when she was a child. Today, she continues to make her grandmother's Italian-American recipes, grows and studies herbs, and spends time at her farmhouse across from the ocean in Prince Edward Island, Canada.

Mireille Blacke, RD, CD-N, is a licensed alcohol and drug counselor, registered dietitian, and freelance health and nutrition writer from the Hartford, Connecticut, area. She has written numerous articles for Llewellyn's annuals since 2014. Mireille worked in rock radio for two decades before shifting her career focus to media psychology, behavioral health nutrition, and addiction counseling. Her Bengal cats consume most of her free time and sanity.

Monica Crosson is the author of *Wild Magical Soul*, *The Magickal Family,* and *Summer Sage*. She is a Master Gardener who lives in the beautiful Pacific Northwest, happily digging in the dirt and tending her raspberries with her family and their small menagerie of farm animals. Monica is a regular contributor to Llewellyn's annuals as well as *Enchanted Living Magazine* and *Witchology Magazine*.

Natalie Zaman is the author of *Color and Conjure* and *Magical Destinations of the Northeast*. A regular contributor to various Llewellyn annual publications, she also writes the recurring feature Wandering Witch for *Witches & Pagans* magazine. When not on the road, she's busy tending her magical back garden. Visit Natalie online at nataliezaman.blogspot.com.

Raechel Henderson is the author of *Sew Witchy* and *The Scent of Lemon & Rosemary*. She lives in Wyoming and writes about living a magical life.

Rachael Witt is a clinical community herbalist, gardener, and teacher. She is the founder of Wildness Within, an herbal business that offers plant-focused classes and workshops, handmade products, and herbal consultations. Rachael is dedicated to simple, seasonal living with the land and teaching people hands-on earth skills. She lives and stewards the Highlands Homestead in Duvall, Washington. Find more at Wildness WithinLiving.com.

Sara Mellas is a multidisciplinary creative living in Nashville, Tennessee. She's authored three books, developed hundreds of recipes for global brands, and written about food, music, and magic for various media outlets. She holds a master's degree in music education and vocal performance and works as a performer and production stylist for television, film, and live events. Outside of her creative pursuits, she can be found spending time with horses and cats and studying astrology.

Susan Pesznecker is a mother, writer, nurse, and college English professor living in the beautiful Pacific Northwest with her poodles. An amateur herbalist, Sue loves reading, writing, cooking, travel, and anything having to do with the outdoors. Her previous works include *Crafting Magick with Pen and Ink*, *The Magickal Retreat*, and *Yule: Recipes & Lore for the Winter Solstice*. She's a regular contributor to the Llewellyn annuals. Follow her on Instagram at @SusanPesznecker.

Suzanne Ress runs a small farm in the Alpine foothills of Italy, where she lives with her husband. She has been a practicing Pagan for as long as she can remember and was recently featured in the exhibit "Worldwide Witches" at the Hexenmuseum of Switzerland. She is the author of *The Trial of Goody Gilbert*.

Gardening Resources

Cooking with Herbs and Spices compiled by **Susan Pesznecker**
Gardening Techniques written by **Jill Henderson**
2024 Themed Garden Plans designed by **Natalie Zaman**
2024 Gardening Log tips written by **JD Walker**